La Vie Parisienne

1852-1870

Joanna Richardson

A Studio Book
The Viking Press   New York

Published in 1971 by the Viking Press, Inc.
625 Madison Avenue, New York, N.Y. 10022

SBN 670-42034-4
Library of Congress catalog card number: 71 - 157975

This book was designed and produced by
George Rainbird Ltd, Marble Arch House,
44 Edgware Road, London W2

Printed and bound by Dai Nippon, Tokyo, Japan

Contents

FOR KATHLEEN
WITH LOVE AND GRATITUDE

Acknowledgments

I must record my gratitude to the late Count Campello, who allowed me to use the Primoli Papers, and to the late Émile Henriot, of the Académie-Française, who gave me permission to publish the letters of Théophile Gautier to Carlotta Grisi. I am much indebted to the staff of the Reading Room and the Periodicals Gallery at the British Museum.

September, 1970   JOANNA RICHARDSON

List of Color Plates

Introduction

On 2 September 1870, Napoleon III surrendered to the Prussians at Sedan. On 4 September, amid scenes of great rejoicing in Paris, the fall of the Bonaparte dynasty and the Second Empire were decreed, and the Third Republic was proclaimed.

In the century which has passed since that momentous day, the Second Empire has come to seem a glittering and splendid age, one to be recalled with fascination and regret. It was the last time when France – which has an admiring sympathy for royalty – was ruled by a sovereign. It was the last time when a Court set the social tone, and invested national life with glamour. The Second Empire had some, at least, of the Bonaparte aura; and that aura has gone for ever. 'The Republic,' said Adolphe Thiers, 'is what divides us least.' But the republics which have followed, the elected presidents who have since governed France, have been unable to restore the element of magic to French life. It is perhaps an element essential to an ancient civilisation.

Hereditary monarchy responds to some deep instinct in human nature: a need for a symbol which transcends everyday politics. Monarchy not only fulfils an emotional need, it intensifies a sense of nationhood, it gives a sense of profound historical continuity. It increases political stability. No other institution can have the same beneficent effect. Baron Haussmann, who created Second Empire Paris, believed in an authoritarian Empire. At the end of his long life, he wrote: ' I had, and I still have, the profound and personal conviction that, in France, the only form of Democracy is the Empire. Our country, the most *single-minded* in all the world, needs a government which is single-minded, too. It must have one man to govern it.'

Speculation is not the province of the historian, but the history of modern France would have been very different if Napoleon III had made a successful marriage, if the Liberal Empire had survived, if the Franco-Prussian War had not occurred. Even after the fall of the Empire, in 1870, the imperial régime might have been restored under Napoleon IV. The death of the Prince Imperial in the Zulu War in 1879 finally ended the hope of a Third Empire. It is easy to see what France has lost as a republic; it is difficult to see what she has gained.

After her resounding defeat at Waterloo in 1815, France went through a period of crisis. She remembered the glories of the Napoleonic era, but she had no prospect of future glory. A generation of young men, brought up on martial legends, eager for renown on the battlefield, found no room for their ideals or for their enterprise. Patriotism was in decline; religion had small influence. Romantic literature reflected the need to escape: to lose oneself in the past or the exotic. Social life – at least among the Paris intelligentsia – showed an escapism of another kind: an escape into Bohemian fashions and Bohemian customs. In the 1840s, French soldiers from Algeria introduced absinthe to France. All too many social misfits, all too many men of potential distinction, were destroyed by their addiction to the pernicious 'green goddess'.

French politics, after the fall of Napoleon, were consistently depressing. In 1814, after the Emperor's abdication, the victorious Allied Powers had restored legitimate monarchy to France: the Bourbon monarchy of pre-Revolution days. It was restored in the person of a younger brother of Louis XVI. This was Louis XVIII. Some called him le Préfet d'Angleterre; and, since he fled from Paris during the Hundred Days, and had to be restored again after Waterloo, others described him, succinctly, as Louis Deux-fois-neuf. Louis XVIII was followed, after his death in 1824, by his younger brother, Charles X; and in 1830, when Charles X dissolved the Chamber of Deputies, ended representative government, and abolished the freedom of the Press, he provoked the revolution known as *les trois glorieuses*. Street fighting began in Paris on 27 July and lasted until 29 July. Charles X abdicated in favour of his grandson, the Duc de Bordeaux (later known as the Comte de Chambord), the posthumous son of the Duc de Berry. However, the Orleanist faction of the opposition engineered the establishment of a constitutional monarchy, and, on 7 August, Louis-Philippe, Duc d'Orléans, was proclaimed king.

Louis-Philippe re-established the tricolour flag, and affected democratic manners; he tried to divest his Court of glamour, and he modelled his life on that of any prosperous family man. During his reign, industry flourished, and the middle classes became the dominant influence in French politics. Louis-Philippe pursued a foreign policy of peace at any price; and, at home, towards the end of his reign, he refused to introduce any liberal or electoral reforms.

In 1847 the opposition party circumvented the law against public meetings; they organised political banquets at which speakers agitated for reform. The Government banned one of these banquets, which was to be held on 22 February 1848; and the Government's refusal provoked the February Revolution. Such was the effect of the insurrections in Paris that, two days later, Louis-Philippe abdicated in favour of his ten-year-old grandson, the Comte de Paris. The insurgents rejected the Comte de Paris, invaded the Chamber of Deputies, and demanded a provisional government. The Second Republic was proclaimed next day, 25 February, and the country proceeded to elect an Assemblée constituante.

The February Revolution was partly caused by the country's discontent with the reactionary government of Louis-Philippe; it was also caused by the acute food shortages which had already caused risings in the provinces. In a wider sense, it was the manifestation of socialist ideas and ideals which had for some years been fermenting in Europe. It was also, perhaps – by a natural paradox – a need for more inspiration in public life. France had been uninspired by the bourgeois monarchy, she still looked back with admiration and regret at the era of Napoleon.

Louis-Philippe had been so sure of his régime that he had encouraged the Bonaparte legend. In 1840, on his orders, his son, the Duc de Joinville, had sailed to St Helena to bring home the mortal remains of the Emperor. On 17 December that year, with all the pomp and panoply which the bourgeois monarchy could muster, Napoleon had been re-buried in the Invalides, in the heart of the country he had loved.

Twenty-five years after Waterloo, his legend kept political force. His nephew, Louis-Napoleon, the son of his brother Louis, King of Holland, had attempted a military coup-d'état at Strasbourg in 1836. In the summer of 1840, he had attempted a second: he had landed near Boulogne, with some fifty followers, and appealed to the garrison to rise in rebellion and follow him. He and his party were arrested, and he was brought to trial. 'I stand before you,' he told the court, 'as the representative of a principle, a cause, a defeat. The principle is the sovereignty of the people. The cause is that of the Empire. The defeat is Waterloo.'

He was sentenced to life imprisonment in the thirteenth-century fortress of Ham, and there he dreamed of the Empire that was to come. He refused an offer of release, because it had been made on condition that he renounced his political ambitions. On 26 May 1846, he disguised himself and escaped to London, to await the moment of destiny.

He did not have to wait for long. The year 1848 brought the fall of Louis-Philippe. There seemed a growing chance of a Bonaparte restoration. In December, Louis-Napoleon stood in the presidential election. Five and a half million voters supported him, a majority of nearly four million. Queen Victoria wrote, perceptively, to her uncle the King of the Belgians: 'The success of Louis-Napoleon is an extraordinary event. It will, however, perhaps be more difficult to get rid of him than one at FIRST may imagine.'

Queen Victoria was right. Three years later, on 2 December 1851, Louis-Napoleon dissolved Parliament, and arrested its principal leaders and many of his opponents. This coup-d'état was followed by a plebiscite in which he was voted dictatorial powers. Within the year, by another plebiscite, and by a majority of over seven million, he was elected Emperor of the French. On 2 December 1852, the forty-seventh anniversary of his uncle's victory at Austerlitz, he became Napoleon III.

The Second Empire was proclaimed that day at the Hôtel de Ville in Paris, and, through the Arc de Triomphe, the new Emperor rode into his capital. The Second Empire lasted until, on 2 September 1870, he surrendered himself and his army to the Prussians at Sedan. The Second Empire was his creation, and it was he who stamped its social and political character upon it. For eighteen years, France enjoyed a glittering imperial régime. It was politically unsound, it ended in national disaster, but it made a brilliant and distinctive contribution to French history.

1 The Imperial Family

Any study of the Second Empire must begin with a study of Napoleon III.

Louis-Napoleon Bonaparte was born on 20 April 1808: the son of Louis, King of Holland, brother of Napoleon, and of his wife Hortense. Since Queen Hortense herself was the daughter of Josephine de Beauharnais, and the stepdaughter of Napoleon, the boy had a double reason for remembering his ancestry. His childhood was disturbed, for, in 1815, on the fall of Napoleon, all the Bonapartes were exiled from France. Besides, his parents' marriage had ended in separation. King Louis, a remarkably difficult man, led a life apart, and his wife settled with her two sons in Rome. They joined the Bonaparte colony which gathered round Napoleon's aged mother, Madame Mère.

In Rome, the young Louis-Napoleon was watched admiringly by his cousin, Princess Mathilde. She was the daughter of the Emperor's youngest brother, Jerome, the former King of Westphalia, who was now known as Jerome de Montfort. Louis-Napoleon was twelve years older than Mathilde, and he had the prestige of age. When he came to her parents' palace, the Palazzo Nunez, he exhilarated her by doing all the things that she did not dare to do. He was even mischievous during mass. 'Judging by his lack of piety during the service,' she wrote later, 'one might have expected less religiosity from him when he ascended the throne.'[1]

In November 1835, when Mathilde was fifteen, her mother died. Queen Hortense was now living at Arenenberg, on Lake Constance. She immediately asked the Montforts to winter there. It was clear, even now, that she was not simply offering hospitality to her nephew and niece. Louis-Napoleon was twenty-seven, and it seemed time that he married. He might well find a wife in Mathilde.

When Mathilde arrived at Arenenberg, well aware of her family's hopes and feelings, Louis-Napoleon was not indifferent. 'Prince Louis,' she remembered, 'was gay, unruly, a bit of a story-teller, and a little given to banter. He took a great deal of interest in me, and, without actually paying court to me, he showed a great preference for me. This did not worry me, quite the contrary. So I readily joined in our little *flirtation*.'[2]

Louis-Napoleon, the future Napoleon III, at about the time of his engagement to Princess Mathilde. From a contemporary lithograph.

Early in April 1836, after a visit to her uncle, the King of Württemberg, at Stuttgart, Mathilde returned to Arenenberg. In the four months of her absence, encouraged by the Württemberg court, she had changed from an unassured adolescent into a self-possessed young girl, quite sure of her charm. The romance continued. Hortense encouraged it eagerly, and Jerome de Montfort so favoured it that he bought an old castle near Arenenberg. He planned to restore it and live in it, so that he could be near his married daughter. On 21 May, the Montforts left Arenenberg to go home to Florence. Louis-Napoleon had given Mathilde a ring set with a turquoise forget-me-not, and a lock of his hair. Mathilde had promised to have her portrait painted for him. They had sworn to write to one another.

The engagement was announced, and the months went by, but there were no preparations for the wedding. Jerome made certain financial suggestions to his future son-in-law, but he reminded him that he still approved of the marriage. On 11 September Louis-Napoleon wrote to his mother from Thun: 'I've told my uncle that I still consider myself engaged, and that nothing could alter my feelings. I also said that if he didn't think me rich enough for his daughter, I should agree, reluctantly, to wait until the spring, when some of my mother's financial claims would have been settled.' On 3 October he wrote again: 'Do explain to my uncle why I can't return to Arenenberg at once; I hope you'll settle everything with him, and that I'll soon have the happiness of marrying Mathilde.'[3]

Whatever the reason which Hortense gave for the delay, it was not the right one. Louis-Napoleon was intent on winning back the Bonaparte throne by a military coup-d'état. At 6 o'clock on the morning of 30 October, wearing Napoleonic uniform, he presented himself to the garrison at Strasbourg. He invited the 4th artillery regiment, whose colonel he had won over, to follow him and to restore the Empire. There were shouts of 'Long live the Emperor!', but some of the garrison still hesitated, and others thought that the revolt was a hoax. Louis-Napoleon was arrested. King Louis-Philippe was unwilling to give publicity to a Bonaparte pretender. He did not even trouble to have a trial, he quietly deported him to America.

Louis-Napoleon's wild venture broke his engagement to Mathilde. It ruined the chance of a splendid dynastic marriage, and it changed the course of French history.

However, his faith in his destiny was not changed by his failure at Strasbourg. The following spring he returned to Europe, and resumed his plotting in Switzerland. The French government demanded his expulsion, and he went to England. In early Victorian London he became a man of fashion. He had many friends in social and political circles; he impressed them all by his unshakeable confidence that, one day, he would be Emperor of the French. On 6 August 1840 he landed near Boulogne, and attempted another coup-d'état; this time he was sentenced to life imprisonment.

It was in the fortress of Ham that he heard that Mathilde was married. He could not know, at the time, how her father had virtually sold her, in order to pay his debts, to a dissolute Russian multi-millionaire; but it is reported that he wept, and said:

THE BONAPARTE FAMILY

Charles-Marie Bonaparte *m* Maria Laetitia Ramolino
1746–1785   1750–1836

12 children
of which

Napoleon I   Louis Bonaparte   Jerome Bonaparte
1769–1821   *King of Holland*   *King of Westphalia*
                          1778–1846   1784–1860

m 1. Josephine de   *m* 1. Elizabeth
Beauharnais - - - - - *m* Hortense de   Patterson
née Tascher de   Beauharnais   1785–1879
la Pagerie   1783–1837
1763–1814
                                                   m 2. Catherine of
m 2. Marie-Louise of   Württemberg
Austria   1783–1835
1791–1847

Napoleon II   Jerome-   Mathilde-   Napoleon-
King of Rome   Napoleon   Laetitia-   Joseph
1811–1832   1814–1847   Wilhemina   *Prince*
                                            1820–1904   *Napoleon*
                                                             1822–1891

                                            m Anatole
                                                Demidoff   *m* Clotilde
                                                1813–1870   of Savoy
                                                                 1843–1911

Napoleon-   Louis-Napoleon
Louis   1808–1873
1804–1831   **Napoleon III**   Napoleon-
                    Emperor of the French   Jerome-
                                                             Victor
                    m Eugénie de Montijo   1862–1926
                        de Guzman
                        1826–1920

                        Eugène-Louis
                        Prince Imperial
                        1856–1879   17

'This is the last and heaviest blow that fortune had in store for me.' Caroline Murat, the niece of Mathilde, was to record the words. She added: 'It is possible, indeed very probable, that had my aunt been Empress of the French, the Franco-Prussian War would never have taken place. She would have made an admirable Empress.'[4]

Ten years later, Louis-Napoleon was President of the French Republic, and Mathilde's disastrous marriage had ended in separation. Once again he thought of making her his wife. 'In 1850,' she remembered, 'there was a question of my obtaining my divorce so that I could marry the President of the Republic. I refused outright, for I preferred the situation I had to the quite exceptional one which I was offered. I did so without any hesitation, and without the least regret. I could not have forfeited my independence when I felt that my heart was not involved. I have congratulated myself on my decision.'[5] She was in fact in love with the Comte de Nieuwerkerke, a sculptor and careerist whose good looks and charm were almost legendary. She could hardly exchange him for an unattractive middle-aged cousin.

Dr Evans, who was to be the Emperor's dentist, drew an honest likeness of him.

'Napoleon III was not a handsome man . . . His head was large, usually slightly inclined to one side, and his features were strongly pronounced. The forehead was broad, the nose prominent, the eyes small, greyish-blue in colour, and generally expressionless, owing to a somnolent drooping of the lids; but they brightened wonderfully when he was amused, and when he was aroused they were full of power; nor were those likely to forget it who had once seen, through these windows of the soul, the flash of the fire that burned within. His complexion was blonde, but rather sallow; the lower part of his face was lengthened by a short "goatee" – called in honour of his Majesty an "imperial" – and broadened by a very heavy, silky moustache, the ends of which were stiffly waxed. His hair was of a light brown colour, and, when I first knew him, was abundant and worn rather long; at a later period it was trimmed short, and was habitually brushed in the style made familiar by the effigy on the coinage of the Empire. In complexion, in the colour of his hair, and also in the shape of his head, Napoleon III was a Beauharnais, not a Bonaparte, and a Frank, not a Corsican. He was a little below the average height, but his person was marked with dignity and distinction, and his deportment with ease and courtliness. No one could fail to observe that he was not an ordinary person.'[6]

Many of those who knew him – including Queen Victoria, who was a sound judge of character – bore witness to his charm, and to his extraordinary faith in his imperial destiny. Only the most violent republicans would have denied his desire to do good. Dr Barthez, who was to be the Prince Imperial's physician, had occasion to study the Emperor at close quarters, and he was, above all, impressed by his benevolence.

'It is curious to see how strongly this man has the instinct of practical well-doing and the satisfaction he feels in doing good . . . The more I see this man, the more closely I study him and the more attached I grow. I have looked for his worse side in everyday life and I have not found it . . . With the Emperor, his only fault, if it is one, is that his

18   *The Napoleonic legend continues. An Épinal print.*

Escadron des cent Gardes.

Cuirassiers 1.ᵉʳ et 2.ᵉ régiment.

Gendarmes à cheval.

Lancier.   Dragon de l'Impératrice.

Guide.   Chasseur à cheval.

Artillerie à cheval.   Train des équipages.

...darme.   Génie.   Voltigeur.   Grenadier.   Sapeur.   Sapeur.   Chasseur.   Artillerie.   Zouave.   Tambour.

...rie Lith. de Pellerin à Epinal.   Propriété de l'Éditeur.   Dépôt.

kindness errs to the verge of weakness. Of course it is of the private man I speak.'[7]

He was to carry his benevolence into his public life. As he had written in his youth: 'The Napoleonic idea is not an idea of war, but a social, industrial, commercial, humanitarian idea.'[8] The Second Empire coincided with the industrial revolution, and Napoleon III determined to accelerate this change. He encouraged the building of railways, the holding of international exhibitions, the reclaiming of waste land and the extension of public works; the transformation of Paris remains his most obvious achievement. In *The Second Empire*, G. P. Gooch wrote wisely of its founder: 'He is an echo of the mighty Emperor, but an infinitely better man. Close acquaintance reveals the most humane of dictators, part idealist, part adventurer, sincerely desiring the welfare of his country and a fairer lot for the common man. Émile de Girardin, the most influential journalist of the time, described him as *Napoleon the well-meaning*, a title subtly blending compliment with criticism. No-one could have been more different from the popular conception of a ruthless autocrat than this kindly ruler who never lost his temper nor raised his voice . . . Though there were other Bonapartes of the second generation, he alone possessed the drive and the quasi-mystical faith to secure a niche in the temple of fame.'[9] Such people, as Gooch himself observed, half idealists and half adventurers, rarely make satisfactory rulers, and dictators usually end by destroying themselves through military ambition or blind folly. One of the most perceptive, most provocative comments on Napoleon III was made by the Austrian Ambassador to Paris. Napoleon III, he said, had only one principle, and that was a superstition – a belief in his star.[10]

An English biographer wrote that he had the will to be great and the wish to do good, but that he was too small for the great things he set out to do.[11] As age and ill-health took their toll, his benevolence sometimes degenerated into weakness. Arsène Houssaye, at the end of the century, declared that the Emperor had been lost by his love of conciliation. 'Conciliation is already indecision; and indecision is the anaemia of power. After Sadowa the Emperor suffered from this anaemia, and he did not recover. He went from one failure to another until 4 September.'[12] But it is probably true, as Dr Evans wrote, that if his reign had ended successfully, his personal qualities would have exalted him to the skies.[13] General Comte Fleury, his equerry, recorded that, in the days of the presidency, Louis-Napoleon had enjoyed throwing off his police escort and paying some unexpected visit to a poorhouse or a factory. After the first surprise, he would be greeted warmly. 'This popularity lasted until the final days of the Empire. It was the result of a quite personal sympathy which was felt for the prince as much as the Head of State.'[14]

Napoleon III had small appreciation of art; he understood little about aesthetic feeling or the poetic imagination. He preferred facts to fancies. He was a philosopher and not a poet. 'He was called a dreamer,' wrote Dr Evans. 'And so he was in the sense in which the word can be applied to a political idealist . . . whose mind is engrossed and preoccupied by social and economic problems. But he was very far from being a dreamer who cherished illusions or wasted his time in idle speculations.'[15]

Napoléon le bien-intentionné: *the Emperor, from the portrait by Flandrin, 1867.*

On 30 January 1853, a few weeks after the Empire was restored, the Emperor married a shallow, ambitious, and exceedingly beautiful Spanish countess: Eugénie de Montijo. It was, on his side, a marriage of love; but it was far from splendid.

Nor did it prove to be satisfactory. After the difficult birth of the Prince Imperial – Bébé-Empereur, some called him – in 1856, Eugénie was forbidden to have more children: a ban which hardly increased her husband's fidelity. As the Emperor's health declined, Eugénie asserted herself increasingly. Perhaps she found politics some compensation for the failures of her private life. At the end of the century, Maxime du Camp concluded: 'The downfall of the Empire, the collapse of French power, prove that Napoleon III made many mistakes; the most serious fault with which we can reproach him, the one which was mortal, is that he married Eugénie de Montijo. Never did a more futile creature put a more indifferent mind to the service of an immoderate ambition. She exercised a detestable influence on superficial manners, she had her camarilla, her court, her partisans; she had her politics and she pushed the country into adventures of which she could not calculate the scope or foresee the end. She was disastrous, and her beauty, which was marvellous, does not absolve her.'[16] Eugénie encouraged the Emperor to support the Mexican enterprise. The Archduke Maximilian of Austria was sent, with French support, to rule a new and turbulent empire at the other side of the world. French support was at last withdrawn, Maximilian was shot by the rebels, and his wife went insane.

'The Emperor seems persuaded that we ask him for glory,' wrote Ludovic Halévy in 1866. 'All we ask is peace with honour . . . We have made enough stir in the world in the past ten years. Sebastopol and Solferino have avenged us enough for Waterloo. We no longer cut the figure of a humiliated nation in history . . . Peace, peace, peace, that is what we want.'[17] It was partly Eugénie's fault that, in 1870, the Emperor allowed himself to embark on the Franco-Prussian War. Eugénie declared that their son would not reign unless they destroyed the military supremacy of Prussia.

Early in June 1870, Count Bismarck advanced a Hohenzollern candidate for the vacant throne of Spain. France expressed such alarm at this threatened act of 'encirclement' that the candidate was promptly withdrawn. But France needed war. In 1866, at the Battle of Sadowa, Prussia had defeated Austria, and the balance of power in Europe had been changed. Ever since then, France had been aware of the Prussian challenge to her grandeur. No French government could idly watch while Prussia united Germany under her, and the French Press began to stir up warlike feeling. The Emperor was sixty-two and in lamentable health; he had no wish for war. Nor had his Prime Minister, Émile Ollivier, who had recently come to power. But the Emperor was being pushed by his Foreign Minister, the Duc de Gramont; he was also being pushed by Eugénie.

Gramont now assumed a hectoring tone. It was not enough that Prussia had withdrawn her candidate, she must be humbled for her presumption. He cabled Count Benedetti, the French Ambassador to Berlin, to keep the crisis hot. William I of Prussia, who was taking the waters at Ems, received Benedetti on 13 July with the greatest

The Empress Eugénie in 1854, by Édouard Dubufe.

courtesy, and assured him that no one wanted war less than he did. But while the Emperor was being pushed by Gramont, the King was being pushed by Bismarck. Bismarck knew that the French army was pitiably unprepared for modern warfare; and he had trained a massive modern army of his own. He had long since decided that war with France would cement the German federation.

Now that France was trying to humble Prussian pride, Bismarck decided that the time had come. At Ems, the King was irritated by Benedetti's insistence on a guarantee that the Hohenzollern candidature would not arise again. He declined to give such a guarantee, and refused Benedetti's request for a further audience. A telegram describing his refusal was then despatched to Bismarck in Berlin. Bismarck sharpened the tone, and stated that the King had 'refused to receive the Ambassador again, and he had had the latter informed by the adjutant on duty that His Majesty had no further communication to make.' Bismarck sent his version of the Ems Telegram to the Berlin Press and to every capital in Europe.

Even with Bismarck's editing, the Ems Telegram was hardly a sufficient reason for war; but it was enough to entice Napoleon III into the trap. On 15 July, the French Minister for Foreign Affairs gave the Senate the official account of the talks between the King and Benedetti. 'We have done everything to avoid a war; we shall prepare to fight the war which is offered to us.'[18] At half-past nine that night, the Emperor presided over a council of ministers at Saint-Cloud. At midnight the ministers left the palace. 'It is war!' cried *Le Moniteur universel*. 'God save France!'[19] The following evening, Thiers and a friend were driving down the boulevards. Excited crowds were singing *La Marseillaise*. 'Mark my words,' said Thiers to his companion, 'I know the military positions of France and Prussia. *We are lost!*'[20]

On 28 July, with the Prince Imperial, a boy of fourteen, the Emperor left Saint-Cloud to join the Rhine army headquarters at Metz. Eugénie had urged the Emperor to assume command of the armies, so that Marshal MacMahon would take orders from him. She had urged him, with only book knowledge and the brief Italian campaign behind him, to command a Marshal of France. The Emperor was in such pain from the stone in his bladder that he could hardly sit his horse; he was forced to direct a campaign which needed the tactical genius of the great Napoleon in his prime.

On 2 September, debilitated by the stone and by prostate trouble, worn by the fatigues and trials of the campaign, he surrendered with his army at Sedan.

'Paris, 3 September,' recorded *The Times* correspondent. 'I only once heard "À bas l'Empereur!" although throughout the evening – especially since the news of his capture has arrived – the orators of the Boulevards have not spared to speak of him with the profoundest contempt, a feeling which has been gathering for weeks, and has now come to a head.'[21] Two days later, he added: 'On 3 September, the bad news began to come out about mid-day. By 8 o'clock the Boulevards were crowded. The crowds on the pavement on either side of the Boulevard were wonderfully still and quiet, moving about slowly and gently, speaking in undertones to each other, like men oppressed with a great calamity. They were stupefied and knew not what to think. Suddenly down the roadway came a troop of men, at a rapid pace. They were repeating in sing-song fashion, like children learning a lesson: "Depose him! Depose him!" '22

On Sunday, 4 September 1870, the fall of the Emperor and of the Bonaparte dynasty were decreed, and the republic was proclaimed. 'Great enthusiasm in Paris,' reported *Le Moniteur universel*. 'Vive la France!'23

The traces of the past were removed with almost indecent speed. At half-past three that afternoon, the flag which flew over the Tuileries was hauled down. Workmen, armed with rifles, stood at the great door of the palace, and shouted: 'Entrance free!' while the mob surged up the stairs. The Prussians were marching on Paris, but their advance was forgotten. Someone scribbled 'Rooms to let' on the palace wall. The Crown jewels were already hidden in the naval arsenal at Brest; in 1887 they would be auctioned.24

The Empress, with the help of her American dentist, escaped across the Channel, and settled at Camden Place, an imposing mansion at Chislehurst, in Kent. The Emperor was imprisoned at Wilhelmshöhe – in what was now Germany – until 19 March, when he was released to join his family. On 20 March he reached Camden Place, where he was still to live with the Bonaparte legend. In his bedroom, overlooking the park, was a canopied bed in carved oak; its white satin bedspread was embroidered with the imperial cipher, and the Bonaparte emblem, golden bees. On the wall hung a portrait of the King of Rome – whom some still called Napoleon II. Next to the bedroom was the Emperor's small study; and here, in the stifling atmosphere which he found congenial, he would work at his papers.

He was rarely seen in the village, but villagers who attended fêtes in the grounds of Camden Place were impressed by his dignity and kindness, and local children soon discovered that the Emperor's pockets were full of pennies. Occasionally, in the summer, the Imperial Family would drive to the West Kent cricket field nearby, and watch the play. And once, when long-on made a brilliant catch, a member of the imperial staff was sent with a message from the Emperor, thanking him and asking him to do it again.

Occasionally he and Eugénie would take a holiday at Brighton, Cowes or Torquay; but usually they remained at Chislehurst, where the marriage took on a new serenity. The Empress remembered: 'I always found him simple and good, charitable and full of kindness. He endured contradiction and calumny with admirable equanimity, and when disaster overwhelmed us he carried his stoicism and meekness to the point of sublimity. If you could have seen him during his last years at Chislehurst! Never a word of complaint or recrimination!'25 Lord Malmesbury found him more depressed by the sufferings of France than by his own misfortunes. 'His quiet and calm dignity and absence of all nerviness and irritability, were the grandest examples of moral courage that the severest stoic could have imagined. I confess I was never more moved.'26

He still suffered from the stone in the bladder which had afflicted him at Sedan, and two operations were performed in the hope of curing him. He seemed strong enough to undergo a third, and it was arranged for noon on 9 January 1873. That morning, while his doctor was sitting with him, the Emperor whispered: 'Conneau, we were not cowards, were we, at Sedan?'[27]

They were his last coherent words. He died before the operation could take place – at a quarter to eleven that Thursday morning. He had planned to return to France, in the hope that his return would lead to his restoration to the throne; but his death, and the death of the Prince Imperial, six years later, deprived the Bonapartes of any future.

PRINCESS MATHILDE

One member of the Imperial Family earned a place apart, and exercised a unique and beneficent influence on the cultural life of the time. This was Princess Mathilde, first cousin of Napoleon III. She had been born in exile in Trieste, in 1820, when the Bonapartes were banned from France, and she had spent her early childhood with the Bonaparte colony in Rome. She developed an admiration which was little short of religious for the uncle she had never seen, the uncle who had died on St Helena. In 1836 she was briefly engaged to her cousin, Louis-Napoleon; in 1840 she married Anatole Demidoff, a dissolute Russian multi-millionaire, but the marriage ended in predictable separation. Mathilde became the mistress of Émilien de Nieuwerkerke; in 1850 she rejected the suggestion that she might obtain a divorce and marry Louis-Napoleon, then President of the Republic. She never felt respect or sympathy, let alone affection, for his wife. To her, Eugénie de Montijo was a shallow, foreign parvenue.

When the Second Empire came into being, Mathilde had already established a *salon* at her *hôtel* in the rue de Courcelles and at her country house, Saint-Gratien, near Lake Enghien. She now determined to complete her cousin's reign by exercising sovereignty over the realm of art and intellect which the Tuileries so little understood. She chose her rôle instinctively, and she chose it out of patriotism. Fortune had smiled upon her, and all that was most distinguished in France must share the imperial favour which she enjoyed. During the Empire, and during the thirty years she lived on in the Republic, Princess Mathilde presided over a *salon* which the Goncourts called 'the true *salon* of the nineteenth century'. No *salon* had ever given France so much as the *salon* of *la bonne princesse*.[1]

Princess Mathilde was the most distinguished hostess of Second Empire Paris. She did not only give conventional dinners and receptions, she gave spectacular fancy-dress balls, and she gave frequent theatrical soirées. Bressant and Madeleine Brohan acted

Two habitués of Princess Mathilde's salon: LEFT *Alfred-Émilien, Comte de Nieuwerkerke, from a drawing by Ingres, and* RIGHT *Victorien Sardou, the dramatist, from a photograph by Nadar.*

one of Musset's proverbs in her *salon*; Coquelin and Emma Fleury performed *La Revanche de Scapin*, by Théodore de Banville, to an audience which included the Emperor and Empress. Occasionally the Princess would give a ball, which diplomats would attend in all their splendour; and in 1870 the Prince Imperial was reported to have danced at the rue de Courcelles the whole night through.

Every year, the Princess held some special celebration in honour of the Emperor's birthday. The Goncourts were dazzled by the fête in 1866.

'The garden full of electric light. Lawns and trees lit up by the light of the Shake-spearean world, the light of a dream. Here and there, the edges of the leaves seem like rows of gaslight, brilliant against the blue sky, and the grey bats turn quite white and pass by like huge butterflies. In the background, through the windows, the blaze of chandeliers against purple hangings. And here and there, in the warm haze, something black is cut in two by something very red: a Grand Cross of the Legion of Honour on a sofa.'[2] In 1869 François Coppée's verse-play, *Le Passant*, was performed at the rue de Courcelles, with the young Sarah Bernhardt as the minstrel boy. In March 1870, the Emperor and Empress attended another of Coppée's plays, *Deux Douleurs*. All Paris was present. 'Princes, ambassadors, ministers – ministers of yesterday, ministers of to-morrow.' The correspondent of *L'Artiste* noticed Maurice Richard, the new Minister for the Fine Arts, who was surrounded by artists: Meissonier, Gérôme, Cabanel, Baudry. 'Men of letters were numerous: Augier, Renan, Arsène Houssaye, Dumas, Sardou, Feuillet, . . . Théophile Gautier, Gustave Flaubert. The Emperor was very gay, and he

Dramatist and actress: François Coppée, and the young Sarah Bernhardt as Zanetto *in his play* Le Passant, *1869.*

talked a little with everyone whom he happened to meet in those splendid salons filled with masterpieces, those magnificent conservatories where you believed in the spring.'[3]

The Press recorded Mathilde's unremitting interest in the cultural life of the age. They observed her at the revival of *Giselle*, where she 'frequently gave the signal for the applause' (Gautier, who had written the ballet, was her friend, her librarian, and her accredited poet).[4] Mathilde attended one of the popular Pasdeloup concerts, and heard Pasdeloup conduct Berlioz (despite her inability to enjoy music).[5] She went to the première of *L'Ami des femmes*, by her friend Dumas *fils*, and to the première of *Le Lion amoureux*, by her friend Ponsard.[6] She was present at the first performance of Verdi's *Don Carlos*, with all the 'upper 5600 of Paris'.[7] Early in November 1864, *La Presse* gaily told its readers that Mathilde was back from her country house at Saint-Gratien. 'Her return to Paris is always good news for all the conversationalists, who meet in the evening at the *hôtel* in the rue de Courcelles; nowadays, this is the *hôtel* where most wit is spent, though the wit becomes no rarer for that.'[8] No-one delighted in the wit more than Mathilde herself. 'I never went to the Tuileries without yawning,' she recalled. 'I used to say to the Emperor: "But it's stultifying!" To which the Emperor would reply in his kindly way: "Never mind, you'll soon be home again . . ."'[9]

'The artist-highness,' a journalist said, '*reunites* rather than receives. She reunites all those who are separated outside the rue de Courcelles. She reunites the painters and critics, the poets and the ministers, the Academicians and the candidates . . . The *re-unions* of the rue de Courcelles . . . will remain celebrated in the memoirs of the time.'[10]

29

The Goncourt *Journal* records her reunions, and Mathilde herself, with growing admiration and affection. The diary of her nephew, Joseph Primoli, then a *collégien* of sixteen, records Saint-Gratien at the height of the Second Empire. Gégé – as the Princess called him – gives an intimate and vivid impression of life with Notre Dame des Arts. He draws a décor familiar to most of the celebrities of the age.

'1 September 1867. Saint-Gratien. This is Princess Mathilde's country house, where I have been staying . . . It is an hour from Paris, and ten minutes from Enghien . . . At either end of the house is a large room, almost entirely glazed in; one is the dining-room and the other is the studio. Over these two wings are two large terraces, one of them next to the Princess's room, with a view across the lake . . . The château is surrounded by vivid, sweet-smelling flowers. On every side there are varied and delightful views . . . At 7 o'clock, the château stirs, the green shutters open, the valets sweep and dust; the gardeners water the shrubs, and change the flowers in the vases. At 11 o'clock, they ring the first bell for *déjeuner*, at 11.15 they ring the second . . .'[11] After *déjeuner*, the Princess painted in her studio, where her guests were free to talk to her, and in the afternoon there were walks and carriage-drives. At half-past six the guests returned to dress for dinner (punctually at seven). There were always visitors from Paris.

Primoli noted two of them. One was Hippolyte Taine, the philosopher, critic and historian. 'M. Taine is not much more than 38 [he was 39], but he wants to seem older . . . He was very witty; I think he listens to his own conversation.'[12] Taine was followed by Théophile Gautier. The poet who enchanted Mathilde enchanted her nephew, too. 'He's certainly the pleasantest man I've ever met,' wrote Gégé. 'He has all the qualities of the great genius without his arrogance . . . I've heard him talk clothes with women, and turn philosophers into poets. He is a master of the art of conversation, and – while he sometimes delights in toying with the fan of paradox, which he does with incredible dexterity – he expresses sound new ideas in poetic and original forms . . .'[13]

The eminent visitors continued to arrive in an endless stream. 'M. Émile Augier is coming here to read his play next Wednesday,' wrote Mathilde to Sainte-Beuve. 'He asks to read before dinner and he will therefore take the train which leaves Paris at 3.30. You should join him and double my pleasure in the reading.'[14] Another visitor (who managed, dexterously, to remain in favour at the Tuileries and at Saint-Gratien) was 'His Literary Majesty', the novelist Prosper Mérimée. In 1868, Joseph Primoli duly recorded:

'Prosper Mérimée wrote to the Princess that he would like to watch her painting in watercolours. She replied at once; she invited him to *déjeuner* next day at Saint-Gratien, and said that she would then sketch his portrait.

'He therefore came by the 10 o'clock train – I might have said the hearse, because he looked exactly like a stuffed corpse. His movements are slow, and when he moves you seem to hear the cracking of bones . . . His thin white hair is brushed up over his ears. He has a huge, creased forehead, ending in two bushes of black eyebrow; the brows which shook Olympus could not have been more terrible . . . As for his glance, it is lacklustre, only his smile keeps its youthful, mocking expression.

'If it were not for the size, which is either too large or too small, the watercolour would have been quite successful. As for the model, I have never seen him pose worse than he did during the sitting. At the beginning I gave him a packet of twelve cigarettes, and two hours later he had smoked them all. And so my poor asphyxiated aunt was obliged to quit her easel, to go out and leave the rest for next day.'[15]

In August 1869, Primoli spent a memorable day at Saint-Gratien, with Gautier, the Goncourts, and François Coppée. 'Coppée,' he wrote, 'is 26, but to judge by his beardless face and his timid manners you wouldn't think that he was more than twenty. He looks like Sardou and Bonaparte . . .

'The Goncourts have come to Saint-Gratien for a few days, at last. The younger one is in great pain from a liver complaint . . . Edmond himself seems even more ill when he sees him suffering, and Jules controls himself so as not to frighten Edmond. No mother would show more concern for her child . . . After dinner they both played billiards, and then Mother sent Baby to bed with a poultice on the stomach. But I think that this very union is the cause of the illness . . .'[16]

'You are Notre Dame des Arts,' Sainte-Beuve assured Princess Mathilde. 'You know how to suit your sort of kindness to every situation and every need.' It was in her *salon* that decorations were duly demanded, sinecures bestowed, pensions and Chairs and Academic uniforms ensured. It was there that plays were first performed, sonnets were composed, novels read aloud, and music played. The Court of the Tuileries was frivolous, ignorant of lasting values. Princess Mathilde recognised and fostered them. She died in 1904, after a long life which had been inspired by her relationship to Napoleon, and largely spent in the service of France.

Two luminaries of the salon *of Princess Mathilde:* LEFT *Théophile Gautier, painted by the Princess in 1870, and* RIGHT *Sainte-Beuve, from a drawing by Heim, 1856.*

PRINCE NAPOLEON

Un César déclassé. So the Goncourts defined Mathilde's brother, Prince Napoleon: one of the most controversial, gifted and significant figures in the Second Empire.[1]

Napoleon-Joseph-Charles-Paul had been born at Trieste on 9 September 1822: the third and youngest child of Jerome and Catherine de Montfort. He spent his early childhood in Rome and Florence, and in 1837, at the age of fifteen, he was sent to Louisburg, to enter the military service of his uncle, the King of Württemberg. He earned his commission, and remained in the army for two years; then, conscious of the German antipathy to France, and increasingly aware of his Bonaparte inheritance, he left Württemberg and returned to his father. In 1845 the government of Louis-Philippe allowed him, Bonaparte though he was, to cross France on his way to England. In May he found himself in Paris, where he moved the faithful of the old Empire by his astonishing likeness to Napoleon. On 22 May, M. Vatry, a Deputy, reported from Paris to Jerome: 'The day before yesterday he deigned to do me the honour of dining and spending the evening with me. I tried to gather some men of substance and some pretty women, and he was a great success with both: on his own account, because of his striking resemblance to the Emperor, and because of the memory of his father. It was the same at the Hôtel des Invalides. Old General Petit wept to see the son of Prince Jerome kneeling by the tomb of the Emperor Napoleon.'[2] The Prince spent several months in England; there he met his cousin, Louis-Napoleon, who had just escaped from the fortress of Ham.

In 1848, when Louis-Napoleon was elected President of the Republic, Prince Napoleon had already been elected Deputy for Corsica. At the age of twenty-six, he was the youngest member of the Assemblée constituante. *Le citoyen Napoléon Bonaparte*, as he was called, already showed himself to be a champion of democracy. He chose to sit on the extreme Left. His political beliefs would remain a problem for his cousin, all the more so when the Second Empire came into being and Prince Napoleon became an Imperial Highness and a Senator.

His gestures were at times as controversial as his speeches. Marshal Canrobert refused to give him command of the assault troops at Sebastopol; and, vexed by this refusal, and by the indecision and activity, Prince Napoleon left the Crimea and returned to Paris. His return was a gift to his enemies, who had not forgotten his outspoken comments on fools and place-seekers, his public dislike of the Empress, and his frank independence of the Emperor. Prince Napoleon was accused of cowardice, and his childhood nickname, Plon-Plon, was changed to Craint-plomb.

His private life was as controversial as his public behaviour. His mistresses were legion, and they were flaunted in full view of Paris. When Rachel was dying near Cannes, in 1857, he left a warship, on an official cruise, to visit her. The incident brought a sharp rebuke from the Ministre de la Marine. And yet, perhaps, it showed the fundamental gravity, the real depth of feeling, in the Prince's nature. 'Can they say I have no sense of duty?' he asked. 'I don't always perform the duties I've been given, but I have always fulfilled the ones dictated by my conscience.'[3]

In 1859 he married Princess Clotilde, daughter of Victor-Emmanuel of Savoy. It was a political marriage, contracted to bind France and Italy together. No couple could have been more unsuited to each other than this turbulent prince of thirty-six and this pious princess of sixteen. He was fond of her, he gave her three children, but his marriage did not modify his ways. The Princess, wrote Maxime du Camp, 'was not at all pretty, but she was gentle, extremely virtuous, and devoted to her husband, whom she loved. She was pale and heavy, with thick lips and a far-away expression in her eyes, and she was exceedingly devout.' She followed the Catholic practices in their most minute detail, she was constantly engaged in good works, and she was endlessly charitable and forgiving. 'She was the most saintly woman I have met,' du Camp continued. 'Her husband remained what he liked to be, a bachelor . . . In the mornings there was always some or other petticoat trailing in his private apartments.'[4]

And so Plon-Plon continued to earn the affection of his friends and the harsh criticism of the conventional. He had some of his father's fecklessness and some of his sister's love of the arts, her bluff spontaneity.

Rachel, the actress, in day dress; Prince Napoleon, her admirer, with his wife, Princess Clotilde.

A rehearsal of Le Joueur de flûte *in* le Palais Pompéien. *Gautier is standing in the centre of the stage;*
Émile Augier, the author of the play, is seated on his right.

'Like Napoleon I,' explained Arsène Houssaye, 'he talks in a language which is
picturesque and concise, learned and original; he does not always convince you, but
he always carries you away. That is because he is always honest, even when he revolts
his listeners. He is an enemy of idle fancies, but if he had found himself in power he
would have attempted great things . . . Prince Napoleon is the charmer *par excellence*
when he can control his brusqueness – the brusqueness of a spoilt child. At our first
meeting in 1848 the Prince proved to me that no artist in France knew the history of
art like he did. At the Théâtre-Français, to which he often used to come, we used to
meet each other at all the outstanding performances, especially on the great days of
Rachel. There again the Prince was a sovereign judge . . . Prince Napoleon has loved
classical and modern art with the same passion . . . How often we have lingered on in
his Pompeian palace until the middle of the night, discussing a fresco, a bas-relief or a
bronze! . . . Perhaps those who saw the Roman house lit up, from afar, imagined that
we were enjoying noisy nocturnal revels . . .'[5]

The Villa Diomède, or Palais Pompéien, in the avenue Montaigne, was listed
among the wonders of Second Empire Paris. It was a diligent reconstruction of a
Roman villa. It was there, in 1860, that Gautier and Augier, the critic and the dramatist,
performed in a classical play with Madeleine Brohan, Samson, and Got from the
Comédie-Française. The programme explained that the occasion was the re-opening
of the theatre at Pompeii, 'which had been closed for repairs for 1800 years'. The
entertainment began with Gautier's prologue, *La Femme de Diomède*; and then, recorded

Prince Napoleon's country seat: the château of Meudon. From a drawing by Anastasi.

Mme Baroche, 'the artistes of the Théâtre-Français, naturalised Romans of the Empire, performed *Le Joueur de flûte,* by Émile Augier, a comedy of manners which was rather too Anacreontic . . . Princess Clotilde, wearing Pompeian jewels out of respect for local colour, did not dare to raise her eyes from the ground.'[6] Houssaye maintained that 'the enthusiasm was indescribable . . . And when all the ladies thanked their host, they asked to put on peplums and sign engagements with the Théâtre du Palais Pompéien. It was agreed that I should write a classical comedy: *The Dancing Women of Herculaneum.*'[7]

Prince Napoleon was sometimes obliged to hold grand receptions; otherwise he chose his guests for their wit, distinction and beauty, and society coveted invitations. But while he entertained splendidly at the Palais Pompéien, he rarely lived there; and in time he decided to sell it. In June 1865 the *Daily Telegraph* reported that he had sold it, 'minus all its decorations, for £32,000'. The following March, the same paper recorded that it had now been 'really sold, for about £70,000'.[8] Arsène Houssaye, the Marquis de Quinsonas, the Comte de Beauregard and Jules de Lesseps had combined together to buy it.[9]

Since the death of his father, King Jerome, in 1860, Prince Napoleon had lived increasingly in his official residence, the Palais-Royal. He also had a château at Meudon, ten miles from Paris. The gardens at Meudon had originally been laid out by Le Nôtre; and now the *Daily Telegraph* correspondent recorded that 'up the long avenue which leads to the château we have parterres after parterres of flowers . . .'

The flowers, which owed much to Princess Clotilde's love of gardening, were not the only attraction. The Prince, continued Felix Whitehurst, 'has a great zoological garden. There the bear bores you by his brutal efforts to beg for bread. The elephant packs and unpacks his trunk. The armadillo potters peacefully in his fussy fashion . . .' As for the Prince himself, declared Whitehurst, he was 'admirably instructed on every subject which attracts public attention, with a keen perception of ingenuity, a quick eye for practical utility, a more than ordinary appreciation of art, speaking all languages, of fascinating manners and an unbounded hospitality.'[10]

Whitehurst was fulsome; but even Maxime du Camp, a critical intellectual, who was not a supporter of the Empire, took pleasure in the Prince's company.

'I have dined with him several times in a restaurant, together with George Sand and Gustave Flaubert, of whom he was very fond. The intimacy was complete; there was no subject which was not discussed. As the Prince was a convinced Classic, and Flaubert gloried in being an out-and-out Romantic, they got carried away, they didn't moderate their answers, and you would have thought yourself back in the days of *Hernani* . . . George Sand, as placid as Isis, smiled at such vivacity . . . We spent more than one good evening like this at Magny's or at the Café Anglais. We hardly talked about politics; Ingres, Delacroix, Victor Hugo, Ponsard, Alfred de Musset, Pradier and Guillaume supplied the subjects of the conversation . . .'

Du Camp considered that Prince Napoleon's worst fault was his intemperate language.[11] The Vicomte de Beaumont-Vassy wrote: 'He brought together the elements of a rather compromising intimacy, where free-thinking, absolute atheism, political utopia and social dreams attempted to live happily together. Never has an intelligent man been so dangerous – but, luckily, so unpopular – in our country.'[12] Anna Bicknell, the governess to the Tascher de la Pagerie children, who lived at the Tuileries for nine years, decided that 'his will was despotic, his temper violent and brutal; his tastes were cynically gross, his language coarse beyond what could be imagined . . . He was jealous of the Emperor's pre-eminent position, as of something stolen from himself; but, though in a state of chronic rebellion, he never hesitated to accept all the worldly advantages which the title of "cousin" could obtain for him. The Emperor felt a sort of indulgent affection for Prince Napoleon.'[13]

Plon-Plon remained the *enfant terrible* of the régime, and the most frustrated of the Bonapartes. His gallantry was proverbial, his political outbursts were frequent, his intelligence and dynamism and his love of the arts were not in doubt. But when, at last, the Emperor and the Prince Imperial had died, and, in his late middle age, Prince Napoleon became the head of the family, the Bonapartists could not accept him as their natural leader. He died in exile, in Rome, in 1891, a would-be Emperor, a man who had been frustrated by the accident of birth, but condemned by his personal shortcomings.

Un César déclassé : *Prince Napoleon in old age. From a photograph by Joseph Primoli.*

2 Life at Court

The Tuileries, the old palace of Catherine de' Medici, was the heart of Imperial Paris. For three hundred years it had housed a succession of French sovereigns. It had been built at various times, and re-planned according to the demands of the moment, and it was not a comfortable place. Several of the large galleries had been divided into apartments for the numerous children of Louis-Philippe; these apartments were separated by windowless, ill-ventilated corridors, lit by smoking oil-lamps day and night. Some lofty salons had been divided, horizontally, into two claustrophobic rooms with low ceilings. Anna Bicknell's first impression was 'strangely lugubrious and funereal.' She added that, 'during the greater part of the Emperor's reign, there was not even water put in, and the daily supply of the inmates was brought up in pails to the various apartments. The sanitary arrangements and drainage were very bad; in the upper regions inhabited by the servants the air was absolutely pestilential.'[1]

There were extensive alterations to provide the Empress Eugénie with an adequate décor. Her apartment was on the first floor. The Emperor's was directly underneath. In 1858 the Emperor asked the architect, Lefuel, to design the private apartments, and in 1860 the furnishing and decoration were finished. The private apartments, and some of the state apartments, were to be destroyed by the Communards in 1871.

When the Second Empire came into being, the Emperor had to create a Court. He himself had simple tastes, but he saw that the new régime must conciliate political extremes: it must proclaim its democratic principles, and it must provide a décor for the aristocratic and the conventional. He was still uncertain of his prestige, and he saw that he must enhance it with the outward signs of majesty.

General Comte Fleury, his equerry, found the regulations which had governed the Court of Napoleon I; he modernised them, and his version was accepted in principle. Napoleon III restored the pomp and ceremony of his uncle's Empire; and such were the brilliance and the vitality of the age that this, the last French Court, was among the most resplendent ever known.

An official reception at the Tuileries. The Cent-Gardes may be seen lining the stairs.

Some of the Imperial Household performed general services, some belonged to the Households of the Emperor, the Empress, and, in time, the Prince Imperial. The general services included those of the Chaplain-in-Chief and the Grand Marshal of the Palace. There were also a Grand Chamberlain, a Grand Master of Ceremonies, and the Master of the Horse and the Master of the Hunt. All these were under the jurisdiction of the Minister for the Imperial Household.[2]

The revenues of the Civil List were twenty-five million francs, and a further two million from the produce of the Forest of Compiègne. One million three hundred thousand francs were divided into allowances for the imperial princes and princesses; six million were allotted for the expenses of the Imperial Household. These included the salaries of the equerries and the ladies-in-waiting, the Emperor's secretariat and the medical officers, the cost of music for the chapel, entertainment, food and linen and additional services. Twelve million francs were set aside every year for the decoration or improvement of the imperial palaces, libraries, museums, factories, estates and forests. Six million were reserved for charities. The Emperor paid a hundred thousand francs for his box at the Opéra. The Cent-Gardes cost between three and four hundred thousand francs a year.

This élite cavalry corps was created by a decree of 24 March 1854. L'Escadron des Cent-Gardes à cheval – as it was officially called – was to consist of eleven officers and one hundred and thirty-seven men. In 1858 its strength was raised to two hundred. The Cent-Gardes enjoyed both social and military distinction. They did not line processional routes, they simply provided a ceremonial guard for palace duty, and a bodyguard for the Emperor. Indeed, until 1858, one of their officers slept outside the Emperor's room every night. In 1870, at the time of the Victor Noir affair, when anti-imperial feeling was running strong, the officers of the Cent-Gardes asked to

resume this duty; the Emperor refused their request. Apart from Napoleon III, who received a distinctive salute, only foreign sovereigns and princes of the Imperial Family were entitled to honours from the Cent-Gardes (a rule which enraged at least one Marshal of France).

The Cent-Gardes were chosen for their physique. Recruits had to be at least six feet tall. In their sky-blue tunics, white breeches, and black top-boots, their helmets with flowing horsehair manes, their breastplates of burnished steel, they lined the staircase on gala occasions, and stood at statuesque and magnificent attention beside the throne. These military Leviathans symbolised the glory of the régime. They were disbanded by a decree of 1 October 1870: within a month of the fall of the Second Empire.[3]

The Grand Marshal of the Palace was the bluff but competent Maréchal Vaillant (who later combined the office with that of Minister for the Imperial Household). He had the command of the Emperor's military household, and he was in charge of all the palaces, their maintenance and decoration, the food, the heating and lighting. He was responsible for allotting apartments to palace functionaries. Under his jurisdiction was the Adjutant-General of the palace, General Rollin, who controlled the administration of the palaces. The general was responsible for the food and wine which were served at the Emperor's table; and imperial guests sometimes suffered from his conservative tastes.

The fact was substantiated by more than one critic. However, since the Emperor and Empress were far from being gourmets, there was little hope of improvement; it would have been surprising had their table been distinguished. As Boulenger wrote in *Les Tuileries sous le Second Empire*: 'The cooking was the simple, plentiful and slightly dated cooking of a conscientious hotel.'[4]

Albert Verly, the son of the colonel commanding the Cent-Gardes, was later to record an illuminating occasion. At one imperial dinner, '. . . the turbot had just been served (with hollandaise sauce, of course), and the sauce-boats were beginning to circulate; but, thanks to some mistake by a cook, the condiment sent up was vanilla custard . . . The Emperor was the first to become aware of the mistake; . . . and he immediately decreed that turbot with vanilla custard was delicious, and that the hollandaise sauce would go with the pudding.'[5]

Under the jurisdiction of Maréchal Vaillant came not only the Adjutant-General of the Palace, but the First Marshal of the Household, who was in charge of the furniture. There were also four Prefects of the Palace, who were responsible for internal administration. They wore a wine-red uniform with white waistcoat and white breeches. The Grand Chamberlain, the Duc de Bassano, was responsible for all the ceremonies and entertainments. *Partant pour la Syrie*, composed by the Emperor's mother, Queen Hortense, became a sort of national anthem during his reign. He himself had no love of music, but he particularly disliked this tune, which followed him wherever he went. The First Chamberlain, Comte Bacciochi, supervised the imperial theatres, music in the chapel, and palace concerts. (It was also Bacciochi, so tradition says, who arranged more personal pleasures for the Emperor.) At first there were eight chamberlains, finally there were twelve. They wore scarlet tail-coats, solidly embroidered in gold; on the left tail, attached by a bow of green and gold lace, was a small gold key. In the evening, like all the officers of the Imperial Household, the Grand Chamberlain and his subordinates wore a blue uniform with a velvet collar.

The Grand Master of Ceremonies was the Duc de Cambacérès, who had been a page to the great Napoleon. He wore a violet uniform, embroidered in gold, as did the two masters of ceremonies beneath him. One of these, the Baron Feuillet de Conches, was responsible for introducing ambassadors into the presence. He performed his task with urbanity, but – unlike most other members of the Household – he agreed to continue it under the Third Republic, during the presidency of Thiers.

The Master of the Horse, for the greater part of the Second Empire, was General Comte Fleury; under him were the equerries – nearly all cavalry officers – who wore their green-and-gold uniform with particular style. Among them were the Marquis de Caux, who later married Adelina Patti, and – in the last years of the Empire – the Vicomte Pernéty, son-in-law of Baron Haussmann. The duties of the Master of the Horse included the supervision of the Imperial stables and carriages. The most famous of the sixty horses in the stables were Buckingham, which the Emperor rode at the Battle of Magenta, and Ajax, which he rode at Solferino. The state coaches dated from the days of Napoleon and Charles X, and they had been restored by order of Napoleon III. The oldest was *la voiture du Sacre*, which had taken Napoleon to Notre-Dame for his coronation. *La voiture du Baptême* had first been used at the baptism of the King of Rome. The other coaches were Topaze, Turquoise, Victoire, Brillante and Opale. For less formal occasions, there were twelve barouches, eight landaus, a park phaeton and a *coureuse*. Seven berlins for everyday use were kept in constant readiness at the Louvre.

The Emperor's personal Household was largely composed of his military Household and his secretariat. The first was under the control of the Grand Marshal, and included the Emperor's aide-de-camp, his orderly officers, and the Cent-Gardes. For most of the reign, the Emperor's secretariat was under the direction of his *chef de cabinet*, the unshakably discreet Constant Mocquard. The Empress's Household was supervised by the Grand Master, General Comte Tascher de la Pagerie; under him were a First Chamberlain, four assistant chamberlains, a private secretary, M. Damas-Hinard, and a librarian. The Grand Mistress of the Empress's Household was the Princesse d'Essling; she arrived at the Tuileries every day, at one o'clock, to take orders. She attended the Empress on all official occasions. The Duchesse de Bassano bore the title of lady-in-waiting; then came the *dames du palais*, among them Mme Carette. Her *Souvenirs intimes de la Cour des Tuileries* were to be a roseate but valuable memorial to everyday life at the heart of the Second Empire.

Two members of the Emperor's Household: LEFT *the Grand Master of Ceremonies, the Duc de Cambacérès, and* RIGHT *the Grand Chamberlain, the Duc de Bassano.*

On New Year's Eve there was always a dinner at the Tuileries for the senior members of the Household. Next morning the drummers of the Garde Nationale would parade in front of the Pavillon de l'Horloge, and give the Emperor a serenade. The Emperor, in the full-dress uniform of a general, would make his appearance on the balcony. Then mass was said; and, at one o'clock, the Diplomatic Corps were received. Next day, the Emperor received the officers of the Garde Nationale and the Army; in the evening, he and the Empress would receive the ladies of the Diplomatic Corps and the Household, and ladies who had been presented at Court.

Between January and Lent, Napoleon and Eugénie would give four grand balls, to which four or five thousand guests would be invited. Some twenty years after the fall of the Empire, Mme Carette recalled these imperial evenings with emotion. Sometimes she had slipped into the gallery which ran round the Salle des Maréchaux, and she had gazed on the fairy-tale scene.

'The gilded cupola of the ceiling was supported by groups of caryatids and trophies. The panels were decorated with portraits of the twelve Marshals of the Empire, in their splendid uniforms; the tall windows were hung with red velvet draperies with golden fringes, and they seemed tiny openings in the enormous room.

'The variety and elegance of the men's dress ... gave these balls a character of their own. Many officers wore white knee-breeches with their uniform. The Diplomatic Corps, in full dress, displayed the costumes of every nation: there were English, Russians, Palikars, Hungarians and Persians, some of them bedecked with embroideries and decorations, others dressed with sombre severity. There were the uniforms of all the armies of the world, even the Chinese, whose sabres must not be touched with a fingertip – this, it seems, is a dishonour for them – unless you want to see them disembowel themselves.'[6]

At Carnival time, there was generally a fancy-dress ball at the palace; invitations were restricted to those who had been presented. They danced to the music of Waldteufel, Strauss, and Offenbach. At the first great Tuileries ball of 1869, the consumption of champagne reached a total which *La Presse* did not dare to publish.[7]

During Lent, there was no dancing at Court, but there were four concerts, organised by Bacciochi, and by the composer Auber, who was chapel-master at the Tuileries. After Easter, social life began again, but in a more informal fashion, and the Empress invited the younger generation, who were not seen on official occasions, to her *petits lundis*. Mme Carette remembered that 'there were at most five or six hundred invitations.'[8]

When Napoleon III was in residence at the Tuileries, a tricolour flag flew over the Pavillon de l'Horloge. The Emperor himself would probably be found in his study; and this, the room from which the Second Empire was ruled, was a room of great austerity. On one wall was a huge map of Paris, presented by the Conseil municipal, on which he followed the transformation of his capital with Baron Haussmann. Under the map was a massive filing cabinet; it attested his methodical nature. In the middle

ABOVE Au rendez-vous des grisettes: *the Empress and her ladies-in-waiting. From the painting by Winterhalter.* BELOW *The heart of the Second Empire: the Emperor's study at the Tuileries. From the watercolour by Fortuné de Fournier.* OVERLEAF *The reception of the Siamese Ambassadors at Fontainebleau, 27 June 1861. From the painting by Gérôme.*

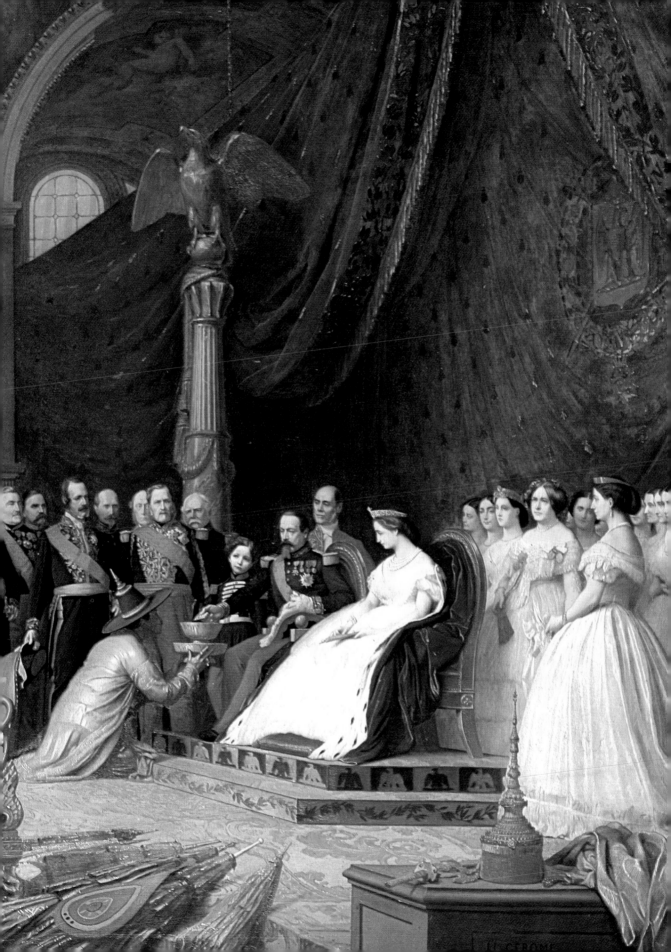

of the room was a desk. Its leaves were always pulled out, and covered with papers. The only ornaments on it were a candlestick and a few family photographs. The Emperor's chair was inconvenient for writing, and it was quilted in green plush, like a chair in some provincial hotel. There was a deep chair, upholstered in leather, for visitors with whom he wanted to talk at his leisure. The visitor would usually find him standing by his desk, his right hand on his dossiers as if he was impressing a seal on them. It was this familiar attitude which Flandrin recorded in his portrait.

In the Salon du Chambellan, waiting for their imperial wearer, were a number of overcoats to suit different weathers and occasions; and on a table lay the Emperor's hat and gloves, and the cane with a head in the shape of a golden eagle: the cane which he always carried when he went out. On a chair lay the tartan rug which an usher would take to the carriage; Napoleon III felt the cold very much, and always wrapped the rug round his knees.

In the morning, he usually wore a dark blue coat and waistcoat, and grey trousers; he wore the ribbons of the Légion-d'honneur and the Médaille militaire in his button-hole. In the evening, he changed into evening dress, with the star of the Légion-d'honneur on his coat. For concerts and official dinners, he wore a tail-coat with black knee-breeches and silk stockings, or, if he needed to 'dress' more, the blue uniform of his Household, with white breeches and white stockings. On gala occasions he wore the uniform of a general of division, with the scarlet ribbon and the star of the Légion-d'honneur. On such occasions, he played his part with diligence, from the moment when Léon Cuxac, his first *valet de chambre*, helped him to put on his uniform. He did not show any satisfaction at being at the centre of power. When he walked towards his throne, he sometimes seemed like a prisoner of distinction who had resigned himself to his fate.

Every night he was reminded of his destiny. Beside his bed, in a casket, was a golden capsule ringed with jewels. In the centre, between two hollowed sapphires, was a fragment of the true Cross. It had been found on a chain round the neck of Charlemagne in 1169, and it had been given to Napoleon by the clergy of Aix-la-Chapelle in 1804. It was said to assure the empire to its possessor.

Visitors who were to be received by the Empress would go to a staircase near the Pavillon de l'Horloge. This led to the ushers' room. There were always three in waiting; they wore maroon coats, embroidered in silver. The ushers would announce the visitor's arrival to the chamberlains or ladies-in-waiting in the adjoining room, le Salon Vert. In this engaging room, green woodpeckers and parrots were painted above the doors, and painted foliage ran riot round the doors and windows. A large mirror at the back of the room reflected the Tuileries garden.

'The garden was so beautiful then,' remembered Anna Bicknell, 'with its groves of horse-chestnut trees . . . The foliage of the splendid old trees formed an impenetrable canopy overhead, and the great central avenue leading to the Champs-Élysées, with the Arc de Triomphe in the distance, was bordered in May by a gigantic wall of

A gala ball at the Tuileries in 1867. In this painting by Tetar van Elven,
the Empress is seen with the Czar of Russia; Napoleon III stands behind,
with the King of Prussia.

blossoms on each side. It is impossible, at the present time, to form any idea of what the garden was then, with the splendid palace in the background, the walks bordered by orange-trees, with their sweet perfume, the well-kept parterres, the terraces, the statues, and the elegantly dressed crowd listening to the military band.'[9]

From le Salon Vert the visitor was taken to await his audience in le Salon Rose, where the pink hangings on the walls cast a roseate light, and, on the pink-toned ceiling, Chaplin had painted the Triumph of Flora. The goddess – a tacit compliment – had been given the features of the Empress; and, beside her, an allegorical figure bore the infant Prince Imperial cradled in flowers.

From le Salon Rose the visitor finally passed into le Salon Bleu. It was here that the Empress received him. The room was decorated in tones of blue, skilfully orchestrated; and over the doors were portrait-medallions of the Empress's friends, among them the Comtesse Walewski and the Duchesse de Morny. All three rooms were cluttered with Sèvres and lapis-lazuli vases, bronzes and statuettes; they were lit by great rock-crystal chandeliers.

After le Salon Bleu came the Empress's study; and in this private, somewhat bourgeois room, with its green-striped walls, the Emperor would come and smoke his eternal cigarettes, and, in time, the Prince Imperial would play. It was a refuge from official life. The study led into an ante-room which, in turn, led into a dressing-room. Here was Eugénie's simple bath; on the dressing-table was the silver-gilt toilet set which had once belonged to Queen Hortense. Eugénie's dressing had been very much simplified, for above this room, explained Miss Bicknell, were several rooms, 'entirely surrounded by wardrobes in plain oak, with sliding panels, in which all the various articles of clothing were arranged in perfect order. Four lay-figures, exactly measured to fit the dresses worn by the Empress, were used to diminish the necessity of too much trying on, and also to prepare her toilet for the day. Orders were given through a speaking-pipe in the dressing-room, and the figure came down on a sort of lift through an opening in the ceiling, dressed in all that the Empress was about to wear.'[10]

Eugénie's bedroom was decorated in oppressive, sumptuous style; the bed, on its dais, hung with heavy curtains, lit by a monumental chandelier, was unpleasantly theatrical. Next to the bedroom was a little oratory. It was here, at seven o'clock on the morning of 4 September 1870, that she heard mass for the last time at the palace.

In this apartment, Eugénie lived as simply as she could. When she was not making an official appearance, she generally wore a plain black dress. She has often been criticised for her extravagance, but in fact the Emperor used to reproach her for her simple tastes, and those who knew her emphasise that she was not fond of clothes. Nor was she particular about the fate of her wardrobe. Her ladies-in-waiting earned comfortable incomes by selling the cast-off dresses which she gave them, often to buyers in America.

Eugénie rarely went to bed before one o'clock in the morning, and she usually rose before eight. She often gave the first audience of the day to her hairdresser, Leroy,

The Imperial Family in the late 1850s.

'a stout, middle-aged man,' remembered Miss Bicknell, 'who, when he chose to come, rushed in like a conqueror, waving his comb, dressed in a brown linen oversuit, ordering the servants about.'[11] On other occasions, she might give her first audience to one of her couturiers. Princess Metternich, the wife of the Austrian Ambassador, had recommended Worth to the Empress, and after 1864 he made all her evening dresses. Mme Laferrière, who had been launched since 1860, made her morning dresses, Félicie made her coats, Mme Virot or Mme Lebel made her hats. They all came to the Tuileries to show her their sketches, and she chose with little hesitation. Incidentally, she once boasted that very few of her dresses, even her dresses for state occasions, had cost her more than 1500 francs, and that she had had them mended, and sometimes even cut out and made up at the palace.

After the couturier's visit, Eugénie would see her husband and son; and then she would summon her secretary, and examine the latest petitions which had been sent to her. Then she would give her orders, and settle down to her correspondence. She wrote every day to her mother, but her Readers helped her with her less personal letters. They also attended her when she paid her morning visit to some hospital or charitable institution. If she stayed at the Tuileries, she would read, or paint in her studio.

After *déjeuner*, she returned to her work. Then she went for her carriage-drive. An equerry cantered beside the daumont; the senior lady-in-waiting sat on Eugénie's left, and they gossiped gaily until they returned to the palace to dress for dinner.

The Emperor himself had to have a more flexible routine; but, as far as possible, he kept to a plan. Every morning, when he had dressed, he would ride to the Bois de Boulogne, attended by an aide-de-camp and an equerry. Then came his audiences, and his meetings with ministers and officers of state. He used to work for most of the afternoon. If he had any leisure, he would read books on archaeology (his enthusiasm helped to make his reign a golden age for the archaeologist). When he went out in the afternoon, he would generally drive his own phaeton, with an aide-de-camp sitting beside him and two grooms sitting rigidly, arms akimbo, on the back seat. He might go to inspect the new artesian well at Passy, or the houses being built in the boulevard Malesherbes. His departure and return were heralded by a roll of drums, and spectators at the palace gates would cry: 'Vive l'Empereur!'. Napoleon III, unmoved, would touch the brim of his hat. When someone expressed their surprise at his cool response, he gave a disenchanted smile, and said: 'I know mankind.'[12]

Miss Bicknell remembered that when he went out, informally, like this, '. . . . an unpretending coupé or brougham was always seen to follow at a short distance; this contained the chief of the police attached to the Emperor's person, whose myrmidons were scattered along the way. There was one, especially, a Corsican named Alessandri, who was devoted to the Emperor with a sort of canine fidelity, and was always near him when he went out; so that to the initiated the presence of Alessandri was symptomatic of the approach of the sovereign.'[13] There was no lack of security precautions. Besides the soldiers at the palace, there was 'a strong force of detectives always standing about the principal doors,' and, at fancy-dress balls, all the guests who were wearing masks had to remove them for a moment before they entered the ballroom. 'Detectives stood about the entrance and mingled with the guests; many of them were dressed as attendants, and carried trays of refreshments through the rooms.'[14]

Déjeuner, at the Tuileries, was originally set for half-past eleven; it was later served at noon. The Emperor and Empress ate alone in the Salon Louis XIV. Dinner was served at seven o'clock in the early years of the Empire; it was later served at half-past seven. Napoleon III would usually have a brief talk with his wife before they made their appearance in the Salon des Tapisseries (later the Salon d'Apollon). There the Emperor's aide-de-camp was waiting, with his chamberlain, his equerry, his orderly officers, the prefect of the palace, the Empress's equerry (if he had escorted her during the day), and the two ladies-in-waiting. The women wore full evening dress, and the men wore tail-coats and decorations.[15]

When dinner was served, a maître-d'hôtel would inform the prefect of the palace, who would make a low bow to the Emperor. Then Napoleon III would give his arm to his wife, and, preceded by the prefect, they would go in to dinner. Behind them came the Prince Imperial who, from the age of eight, was allowed to leave his goldfish and his magic lantern, and to dine with his parents. After the Prince Imperial came the aide-de-camp and the Emperor's chamberlain, escorting the ladies-in-waiting. Joseph Primoli, one of the younger generation of Bonapartes, found the family dinner as artificial as a play by Marivaux.

The Court remained theatrical. At the end of the Empire, an exotic figure would sometimes be seen behind the Empress: this was Scander, her Nubian attendant. He stood there, in gold-embroidered robes, as if he had swaggered out of some eighteenth-century painting. The table itself hardly suggested informality. In the middle was a Louis Seize silver basket, full of flowers from Bourjon, the Court florist; at each end were Louis Seize silver candelabra, and here and there, on silver stands, were plates of petits-fours, compotiers, and dishes of fruit. On other stands were the two main dishes and the four *entrées* which were soon removed to be carved. There was the same ceremony for the two *rôtis* and the four *entremets* which followed. The soup plates and dessert plates were silver, or silver-plated. However, when Primoli compared a Tuileries dinner to a comedy by Marivaux, he was unduly flattering. Nearly half a century later, Caroline Murat would look back with distaste on those Sunday dinners, strictly confined to members of the family. 'Oh! the boredom of those gatherings! . . . There was no thought except as to who should have precedence – a struggle which was renewed every Sunday during the fifty-two weeks of the year.'[16] Boulenger, in his book on Court life, said that the conversation was dreary. The Empress – who was not a professional sovereign – hardly made any effort; the Emperor attempted to talk, but there was little to say. Politics, and all delicate subjects, were forbidden in front of the servants, and art and literature were not yet socially acceptable, and, anyway, nobody knew very much about them.

After the more intimate dinners, the Emperor would turn the handle of a mechanical piano while the guests attempted the latest dance. Sometimes he suggested a game of lotto. But all too often the evening would drag on in the salon, in the enervating heat emitted by four chandeliers and a fire. The Empress talked trivialities with her ladies-in-waiting; the Emperor played patience. The men talked to each other in low voices. At ten o'clock, to the general relief, the servants would bring in tea.[17]

But, whatever the tedium of lesser occasions, State occasions were dazzling. Chroniclers long remembered how the Emperor had received the Siamese Ambassadors, 'a set of fellows in long silk dressing-gowns, looking as if they had been moulded in greenish chocolate.'[18] The Emperor and Empress were constantly entertaining foreign sovereigns: the Queen of Haiti, the King of Spain and the Emperor of Austria. In 1855 Queen Victoria paid a state visit to France. 'I am,' she wrote, 'DELIGHTED, ENCHANTED, AMUSED, and INTERESTED ... The Emperor has done wonders for Paris ... Everything is beautifully MONTÉ at Court.'[19] In March 1864, the Emperor gave a banquet in honour of the Archduke Maximilian and his wife, soon to be the unhappy Emperor and Empress of Mexico. The whole imperial family attended, and after dinner Adelina Patti sang airs from *La Sonnambula.* Auber was commissioned to write the Mexican national anthem.[20] In June 1867, when most of the sovereigns of Europe came to see the International Exhibition in Paris, Napoleon III gave a ball for the Czar of Russia and the King of Prussia.

'It would be difficult to describe the prodigious appearance of the Tuileries garden last night,' observed *La Presse* on 12 June. 'Long garlands of light in white glass globes, thirty thousand gas-lamps illuminating the private garden ... The fountains and pools were lit up by hundreds of electric lights of different colours. All the trees were lit up by luminous balloons, and ... seemed to be aflame with Bengal lights. A huge temporary staircase was erected on either side of the balcony of the Salle des Maréchaux, and it connected the palace with the garden. Dancing began at eleven o'clock, under the masterly baton of Strauss, and it continued until three o'clock in the morning.'[21] In 1869 came a banquet for the Queen of the Netherlands, followed by a performance of François Coppée's *Le Passant.* Early in 1870 there was a dinner for seventy in honour of the Archduke Albert of Austria; and afterwards, in le Salon Blanc, there was a reception for *les intimes,* to which three hundred guests had been invited. Christine Nilsson sang, and the young Sarah Bernhardt recited from Musset.[22]

While the Tuileries remained their official residence in Paris, the Emperor and Empress enjoyed four other palaces near by. If Versailles was little used, Saint-Cloud, forty minutes from Paris, was a familiar habitation. The Court usually moved to Saint-Cloud in May or in June. The palace was almost a retreat. There was little etiquette, and few people were received in audience. The Emperor 'was never so happy as when he could get away from Paris and be in the open air. I have heard him say,' wrote Dr Evans, 'that he would have liked nothing better than to be a farmer. He was

Two pictures of a vanished palace: ABOVE *the Empress's dressing-room at Saint-Cloud, from a watercolour by Fortuné de Fournier, and* BELOW *Saint-Cloud, by Pierre-Eugène Grandsire. A painting from the Souvenir Albums presented to Queen Victoria after her visit to France in 1855.*

pleased to see the broad fields, and orchards, and the gardens; he would have been still more pleased could he have cultivated them or laid them out.'[23] At Saint-Cloud, the Emperor and the Prince Imperial played with the model railway in the private park. The Empress drove round the neighbourhood with only a groom in attendance. Near Saint-Cloud was a small country house called Villeneuve-l'Étang, which the Emperor had given her; and there, in imitation of her heroine, Marie-Antoinette, Eugénie had set up a dairy.

Saint-Cloud was to be destroyed during the Franco-Prussian War. The Prussians claimed that it was a French shell, fired from Mont-Valérien on 13 October 1870, which fell on the Emperor's bedroom; it began such a blaze that the palace could not be saved. The explanation seems improbable. Despite this so-called inferno, the Prussians were able to pillage the palace; their commanding officer, Strauss, told all his subordinates to choose a memento of Saint-Cloud before he gave the order to burn what was left. The blackened walls and twisted metal, the roofless state apartments, were finally demolished in 1891.[24]

But, whatever its charm, Saint-Cloud was not the Emperor's favourite palace. Napoleon III always felt particularly drawn to the Renaissance palace which his uncle had called 'the proper dwelling for kings'. During the Second Empire, the Court went into residence at Fontainebleau every June, and stayed there for a month or six weeks. If Saint-Cloud offered an escape into informality, Fontainebleau was a glittering social centre.

When the Emperor and Empress arrived for the summer, the town was all astir. The Garde Impériale were drawn up in the courtyards of the palace, the military and civic dignitaries prepared to receive their Sovereigns. Then the drums rolled, the bugles blared, and a salvo of gunfire announced that the imperial train had stopped at the station. Napoleon III stepped out of his personal carriage, and led his wife to their waiting daumont. Escorted by the Cent-Gardes, they drove to the palace.

They were followed, within the first few days, by the flower of French society: a Winterhalter procession of women, wearing the latest creations of Worth, bringing trunks of majestic crinolines and fairy-tale collections of jewels. Guests at Fontainebleau were given freedom of movement; but most of them enjoyed boating on the lake. It was full of carp, one of which was said to date from the days of François I. A whole flotilla of small craft was constantly at the guests' disposal. There was a caique from the Bosphorus, with its Turkish boatman; there was a gondola from Venice, reserved for the Empress, complete with a gondolier from the Piazza San Marco. There was even a frigate, with a crew of two from the imperial navy, flying the standard of the heir to the throne; it was just large enough to carry its passenger. A tiny steam-ship was always ready to take the guests in tow; and, on fine evenings, it took them to a miniature island at the far end of the lake. Here, in a kiosk, in the peaceful summer weather, Prosper Mérimée would recite poetry. Octave Feuillet, the novelist and dramatist, who was librarian at Fontainebleau, recorded a June evening in 1868. 'A steam-ship

Fontainebleau: the Cour de la Fontaine and the famous Étang des Carpes. On the left is the kiosk in which Mérimée recited poetry to his fellow-guests.

was chuffing on the lake, among the little sailing-boats. Some of the ladies had embarked. Night was falling, but in splendour, and what with the boats, the dresses, the lights reflected in the water, and the sombre verdure in the background, it looked a real Court festivity.' The palace itself was magnificent, but strangely melancholy; and Feuillet found it so as he took an evening walk in the park, 'under the old trees which were contemporaries of the Valois. It was a little sad and solemn, and yet quite sweet, with the smell of new-mown hay and especially of the lime-tree flowers which saturated the air.'[25]

When the hunting season came, the courtyards of the palace would be filled with impatient hounds and horses; and, in the evening, the whole neighbourhood would come to watch the traditional climax of the hunt, when the hounds devoured the stag's head by flaming torchlight. Sometimes there were excursions into the surrounding countryside; there were picnic parties, and the guests danced, in the open air, to the music of some military band. There were visits to the studios of local painters, like Rosa Bonheur, and Decamps, and one day the Empress decided to visit Père Ganne's inn at Barbizon: the headquarters of the rustic school which produced such artists as Millet and Rousseau. The old tavern-keeper was nearly struck dumb by the honour. The evenings at Fontainebleau passed in charades, parlour games and lotteries, or in dancing to the music of a barrel-organ. It was hardly the Tiberian depravity which was condemned by republican journalists.[26]

In the first days of September, the Imperial Family moved to their seaside home at Biarritz. The Villa Eugénie had been built to the Emperor's designs; it combined princely proportions with English comfort and simplicity. Years later, when the Empire had fallen, it became a casino.

Biarritz was sometimes known as Eugénieville; and indeed it owed its popularity to the Empress. Eugénie welcomed informality; and she was fond of the place, which was so near the frontier of her native Spain. Late in September 1867, Felix Whitehurst, of the *Daily Telegraph*, visited Biarritz for the first time. He found it 'wonderful – a lovely sunset, a calm sea, music, the perfume of heliotrope, the absence of noise . . .' A few days later, he sent his readers a detailed and appreciative account of this Second Empire resort.

'Twenty years ago no Frenchman would have believed that this little Basque village of Biarritz could ever become the seat of an Imperial Court . . . Yet on this very day it really seems to have advanced to such an eminence . . . The Villa Eugénie is a square, unadorned, not to say ugly building, situated on a slope which leads down to the sea; the background is covered with a sort of juniper, and there are a few dwarf trees . . . The look-out from the villa is grand, and in wild weather it must be a splendid spectacle to see waves break over the stupendous rocks . . . It may amuse some to know that the land on which the Villa Eugénie is built was a waste half reclaimed from the sea, and that His Majesty bought the fee simple for £12. Just beyond the villa to the east is a model farm, worked by Louis-Napoleon, proprietor, *rentier*, and Emperor . . . The very streets of Biarritz are lined with sycamores, under the leaves of which Biarritz in hot weather lives and breathes, but does not move. A more picturesque little place I have never seen . . . Twenty years ago, not many people knew that there existed on the shore of the Bay of Biscay a little sardine-fishing village. In twenty years more it may perchance be the Brighton of the Continent . . . The Court lives quite a primitive life, going on excursions, eating picnics, and walking about the town.'[27]

On about 10 October, the Court would tear themselves from Biarritz and return to Saint-Cloud. On 10 or 15 November, they would move for a month or so to the palace of Compiègne.

Compiègne became a feature of social life in the Second Empire. There were five *séries*, or house-parties, every season, and some eighty guests attended each of them. The formal programme for these *séries* varied very little. It generally included a hunt or shoot, a banquet and a ball, and a visit to the medieval castle of Pierrefonds, which Viollet-le-Duc was restoring. The visitors included foreign royalty, statesmen, diplomats, generals, artists and men of letters: all who were distinguished in society. Pasteur arrived with a number of frogs: presumably he intended to entertain his fellow-guests with scientific experiments. Unfortunately the frogs escaped from their boxes, and scattered in all directions. 'It was like one of the plagues of Egypt,' wrote Bouchot, in *Les Élégances du Second Empire*.[28]

Octave Feuillet gave more cheerful accounts of Compiègne in his letters home to his

A hunt at Compiègne. The Emperor and Empress may be seen on horseback in the foreground.

wife. He delighted in his room, overlooking the park, 'the long avenues lost in the mornings in a golden, radiant mist, the marble gods and goddesses.' He enjoyed his conversation with his fellow-guests. 'I've spent the morning with Mérimée, whom I found in bed,' went one of his letters. 'I finally broke the envelope of ice in which he usually seems to be crystallised; and, after we had chatted for three-quarters of an hour, we parted from each other on really cordial terms.'[29]

The most vivid and engaging description of Compiègne was written by an American socialite, Lillie Moulton. She was the wife of Charles Moulton, a banker's son who was living in Paris, and she was renowned for her beauty and for her singing. On 22 November 1866, she reported excitedly to a friend:

'Dear A.,

'You know it has always been my wish to see the life at Compiègne, and behold, here I am! . . .

'We received the invitation twelve days ago . . . This gave me plenty of time to order all my dresses, wraps, and everything else that I needed for this visit of a week to royalty.

'I was obliged to have about twenty dresses, eight day costumes (counting my travel-ling suit), the green cloth dress for the hunt, which I was told was absolutely necessary, seven ball dresses, five gowns for tea . . .

'We arrived at the St Lazare Station at 2.30, as indicated on the invitation.

'We found the Vicomte Walsh (the Chamberlain of the Emperor) waiting to show the guests where the train was. It would have been rather difficult not to have seen it, as it was the only one in the station, and was marked "Extra and Imperial".

'There were several large saloon carriages with large, comfortable *fauteuils*, and some tables covered with newspapers and *journaux illustrés* to beguile the time . . .

'We actually flew over land and dale. I never travelled so fast in all my life; but then I had never been in an Imperial train before . . .

'The Grand Chamberlain received us with pleasant cordiality and waved us towards a *huissier*, who, dressed in a black livery with heavy chains round his neck, looked very important. He, in his turn, passed us on to the particular valet allotted to us, who pompously and with great dignity showed us the way to our apartments . . .

'My bedroom is furnished in white and green with a delightful *chaise-longue* and large *fauteuils* . . . I made my toilette in a maze of excitement . . .

'On leaving our apartment, a little before seven, we found the lackey waiting to show us the way to the *Grande Salle des Fêtes*, and we followed his plump white calves through the long corridors, arriving at last in the salon where all the company was to assemble . . .

'The Grand Chamberlain glanced round the room with an all-comprehensive look, and seemed intuitively to know when we were all present. He then disappeared into His Majesty's private salon.

'There was an ominous hush, a flutter of agitation, a stiff attitude of expectancy, the guests arranging themselves according to their own consciousness of their rank; and presently the doors of the salon were quietly opened and Their Majesties entered . . .

'The Empress looked lovely. She wore a beautiful gown, a white-spangled tulle, with a superb tiara of diamonds, and on her neck a collier of huge pearls.

'The Emperor was in white *culottes courtes*, white silk stockings and low shoes, as were the rest of the gentlemen. He wore the ribbon of the Légion-d'honneur, and on his left breast the star of the same.

'The Grand Maréchal, waiting his opportunity, approached His Majesty, who went up to the Empress and gave her his arm. The Grand Maréchal then led the way slowly and with due stateliness to the banqueting hall . . .

'We marched in procession through the long gallery, trying to prevent ourselves from slipping on the waxed floor, and passed between the splendid Cent-Gardes, who lined both sides of the entire length of this enormous hall . . .

'There the men stood, motionless as statues, staring solidly before them, without so much as a stolen side-glance at the beauty and elegance passing before their eyes . . .'[30]

The description was continued, ten years later, by Émile Zola, in his novel *Son Excellence Eugène Rougon*.

'The entrance into the dining-room was made with great ceremony. Five chandeliers were blazing over the long table, lighting up the different pieces of the silver surtout . . . The silver-plate set a chain of silver moons along the edge of the cloth; while the sides of the dish-warmers, in which the burning candles were reflected, the glasses streaming with flecks of fire, the dishes of fruit and the vases of vivid pink flowers, made the imperial table a splendour, the shimmering light of which filled the vast room. Through the double doors, which were opened wide, the procession flowed in . . . It was an almost loving approach, an epicurean arrival in a setting of luxury, light and warmth, like a sensual bath in which the musky scents of the clothes mingled with a slight smell of game, enhanced by a touch of lemon. When, on the threshold, they came face to face with the splendid vista of the table, a military band, concealed in a nearby gallery, greeted them with a fanfare, like the signal for some fairy-tale festivity.'[31]

'There must have been about one hundred persons seated at the table,' wrote Mrs Moulton. 'I never saw such a tremendous long stretch of white linen . . .

'When Their Majesties had finished they rose, and everyone followed their example. All the chairs were drawn from under you, *tant pis* if you were in the act of eating a pear and had not yet washed your fingers . . .

'On our return to the salon the magnificent Cent-Gardes stood just as we had left them, and I wondered if they had unbent for a moment all the time we had been at dinner . . .

'Waldteufel, *le fabricant de valses*, put himself at the piano, . . . and played some of his charming *entraînante* music . . . Waldteufel has an apartment in the town of Compiègne, where he fabricates his waltzes by day and comes here to play them by night . . .'[32]

Next day, at dinner, in that winter of 1866, Mrs Moulton sat next to Théophile Gautier. He looked, she thought, like the Dickens of the photographs, and he talked a good deal of entertaining nonsense. He wrote a noble sonnet in her honour, and she later found it on her dressing-table. It was an eventful week. She performed in a charade, went to a shoot (which she disliked), and watched a performance of *Le Fils de Giboyer*, by the Comédie-Française, in the palace theatre. She also found herself next to Baron Haussmann at *déjeuner*. Le Grand Préfet enquired how she liked the new boulevard Haussmann; she replied that it had cut off half her garden, and that she could not play croquet any more.

'After a moment's hesitation he asked: "How would you like it if I put a piece of ground in the Bois at your disposal?"

'I could have screamed with joy! What a piece of news to tell my friends after breakfast! I chanted a little *Gloria* under my breath, and asked him if he really meant it. He said: "Of course I mean it, and as soon as I return to Paris I will have the formal papers made out and sent to you, and you can claim the ground when you like." He added, gallantly: "I will have the document made out in your name, Madame, in souvenir of our breakfast to-day."'

Mrs Moulton was delighted, but she was apprehensive. What would happen, she wondered, 'if every time he sat next to a lady he gave her a slice of the Bois de Boulogne?'[33]

Such was the Court of Napoleon III.

3 La Vie Parisienne

For those who belonged to *le tout Paris,* the 'upper five thousand six hundred of Paris,' life had never been more intense than it was in the Second Empire. 'No-one was thinking about the future. Morals were very lax. Sybaritism, coming from above, was then the fashion, and everyone put serious affairs aside.'[1]

A society woman would spend the morning receiving her various suppliers, for she rarely went into a milliner's or a couturier's, and work was done at her apartment or *hôtel.* An elegant woman hardly ever walked, and if, by chance, she took a few steps down the boulevard, her footman would discreetly follow her. In the afternoon, she paid social calls, and then came the sacrosanct rite of the carriage-drive in the Bois de Boulogne. The tour of the lake, which Society made every fine afternoon, was incomparably splendid. In 1885, Henry de Pène, the founder of *Le Gaulois* and *Paris-Journal,* recalled the enchanted scene.

'Do you remember? A hundred years ago – or was it yesterday? – the promenade in the Bois was a fairytale. Crowds of eager spectators were massed along the paths on either side, from the Grande Cascade to the middle of the Place de la Concorde. And in the thick of the coupés, the victorias, phaetons and landaus, . . . Mme Musard's eight-spring carriage with its powdered lackeys was passing the carriages from the Tuileries, . . . in the sparkling crowd all flooded with purple light by the setting sun.'[2] After the drive came a hurried return home to dress for dinner at seven o'clock. In the evening, from December to May, in the elegant quarters of Paris, animated social life continued for the greater part of the night.

'There have been balls or receptions everywhere in the highest circles this week,' reported a weary journalist in 1856. 'They have been at the Tuileries, at King Jerome's, at Princess Mathilde's, at M. Fould's, at M. Walewski's, and probably elsewhere, too.'[3] Early in 1860, another exhausted critic took up the theme. 'We are in the Parisian paradise, or the Parisian hell. Every night, since 1 January, has been spent in festivities, spectacles, concerts and dances. It is a perpetual coming-and-going, a

'The far-famed grisette can be seen in full feather at the Closerie des Lilas.'
A lithograph of the open-air ball during the Second Empire.

63

constant toing-and-froing, a continual volcano. They are dancing at Court, they are acting comedy at Prince Napoleon's, they are singing everywhere, except at the Opéra. I'm wrong, they're singing at the Opéra, too.'[4] Five years later, the tempo of life was as fast as ever. 'The great world of Paris is in full swing . . . Every day of the week brings a new social duty and a new pleasure. On Sunday, Mme la Princesse Mathilde receives men of letters and artists, and Mme Troplong receives the politicians. On Monday, the Duchesse de Pozzo di Borgo opens her salons to the aristocracy of the faubourg Saint-Germain. On Tuesday, the Comtesse de Casabianca entertains official society, and Mme la Princesse Mathilde has her grand receptions . . . I'm not mentioning the dinners and entertainments, large and small . . .'[5] Among them was Prince Napoleon's ball at the Palais-Royal. In 1865 'these salons, famous from the days of the Regency – salons in which the Regent and his lovers used to cook partridges and mull champagne, . . . were opened to the select world of Paris . . . Ambassadors were as plentiful as peas in May.'[6] Early that year, over three thousand guests attended two great balls at the Hôtel de Ville; there were, it is said, one hundred and forty players in the orchestra, which was conducted by Strauss. 'Gaiety is now setting in heavily,' wrote an English journalist in the early summer of 1867. 'Everything indicates a severe and prolonged season.'[7]

For those who moved in official circles, in high society, in the world of the wealthy,

Three elaborate fancy-dresses: the Empress as a gipsy, Mme Gorschakoff as Salammbô, and the Marquis de Gallifet as a cock.

there were balls and dinners and entertainments of astonishing novelty and magnificence. The most distinguished diplomatic *salons* were those of the British Embassy,
in the days of Lord and Lady Cowley, and the Austrian Embassy, after the arrival of the
Metternichs. Comte de Nieuwerkerke, the Surintendant des Beaux-Arts, held musical
and artistic soirées every Friday, in his official apartments in the Louvre.[8]

The towering figure of Nieuwerkerke was also conspicuous at the fancy-dress balls
which were all the rage. On Shrove Tuesday, 1857, the Empress herself attended a
bal masqué which was given by Princess Mathilde at the rue de Courcelles. 'She came
with white-powdered hair, personifying Night under her cloudy veils, starred with a
Milky Way of diamonds.' Mme Baroche, who recorded the occasion, also noted the
famous ball at the Hôtel d'Albe early in 1860. 'Princess Clotilde, as a Watteau shepherd-
ess, all pink and white, was dancing with animation.' Princess Mathilde appeared as a
Nubian woman, 'a disguise which was more artistic than flattering.'[9]

On 9 February 1863 a fancy-dress ball was given at the Tuileries. Four gigantic
beehives were brought in, and out of them stepped four women, dressed as bees – the
symbol of the Bonapartes – to dance in tribute to the Emperor. 'People are putting
bees everywhere,' noted Henri Dabot, the diarist, 'and it is the most difficult thing in
the world to prevent the couturiers from attaching bees to their customers' clothes.'[10]
Bonapartism was in fashion. So was *Salammbô*, Flaubert's novel of ancient Carthage,

The fancy-dress ball at the Tuileries, 9 February 1863. This sketch by Moulin shows the famous Dance of the Bees.

which had just appeared; and, since Flaubert had described his heroine's costume, Salammbôs were constantly observed at Parisian dances. One of the first to wear the costume was the Comtesse de Castiglione.

In February 1863, describing the latest imperial ball, Mme Baroche wrote:

'Princess Korsakoff came as Truth, so true that the Comte de Budberg, the minister, observed that truth was sometimes an indiscretion. On another evening, the Princess represented the Sea. It was a troubled sea, which rolled its green gauze waves around her; they were transparent, and through them you caught glimpses of pearls and shells and corals, mingled with a profusion of sea-weed. It is said that while this beauty was talking to a coco-seller, a passing guest, in a domino, turned on the tap of the barrel; the Sea was inundated (with champagne) and grew very stormy . . .

'Another kind of eccentricity. An artist, G. Doré, represented *The countryside after the rain*, with samples of every species of nature, even insects on his nose. Animals were swarming all over the place. The Comtesse de Brimont, transformed into *A night in the forest*, had decked herself out with butterflies, lizards and beetles; the whole of this little world was disporting itself upon her in the midst of moving foliage, together with a squirrel.'[11]

In 1865, Mme Drouyn de Lhuys, the wife of the Foreign Minister, gave the first private fancy-dress ball of the season.

'There enters upon the scene,' recorded an English journalist, 'an Eastern Prince, with more jewels than the originals ever wear . . . To him succeeds the Rimsky-Korsakoff, in a Russian court-dress, splendid; her robe literally massive with precious stones . . . Here you see a real Anglo-Indian princess; she is dressed not only in fine feathers, but also in fine birds . . . With this feathered songstress . . . walked a thing in pink. I believe he was a *berger*, and looked as if he had just stepped out from a teacup of old china . . . He looked like the ghost of a strawberry ice, and was much admired.'[12]

Early in 1866, at a fancy-dress ball at the Tuileries, the Empress appeared as her heroine, Marie-Antoinette, with the Prince Imperial as her page. Princess Metternich, who once called herself 'the best-dressed monkey in Paris,' came, daringly, as an *incroyable*. 'She wore a hat – a straw-coloured satin – wreathed with flowers and diamonds; her petticoat, of yellow satin, was looped over an undergarment apparently composed of nothing but flowers.' The Marquise de Gallifet drew all eyes as the Archangel Gabriel. Her golden sword was 'grasped tightly in her fairy hand and brandished even while dancing.' The Archangel Gabriel, like the rest, no doubt enjoyed such earthly pleasures as 'pâtés de foie gras, salade de légumes truffés, galantine de gibier truffé, poulet à la glace, grapes, fresh peaches, champagne decanted and a bottle for each guest.'[13] Nieuwerkerke came as Pontius Pilate. Princess Mathilde appeared as a Roman woman; Bapst, in his Life of Marshal Canrobert, also recorded her at the Ministère de la Marine, when she was dressed as Anne Boleyn, after the portrait by Holbein. On this occasion, 'the event of the evening was the opening procession formed by the representatives of the four quarters of the world . . . Africa (Mme Montant) was mounted on a camel admirably constructed . . . America (Miss

Carter), a lovely blonde, reclined in a hammock swung between banana trees, each carried by negroes.'[14] Mme Rimsky-Korsakoff, who rarely missed a party, came as a Roman Empress, Mme de Metternich as a woman of *le Grand Siècle*, and la Castiglione appeared – one would like to know how – as an acacia flower.[15]

There was a certain hypocrisy among *le tout Paris*. La Castiglione was known to be the mistress of Napoleon III; English visitors to Compiègne were 'struck with the freedom in conversation and manners of the Court . . . Their forgetfulness of all *convenances* is,' declared Lord Malmesbury, 'quite incredible.' And yet–apart from Princess Mathilde – no respectable society woman would receive an actress or a singer. 'No public women whatever are admitted into good French company,' wrote the author of *Life in Paris before the War and during the Siege*. 'Once "upon the boards", . . . no matter how irreproachable their character may be, they can never be received by women of character and condition, except in their professional capacity.'[16]

The double standards were all too clear. Actresses and singers remained *tabu* in high society (at least until Adelina Patti married the Marquis de Caux). But high society paraded their liaisons. The Emperor made no secret of his love-affairs; Prince Napoleon flaunted his mistresses, and Haussmann was unashamedly seen driving in his carriage with the young actress Francine Cellier. Comtesse Le Hon, the wife of the Belgian Minister, continued to preside over a brilliant *salon* in her *hôtel* off the Champs-Élysées; and all the world knew that the Duc de Morny was her lover (his *hôtel* nearby was sometimes called *la niche de fidèle*). *Le demi-monde* was all too close to *le tout Paris*. Marie-Anne Detourbey, generally called Jeanne de Tourbey, presided over another *salon* in the rue de l'Arcade; she was the mistress of (among others) Prince Napoleon. She later married the Comte de Loynes, separated from him, kept his name, and became the mistress of the critic Jules Lemaître.

One woman who owed her social status to *la vie galante* was Mme Musard, daughter-in-law of the famous Musard of the Opéra balls. She owed her vast wealth to her infatuated lover, the King of the Netherlands, and she took good care to display it.

'A curious *déjeuner* was given yesterday by Mme Musard,' recorded Felix White-hurst early in 1866. 'Her enormous fortune of a million sterling, her beauty – at least I think so – seat on horseback, horses, carriages, *hôtel*, stables, and the rest, are things daily talked of and displayed on the stage of this vast theatre of Paris. The guests assembled in a long gallery, draped with green curtains. Breakfast was served and eaten; coffee and cigars followed; then a bell rang, and all the draperies were suddenly withdrawn. And where did the guests find themselves? . . . Why, in the stable, where stood eighteen magnificent horses that had also breakfasted, but *not* off truffles and champagne, coffee and cigarettes, and behind curtains. "Eh bien! c'est une idée comme une autre," and, as such, worthy of notice in the chronicle of passing Paris.'[17]

The Second Empire was, not surprisingly, the golden era of the courtesans. The wages of sin would vary according to what part of Paris the courtesan happened to live in. 'And so the protector of a lorette living, for example, in the rue de Grammont, could get away with 300 francs a month (for gloves and flowers). In the rue du Helder,

it was already more expensive: 400 francs a month (with a groom). In the rue Saint-Lazare and the rue de la Chaussée-d'Antin, one had to allow 500 francs a month (a horse and carriage). As for the lorette who lived in the faubourg du Roule (faubourg Saint-Honoré), she needed a protector who was at least a count, if not a duke. He had to assure her an allowance of 10,000 francs a month, a lodge in an *hôtel*, two carriages, two horses, a footman and a chef.'[18]

In Second Empire Paris there were a dozen courtesans who were generally known as *la garde*; they were the queens of their profession. Each of these women, *expertes ès sciences galantes*, considered her beauty as her capital, and made it pay breathtaking dividends. 'When I've been to your *hôtel*,' said Alphonse de Rothschild, to one of the *grandes cocottes*, 'my own *hôtel* seems like a hovel to me.' These were the patricians of gallantry: the women whom visiting princes considered it essential to see.

The most successful member of *la garde*, in material terms, was undoubtedly La Païva. She was also the one great courtesan who appears to have had no redeeming feature.

Thérèse Lachmann was born in the Moscow ghetto in 1819. Her father was a weaver; and, at seventeen, she was married to a young tailor. After a year or two, she abandoned her husband and infant son, and worked her way to Paris. In 1841 she encountered the Viennese pianist Henri Herz; he was rich and famous, and she became his mistress. He brought her the company of musicians, journalists and men of letters; he indulged her fancies for clothes and jewels. But he could not give her the *entrée* to the faubourg Saint-Germain; and, when he took her to a reception at the Tuileries, they were turned back at the ante-room. It did not suit King Louis-Philippe to accept this irregular alliance. The rejection probably explained the profound aversion to France which Thérèse would feel for the rest of her life.

In 1848, Herz set off on a tour of America; Thérèse again took her destiny in hand. She went to London, and ensnared a peer of the realm. She returned to Paris, well aware of the benfits of a title; and, since her husband had tactfully died in 1849, she was free to take a titled husband. At Baden she discovered a Portuguese marquis, Albino-Francesco de Païva-Araujo. In 1851 she married him.

The marriage lasted for some months; she now had to ensure that she was wealthy enough to be the envy of Paris. She discovered a Prussian count eleven years her junior. His name was Guido Henckel von Donnersmarck. He was one day to be a prince, and he happened to be a man of glittering wealth.

Viel-Castel described La Païva's conquest of von Donnersmarck:

'She encountered this prince, or count, or duke, on her travels, and she followed on his trail to Constantinople, St Petersburg, Naples and Paris; the prince always found her in the lap of luxury, dazzling in her strange, voluptuous beauty, a beauty which was a little contrived, and very artificial. La Païva did not seem to pay any attention whatsoever to the prince, but one fine day it was not she who followed the predestined mortal, but the predestined mortal who pursued her. He was in love to such an extent, to such a degree, that he went to her, not to offer her his hand – La Païva would have had no use for it – but the accessories.

'The panache of the courtesans dressed overall': a Second Empire cocotte, *as seen by Constantin Guys.*

LEFT *Mme Musard, whose wealth and beauty were the talk of Paris;* RIGHT *La Païva, the most successful courtesan of the age.*

'"I have three million a year," he told her. "If you'll live with me, we can share it."

'La Païva, who had spent three hundred thousand francs on the conquest of the prince, accepted to recover her expenses . . .

'La Païva displays two million francs' worth of diamonds, pearls and precious stones on her person. She is the great debauchee of the century.'[19]

In a city where manners were hardly puritan, in an age when morals were lax and love was cheaply bought, La Païva could never divest herself of her ugly notoriety. In an age of *parvenues*, she remained the most immoral of *parvenues*; in an age of *nouveaux riches* she remained the most derided of the *nouveaux riches*.

However, there was no lack of celebrities in La Païva's *salon*. The *hôtels* in the place Saint-Georges and, later, in the rue Rossini, seemed too humble to house her guests. Besides, they did not satisfy her love of ostentation. The tailor's wife from Moscow still needed to display her wealth; the pariah who had been rejected by the faubourg Saint-Germain still needed to show some sort of domination over Paris. On 4 May 1856 *L'Artiste* announced: 'The Marquise de Païva's *hôtel*, which will stand in the avenue des Champs-Élysées, after Mme Le Hon's *hôtel* and M. de Morny's *museum*, is beginning to rise from the ground.'

The *hôtel* Païva was to be, as its chatelaine intended, the most luxurious private *hôtel* in Paris. Its architect was Pierre Mauguin; and for ten years he laboured at his creation. As the year 1866 began, the *hôtel* was almost finished. 'The only thing left,' said Dumas *fils*, well aware of the chatelaine's morals, 'is to lay the pavement.'

The *hôtel* Païva (which remains, as The Travellers' Club, today), was listed among the sights of Imperial Paris. It stood out, like La Païva herself, as a symbol of the Second Empire; and whether or not one admired the intensity of its ornamentation, it represented, and that with splendour, the taste of the time. The vast salon, lit by five tall windows, seemed a kind of temple dedicated to physical pleasure; it was hard to take one's eyes off the magnificent ceiling where Baudry had painted Day chasing Night away. The salon walls were hung with crimson damask, specially woven at Lyons for eight hundred thousand francs. The staircase, lit by a massive lustre in sculpted bronze, was made – steps, baluster and all – entirely of onyx. The bathroom, said Gautier, was worthy of a Sultana in the Arabian Nights. Its walls were onyx and marble. The bath was solid onyx, like the lavatory, and the three taps, sculpted and gilt, were set with precious stones. The locks on the doors were said to be worth two thousand francs apiece. The bed, encrusted with rare woods and ivory, delicately wrought, stood like an altar in an alcove, under a ceiling on which Aurora, Goddess of the Dawn, hovered in the empyrean. It had cost a hundred thousand francs. The visitor felt himself in the presence of a single idea: the defiant, obsessive idea of personal glorification.

La Païva's one resource remained her wealth. She was conscious of every franc she possessed, and of every single centime that she spent. Émile Bergerat, the journalist, a son-in-law of Gautier, wrote the simple truth when he called her ' . . . the archetype of those courtesans who are courtesans only for money, and fall in love with money alone. La Païva was a coffer. She was never known to have a passing fancy . . . She had a horror of dogs and cats and birds and children, of everything that is an expense and brings in no reward, and may divert one from the hunt for the Golden Calf. But she would have given herself to a miner for a nugget.'[20]

The *hôtel* Païva was said to be more than a décor for grandiose prostitution. It was rumoured to be a centre for Prussian espionage. Henckel von Donnersmarck was well known to Bismarck; and, though his liaison with La Païva kept him in Paris, his sympathies remained with his own country. La Païva had used France in her career, but she had not forgotten that France despised her; and she and Henckel had long been fostering Prussian interests. In the last years of the Second Empire, La Païva had often talked to Prussian diplomats about the political indiscretions and military weaknesses, the signs of social decadence in France. She had foreseen the coming conflict between France and Prussia; it seemed to her inevitable and not unwelcome. And when, in July 1870, it came, she had no regrets. She went, immediately, to live in Henckel's castle in Silesia. He himself joined the Prussian forces which were invading France. Before hostilities were over, Bismarck made him Prefect of Lorraine. When the peace preliminaries were discussed, Henckel and Bleichroder, on behalf of Bismarck, examined the financial clauses of the treaty with Thiers. Bleichroder suggested that France should pay war indemnities of three thousand million francs. Henckel made the Chancellor demand five thousand million. In March 1871, when the Prussians entered Paris, every *hôtel* in the Champs-Élysées was locked and shuttered but for one. From the steps of the *hôtel* Païva, in full uniform, Henckel von Donnersmarck watched his compatriots march past.

The fall of the Empire brought the final triumph of La Païva. On 28 October, when her marriage to Païva had been annulled, she and Henckel were married at last at the Lutheran Church in Paris. She was fifty-two. Jean-Philippe Worth recorded that Henckel had given her, as his wedding-present, the Empress Eugénie's necklace, which the ex-Empress had been forced to sell. The three rows of diamonds were faultless, and this example of the jeweller's art was considered the finest of its time. It was La Païva's revenge on the faubourg Saint-Germain.

'Vice is seldom clad in rags in Paris,' wrote an English observer. 'Either it is very bad indeed, and clothes itself in cachemires surmounted by diamonds, or is passingly bad, and is clothed decently by charity.'[21] Vice did indeed wear diamonds during the Second Empire. In 1860, *Le Figaro* announced a fancy-dress ball at which the goddesses of Olympus were to be represented by the Parisian courtesans. La Païva had, it was said, arranged to come as Juno. 'The treasures of diamonds, pearls and precious stones she would scatter over her dazzling tunic are valued at not less than 1,250,000 francs. Mme Barucci would come as Pallas, ... with 250,000 francs' worth of various diamonds and jewels. Mme Anna Deslions would come as Venus, with 300,000 francs' worth of precious stones.'[22]

Small wonder that some people asked if morality had progressed as much as science and material prosperity. Early in 1857, the Goncourts declared: 'Never has the low world of gallantry reflected high society as it does now. There are business affairs from top to bottom of the ladder, from the minister to the prostitute ... The prostitute is a businessman and a power ... Today she dictates behaviour, she bespatters opinion; she eats marrons glacés in her box at the theatre, next to your wife. She has a theatre of her own: les Bouffes. She has a world of her own: la Bourse ... It is an abnormal time, the brain and the heart of the country are too disturbed, the material progress of France is being made too fast and too disgustingly for society not to explode. And when it does, it won't simply be a '93. Everything may go.'[23]

There were not many, in high society, during the Second Empire, who paid heed to such a warning. In 1872, when Maxime du Camp came to discuss prostitution in his vast survey of Paris, he expressed his horror at the decadence of society; and he blamed the French defeat in the Franco-Prussian War on the immoral, irresponsible life of *les petits crevés*: on the aristocratic men-about-town of the Second Empire, on the bourgeois who followed their example and '... repudiated all morality, all courage, all generous amibition ... So it was that, when France sought within herself for the men she needed, she saw a void, and she found nobody.

'In this work of social decomposition and degeneracy, *les femmes galantes* were instruments of prime importance. They were female minotaurs, they devoured young men with an evil persistence which one would be tempted to take as an instinct of the

The grand salon in the hôtel Païva.

species. To see them swarming as they did, starting when they were little more than children, and still imposing themselves on the very threshold of old age, one would think that they had been entrusted with some secret and important social mission . . . If, as people have said, prostitution, or rather its external appearance, is the clear expression of the real morals of a society, we are sick indeed.'[24]

There was much wisdom in these words. But, as the century progressed, as France became more sober-suited and republican, as the Second Empire assumed the glamour of more distant history, certain critics changed their tone. The sick society was forgotten; the sparkle was remembered. And some recalled the gallantry of Second Empire Paris with regret.

In 1888, in his *Mémoires d'un Parisien*, Albert Wolff wrote: 'We older men knew the time when a beautiful and intelligent woman, of easy virtue, could make her rooms a veritable *salon*, which no man of doubtful education ever entered; and we were happy to be admitted, because we showed, just by being present, that we were somebody in the streets of Paris. After this thoroughbred courtesan there came another of an inferior kind; since then, the profession has fallen a notch lower still. Today love in Paris is just a bazaar; it is like La Belle Jardinière, the multiple store of French gallantry, where, for a modest sum, you can buy a small kit for a man-about-town.'[25]

In the meanwhile, during the Second Empire, *le tout Paris* continued to spin in its vortex; and 'any dazzled foreigner,' explained the *Revue de Paris*, 'need only go out to dinner to brush shoulders with more poets, artists, millionaires and beautiful women than there are over all the rest of the map of the world.'[26]

Parisians have always enjoyed their pleasures; but even they have rarely enjoyed them with such feverish, blind intensity as they did in those eighteen imperial years. In *Les Plaisirs de Paris*, Alfred Délvau declared that if they had to choose between the classic *panem et circenses*, they would prefer their pleasures to their daily bread. Pleasure, he said, was their mania, their malady and weakness. They loved violent emotions, entertainments which created noise and stir and excitement.[27]

In 1860, they flocked to see the young acrobat Léotard, catching the flying trapeze at the Cirque de l'Impératrice. 'The photograph-sellers are offering the gymnasiarch Léotard in 35 aerial poses,' noted Henri Dabot, that July. 'In Paris, the man who risks his life, no matter how, whether or not it serves a useful purpose, is sure to start a general infatuation.' On 3 September 1863, the same diarist reported: 'Yesterday, to the great stupefaction of the passers-by, a mechanical carriage, going by itself, went triumphantly all along the *grands boulevards* in Paris. There were three people in it, and 300,000 to watch it.' But the mechanical carriage was forgotten almost at once. That autumn, the hero of Paris was Félix Tournachon, better known as Nadar. Author, caricaturist, and the supreme photographer of the age, he was also an intrepid balloonist; and, on 5 October, Dabot reported: 'Nadar has made a colossal balloon in which he took off from the Champ-de-Mars last Sunday, in the presence of the whole of Paris, which had gathered on the quais and bridges. There were thirteen people in the basket

The Queen of Hearts. La Castiglione in fancy dress.

Le Cirque de l'Impératrice, in the Champs-Élysées.

of the balloon, including Nadar, the two Godards, and the Princesse de la Tour-d'Auvergne. The balloon, which took off at 5 o'clock, came down at Meaux at 10 o'clock that evening.' Later that month, Nadar made a second ascent from the Champ-de-Mars, in *le Géant*. This time the balloon crashed at Hanover. *Le Géant* was less damaged than its passengers.[28]

The Parisians did not only revel in such life-and-death adventures; they adored the extravagant and the spectacular, and the theatre catered for their needs. In 1865, Anthony North Peat recorded 'a piece called *Le Déluge*, which fills the theatre with a dense throng of enthusiastic spectators. Palaces of Babylonish magnificence are burnt by roseate fire, Chaldean plains covered by tents and flocks of sheep are submerged beneath the avenging floods . . .' In *Paris-Revue*, the end-of-the-year revue of 1869, the prologue showed a panorama of Paris at midnight, with gaslit shop-windows, passing carriages, and the crowds coming out of the theatres. The first act showed the Gare Saint-Lazare 'with a real train coming out of the tunnel at Les Batignolles. The second act showed the moon. The third showed the celebrations at Suez at the opening of the canal. The fourth act was the final apotheosis, with human flowers.'[29]

Two of the wonders of Imperial Paris: LEFT *Léotard, the gymnasiarch, and* RIGHT *Nadar in the basket of* le Géant.

In the thirst for excitement and novelty, Parisians went from one craze to another. 'One of the characteristic traits of the age,' North Peat observed, 'is the periodical occurrence of a mania.'[30] His opinion was confirmed by the author of *Life in Paris before the War and during the Siege.* 'Among the French it rarely happens that a taste for anything is not carried to such an extent as to become a folly.'[31] Maxime du Camp maintained that infatuation was a French ailment, and that it was especially Parisian. 'Everyone believed in Cagliostro and sat round Mesmer's bucket; they got crushed on the paths of the Jardin des Plantes, seeing the giraffe, and at the gates of the Jardin Turc, seeing the dog Munito; it is as if people's heads were turned by a wind of madness. Parisian enthusiasms are sudden, and they are sometimes tremendous, but they don't last long.'[32]

In 1857, Daniel Hume, the medium, was the talk of Paris. On 2 April, Mme Baroche recorded that Hume 'had only performed, so far, at the Tuileries and at Prince Napoleon's. People have seen tables leave the floor at his command, and rise up, without any strings attached; bells have moved around in circles, an accordion moved across people's legs, playing tunes. A little bell, which the Empress was holding very firmly, went and put itself in the Emperor's hand, in spite of all her efforts to keep it.'[33] 'Everyone is turning tables, or trying to do so,' continued Henri Dabot. 'It's the favourite occupation of the moment. It's people's heads which are turning, not the tables.' In 1863, he added, with incredulity: 'Some time ago, a new mania, a curious form of madness, took possession of the Parisians; they began to collect . . . old stamps, postmarked stamps which had been used.'[34] Dabot was not the only person to marvel at the advent of philately. In 1865, North Peat observed: 'A few years ago, grey-haired people as well as little children were seized with the stampomania . . . Then came the crestomania, then the potichomania, which consisted in converting plain glass jars into magnificent specimens of porcelain and pottery.' The following spring, North Peat reported that 'a new mania has come over the inhabitants of Paris – that of collecting the portraits of great political criminals, murderers, etc. The photograph of Booth, the assassin of Lincoln, is, I am sorry to say, obtaining a very large sale, especially among the fair sex, who think him a very fine-looking man.'[35]

There was a restless need for excitement. 'It is better to die at thirty in Paris,' said Alfred Delvau, 'than to reach a hundred in a village.'[36] Life was so intense among the prosperous in Paris, that there seemed little chance of reaching a comfortable old age. 'In general,' said Philarète Chasles in 1863, 'people believe that luxury is the state most favourable to health; it is a serious mistake, as is clearly shown by the mortality rates in France and Germany. It isn't luxury which makes a man strong and fit, it is the exercise of his physical, intellectual and moral powers . . . According to the mortality rates, the two most dangerous professions are those of the millionaire and the knife-grinder, they give a man only twenty-nine years.'[37] In 1867, discussing Parisian society, Gustave Claudin wrote: 'Question these so-called happy people: they will all tell you that staying in Paris has become fatal to health. Business and pleasure . . . no longer bear any relation to human capacity. In some circles, you would need three stomachs, three brains, and forty-eight-hour days to fulfil the complicated demands of life.'[38]

Once or twice a year, it is true, there came an imperious need to escape. In 1865, the author of *Paris Partout* explained that '. . . one essential of smart life in Paris, an essential as imperious as that of a country visit in the spring, comes over you some fine morning in July or August. It forces you to pack your trunk and go to some spa or other. . . . Every year Vichy . . . sees the victims of the Paris carnival. They come to restore their health and recruit their strength for the following winter . . . They have worked for eleven months to wreck their health, eleven months well spent in dinners, balls, entertainments, and nights at the gaming-table. They have twenty-one days to devote to its restoration.'[39]

Even now, their purpose was not purely medical. Even for these three short weeks, in Vichy, Ems or Homburg, they could not forgo their Paris pleasures. *Le tout Paris*, and its attendant train of *cocottes*, descended on Baden to dance, intrigue, and gamble, and make love. When Paris was deserted, Baden became the summer capital of Europe. As *La Vie parisienne* observed in 1868: 'Baden-Baden is Paris and its *demi-monde*, with a

ABOVE RIGHT *Table-turning: the rage of Paris in May 1853. An impression by Gustave Doré.* BELOW *Potichomania: another Parisian craze. A cartoon by Honoré Daumier.*

Le foyer des Variétés, by Constantin Guys.

few foreigners thrown in to make it look respectable.'[40] The end of the season was announced when the *demi-monde* re-appeared in the Bois de Boulogne. 'A very considerable crowd on Sunday, driving in the Bois,' reported the same publication this autumn. 'All the *haute bicherie*, in their coupés, back from Ems, Spa, or Homburg, made their personal mark once again in Parisian society.'[41]

Some of the sharpest criticism of *la vie parisienne* was made by Taine, in 1867, in his *Notes sur Paris. Vie et opinions de M. Frédéric-Thomas Graindorge.* M. Graindorge, a Frenchman, had left Paris at the age of twelve, and received his education abroad. He had made a fortune in America. Now, in middle age, he came home, and observed the vacuity and the immorality of Second Empire Paris.

When he visited the theatre, he noticed the number of lorettes. He found them 'soiled, degraded, impudent, accustomed to affronts and insolence.' Parisian men, observed Graindorge, were so used to talking to prostitutes that they had forgotten the tone of respect which was due to honest women. Visiting a *salon*, he observed the ominous boredom among the married women.

'One of them kept using the phrase *knowing life*; by that you may understand the intoxication, the intense sensation, the palpitation of heart and nerves, the whirlwind which bears away everything, intellect and senses. These women's words are moderate, but their thoughts! No-one can measure the voids, the bottomless chasms under their cold and uniform urbanity . . . Boredom with the daily casserole, a longing for little suppers. One could lead them a long way down that slope.'

To Graindorge, the only aim of *la vie parisienne* appeared to be pleasure and show. Society was bent on pleasure, and occasionally found it, the bourgeois pursued it, but in vain, and the poor either sold it or stole it.[42] 'Of course everyone has a right to luxury, and everyone can dress and furnish as he chooses,' wrote Jules Claretie in 1867. 'But this appetite for pleasure, this love of dress has grown wildly exaggerated, and this is the piercing wound. It is also inevitable when everyone lives half asleep, cradled by his egoism, and as if the social problems were finally solved.'[43]

'*The need of excitement*,' added Taine. 'The phrase is always on one's lips in Paris.'[44] Life, for the rich, was not only feverish, it was also reckless. Anna Bicknell recorded: 'In the beginning of the Empire, money had seemed inexhaustible . . . The Empress, soon after her marriage, had a fancy for a yacht of her own. Immediately a beautiful little toy was built for her, too small to be of any use, but a little gem, with the greatest luxury shown in every detail. She had the beautiful Hôtel d'Albe built for her sister, and no expense was spared to make it perfect. The Duchess of Alba died there shortly after the splendid ball which had been given for its inauguration. The Empress then could no longer endure it, and it was recklessly pulled down, after only a few months of use.'[45]

Such extravagance was naturally copied, even by those who could not afford it. As Blanchard Jerrold wrote: 'There are people here who stint themselves for months, in order to make a grand appearance, as distributors of gorgeous *étrennes* on New Year's Day . . . Time was when children were content with the rough horse, the bran doll, and the plain battledore and shuttlecock. But the luxury that is unfolded to the sight of Paris children these days! Here are dolls that are to be bought for gold; dolls' furniture at prices that would comfort much living nakedness and suffering of the poor arrondissements; toy boats (to float in the fountain of the Tuileries gardens), at the price of a mechanic's week's labour.'[46]

Thomas Graindorge, leaving a *soirée*, noticed a laundress's boat on the Seine; for some poor woman was still washing linen at midnight to earn a few sous.[47] Such injustice was gaily forgotten by society. The children of *le tout Paris*, and of those with social aspirations, had their dolls dressed in real lace, and in boots which were made by the leading bootmakers of Paris. When Paul Siraudin, the dramatist and confectioner, attempted to humour his fellow-Parisians, he made a doll, 'dressed it in blue velvet, covered it with real English point lace, and sprinkled it with *real* diamonds, until it was worth something more than one thousand pounds sterling! He planted this precious toy upon a pedestal: the *chroniqueurs* went to work – and in a few days there were mighty crowds in the Rue de la Paix. Siraudin was in everybody's mouth – and so were Siraudin's *bonbons* . . .'[48]

Such extravagance, such frenetic love of pleasure, were symptoms of social decadence; they showed the Parisians' complete indifference to reality. 'It was all pleasure, delight in living, in luxurious living,' wrote Henri Dabot, 'and in the meanwhile the chains of Paris were being forged at Essen.'[49] The quality of life was impaired – or, rather, it was ignored.

'Where are the censors who are to deal with this pleasure-seeking, laughing, spendthrift, audacious throng?' enquired Blanchard Jerrold. 'The epigrams are fastened on very high places indeed. Scandal is so general, and covers all society so completely that the splendid subject of the latest damaging anecdote sails into the prefect's or minister's drawing-room, it may be in the character of Aspasia (fancy balls being the rage in a city where many must be delighted to be rid for a time of their own character), the happy observed of all observers! She is welcome, for she is witty – and she is not much worse than many of her friends.

'The lady who invents a new way of spending money becomes a notable presence in the city of Boulevards. It cost a certain great lady £600 sterling for toilettes fit to ruralise at Compiègne with the Imperial Court last autumn, and this for one fortnight!'[50]

In the first months of the Second Empire, at a ball at the Tuileries, Delacroix had observed, with uncomfortable shrewdness, 'that one of the great difficulties about the French character, perhaps the one which has contributed more than anything else to the catastrophes and failures in which our history abounds, is the universal absence of a sense of duty . . . The imagination puts our obligation in the things that please us, or bring us profit. With the English, on the contrary, . . . everyone feels the necessity of duty.'[51] Second Empire society had a false sense of values; and Delacroix expressed the fact succinctly when, in 1854, he was again invited to the Tuileries. The garden was illuminated by coloured lanterns and Bengal lights. 'That is beauty to them!' he wrote. 'An April afternoon leaves them indifferent.'[52]

In 1882, Jules Vallès, the former Communard, wrote with a certain satisfaction: '*Le Tout-Paris* is dead, or, rather, one should say that *le Tout-Paris* has moths in its evening-dress. The time is past when it seemed to dictate the law of taste, to consecrate talent, and to apportion glory.'[53] Others took a different view. In 1905, Dr Henry Evans, who had known the Court of the Tuileries, lamented the decline of society under the Third Republic.

'Left, since the disappearance of the Imperial Court, without a recognised head and arbiter of forms and ceremonies, and procedures and precedents, Paris society has become broken up into circles and cliques . . .

'The tone of Paris society in those days was quite unlike that which has since obtained. It was cosmopolitan and not provincial, and was a reflex of the political prestige of the Empire both at home and abroad. It was a society full of movement and originality, of unconventionality, and gaiety, and charm. . . The women of those days were not more beautiful than are the women of the Republic; but the women of the Empire had *chic*. Everyone then who was somebody in society – man or woman – was *chic*, if not by nature or by grace, then by example and habit . . . Paris is now socially dead.'[54]

'His elegant carriages, with their small horses, recall the equipage of Cinderella.'
A carriage in the Bois de Boulogne, by Constantin Guys.

4 Paris Inconnu

If the upper classes lacked a sense of social responsibility, or a serious interest in politics, they could live a life of unending pleasure. The bourgeois were more concerned with reality, but they were decidedly comfortable. Money was there for the making, and servants were there for the asking.

In his lively book, *Les Quatre Coins de Paris*, in 1863, Léo Lespès explained that there were usually four kinds of servants to whom one paid wages: the coachman, the lackey, the lady's maid and the cook.

'The coachman is a personage; he is as independent as a free city in the Confederation of the Rhine; he has *his horses* and *his carriage* . . . The lackey is a tall young man, as handsome as Antinous, pink-cheeked and fresh. He is given a thousand francs a year, board and lodging and laundry, and epaulettes with large bullion on his shoulders . . . This general officer's task is to clean the knives, lay the table, hold madam's shawl at the Tuileries and look after the master's wardrobe. He is a valet in the morning, a majordomo during the day, and a male escort on a walk or at a theatre . . . The cook is the only Rabelaisian domestic figure . . . Every real *cordon bleu* is over thirty, with a red nose, a double chin, and a fickle heart.'[1] A few years later, an English observer declared that 'the lady's maid is at this moment the same familiar, shrewd, important and ostensible person in a French family as she appears . . . in the inimitable waiting-maids or suivantes of Molière.'[2]

Now that he enjoyed financial prosperity, and the social status and power which went with it, the bourgeois was careful to observe certain *convenances*. 'The Parisian really likes a carriage,' explained the author of *Paris Partout* in 1865. 'He makes it a necessity of life . . . On the boulevard des Italiens alone, according to statistics, 10,750 vehicles pass every twenty-four hours; the Champs-Élysées, which are hardly frequented, except in the afternoon, have an average of 10,000 in the same space of time . . . The height of fashion is to have your winter and summer carriages, your turnouts for day and night.'

Another tradition to which the bourgeois carefully conformed was a love of country

'The vast majority of women working in Paris live by needlework.'
An old woman knitting. From a photograph by Disdéri.

life. The author of *Paris Partout* took a somewhat cynical view of this 'passion'. 'When the month of May comes round, all the friends you meet on the boulevard feel obliged to make excuses for themselves, and to explain why they are not in the country. The Parisian doesn't like the country, but he is very anxious to seem to like it, and he would think himself dishonoured if he couldn't say that he spends at least a week there every year. For him, the ultimate thing is simply a small house with possession or use of a little garden, or even an apartment near a river, lake or pond; the garden and water are not strictly necessary, it's sometimes enough to have a tree nearby.'[3]

Bourgeois pretentions were based on solid foundations. Trade was flourishing. The number of patents taken out for inventions is an indication of industrial enterprise. During the reign of Louis-Philippe it had been only 2,937; during the Empire, it rose to 6,193. The rebuilding of Paris, the improvement of means of communication, and the abundance of capital fostered the concentration of industry, and the creation of the big multiple stores, like le Bon Marché, les Grands Magasins du Louvre, and the Épicerie Potin. In 1852 le Bon Marché was only an unimportant linen-draper's shop in the rue de Sèvres; in 1869 it had a turnover of seven million francs.

The most important enterprise for financiers and speculators was undoubtedly the spreading network of railways. One of the Prince President's first actions after the coup-d'état of 1851 was to have a *chemin de fer de ceinture* built inside the fortifications of Paris. During the year 1852 a series of decrees authorised the building of new lines, the forming of companies, and, most significant, the amalgamation of most of the existing companies into larger concerns which developed a vast railway system. Between 1852 and 1870, there was remarkable progress in developing the means of communication. Men, ideas and products circulated faster and more cheaply. This

LEFT *A department store in Second Empire Paris. From a contemporary watercolour.*

RIGHT *A hazard of the railway age: leaving without one's change. A cartoon from* Le Journal amusant, *1859.*

mobility had a marked effect on everyday life and on international relations, and it is one of the distinctive features of the second half of the nineteenth century.[4]

The Second Empire was a time of unrelenting speed and pressure. 'To arrive in time, and not miss the train, and not get on the wrong train, that is essential in a century of railways . . . In other words,' wrote the author of *Paris amoureux*, 'the success of today is not the success of yesterday, and it will not be the success of tomorrow. Hurrah! Success moves fast.'[5] Some people felt that the railways, which brought so many provincials, so many foreign visitors to Paris, had made the city less Parisian, and they deplored the loss of the Parisian spirit. Yet by the time Benjamin Gastineau finished writing his *Sottises et scandales du temps présent*, he had come to feel that the railways were not, perhaps, after all to be deplored: they were a sign of the future unification of humanity. 'But why are we talking about Parisians and provincials? . . . The railway will destroy the old moulds, the arbitrary agglomerations . . . Steam will create a new humanity, it will make a new map of the world.'[6]

In Paris itself, there were far-reaching changes in the means of transport. Until 1855, there were a dozen different omnibus companies in the capital; that year all the companies were amalgamated, and the service was centralised, to the great advantage of the public. 'The connections are certainly the most important of the many improvements made in the omnibus service for some years.' So wrote the author of *Paris illustrée*, in 1858. 'Thanks to these connections, you can go from one end of Paris to the other by changing omnibuses, and all for six sous.'[7]

In 1866, the author of *Eight Days in Paris* recorded that thirty-one lines of omnibuses were circulating in the capital from 8 a.m. to 11 p.m. A ticket for the *impériale*, or roof, cost 15 centimes, without connection; a ticket for the inside cost 30 centimes, including connection. The various lines were distinguished by different letters of the alphabet, and by their colours: yellow, green, orange, brown and chocolate.[8]

'We must be honest,' so the author of *Paris illustrée* had said. 'Knowing how to use the omnibuses is a real art . . . [But] nothing unbecoming or untoward occurs on omnibuses. A woman may perfectly well travel on one alone. Usually you find more women on omnibuses than men. Smokers and drunks are strictly forbidden. The omnibus is certainly not a fashionable conveyance, but people of the highest social standing do not hesitate to use it. If you leave the Odéon on an omnibus when the Senate (who hold their sessions opposite) have finished their day's work, you have the satisfaction of travelling in an omnibus full of Senators.'[9]

The plebeian might sit next to a Senator in an omnibus; but there remained a chasm between the social classes. As Leroy-Beaulieu observed, in *La Question ouvrière au XIXe siècle*: 'French society has become a society of *parvenus* and adventurers, whose only aim is to eclipse each other and to excite public envy. All the resources of private individuals are spent on outward luxury. Everything has been sacrificed to the splendour of clothes, carriages and furniture. *Society* in Paris is nothing, now, but a collection of *bourgeois gentilshommes*, who have all the eccentricities, all the faults of behaviour, of M. Jourdain, with much more corruption of heart. Most well-to-do families have adopted nomadic habits, flowing towards the big cities and selling their country inheritance. The education of youth has been deplorable in its nullity. Most children to whom the labour of preceding generations had assured the prospect of several hundred thousand francs, have been brought up with a criminal casualness and negligence, accustomed to think of living without effort and without work, of consuming their days in idleness and pleasure . . .

'Who could be surprised that the working people have been affected by the contagion of this malady? They are rightly accused of drunkenness, but what are those rows of cafés doing on our boulevards, overflowing with idlers and absinthe-drinkers? . . . They are reproached for misconduct and immorality. But who supports those elegant courtesans, . . . whose names are repeated and extolled with a sort of deference by our gossip-columnists? . . . Let us open our eyes and confess our faults. The working population of the big cities usually have nothing but corrupting examples before them. Their greatest crime is to be ready to imitate these opulent classes whom they envy.'[10]

Blanchard Jerrold confirmed this view. 'The Belle Jardinière decks the workman out for his fête days in imitation of his master. The jewellers . . . provide his wife with substantial electro earrings . . . The tradesman's wife must, on great days, be dressed like the richest of her customers.' 'French women of the humblest description do not meddle with the mysteries of dressmaking,' wrote another English observer. 'And very humble persons, in shops and public places, may be overheard talking of their couturières their marchandes-de-mode, and their femmes-de-chambre, who have themselves by no means so respectable an appearance as a second-rate housemaid in the family of an English gentleman.'[11]

La fille de comptoir. *From a drawing by Gavarni.*

Gavarni

Throughout the nineteenth century, two evils infected the urban working class; these were drunkenness among the men, easy virtue among the women. 'There are very few natural virtues,' so the Goncourts observed. 'Many virtues are impossible for the common people. Under an income of two thousand livres, certain moral senses do not exist.'[12] Drunkenness and immorality were not peculiar to the working classes, they have always been the vices of humanity. But since the worker did not have a private house like the bourgeois, his faults were more public. In Second Empire Paris, these two evils were all too plain. A decree of 1851 had given the Prefect absolute authority over bars and cafés; he could always order them to be closed, to protect public morals or prevent political gatherings. It was easier to ban a meeting than to stop drunkenness or immorality. Far from diminishing, the number of bars and cafés increased. The creation of retail shops which were licensed to sell spirits, was more regrettable. People did not drink more wine, but they drank more spirits.

In the fifth edition of his popular work, *Livre des classes ouvrières*, the Abbé Isidore Mullois, a Carmelite preacher, had desperately tried to persuade the working classes that there was no need to envy the rich. 'There is one thing you can be sure of. And that is that wealth is not the same thing as happiness; you will find this hard to believe, but it is quite true: you can be very rich and very unhappy. Happiness lies in mediocrity, and in moderate comfort, and happiness is more often found in the working classes than elsewhere. Fear not, Providence is good to you . . . A moral and industrious workman is the favourite, the spoilt child of Providence!' It was an unconvincing sermon; and to those who heard it there must have seemed little consolation for their condition. Working men must have found it hard not to console themselves in the nearest tavern for their irremediable destiny. 'Of course you may take a little recreation on Sunday,' added Mullois. 'The Sabbath is partly made for that . . . If you have something to spend, after you have been to mass, . . . spend it on the family, on your wife, your children, your old father . . . Have you only got dry bread to eat? Well, then, eat the bread with your family, affection will give a relish to it.'[13]

As Corbon, the working-class writer, observed in *Le Secret du peuple de Paris*, moralists were always bourgeois, and they were afraid of social agitation. The moralist, so Corbon wrote, simply told the working class: 'Don't worry about politics; think only of your work. Restrict yourself to this circle, and never try to get out of it. Be very good, very thrifty, just think of your own small concerns, and all will be well.' Corbon made the blunt comment that such advice blew over the workman like a light breeze blowing over granite. Everyone, added Corbon, must ask what light was necessary to illuminate the depths of society. 'Need we say that this light is education, and that we must count, above all, on the primary teacher to prevent the causes of failure in the young generation?' The secret of the people, Corbon concluded, was to be the instinctive force behind the new spirit of redemption. Revolution should complete the work begun by Christianity; it should bring the earthly redemption of all those who were humbled and oppressed. It should raise man up from his so-called indignity, make him the collaborator of God, and 'inaugurate the heroic age of labour'.[14]

Fancy dresses, 1860. On the RIGHT *a boating enthusiast;*
TOP LEFT *Pêcheur napolitain;* CENTRE LEFT *A Caucasian Prince;*
BOTTOM LEFT *Vivandière.*

While Corbon expressed his idealistic socialism, there remained in fact all too much uncertainty. As Leroy-Beaulieu observed, 'the reverse of the medal of magnificent modern industry was an excessive instability. Everyone suffered from it, but especially the workers. People were never sure of the morrow.' And Leroy-Beaulieu anticipated the modern problem of labour and management.

'No occasion should be lost to bring together the workers and their employers, to make their relationship closer and more constant, to ensure that they are no longer like the citizens of two rival and hostile nations. Many prejudices disappear, many animosities lose their edge when there is contact between human beings . . . Education also has a large part to play in easing relations between the different classes of society. It is not an all-powerful panacea, but it can have considerable influence, provided that it is solid and substantial. It must be concerned with useful ideas, and no longer just with words.'[15]

In the meanwhile, the poor in Paris lived in a lamentable state. At the bottom of the social scale were men without aspirations, cast by discouragement into drunkenness and idleness. Above these 'vicious' plebeians came the merely lazy; above these, in the 'proletarian population', came a much larger class of useful and hard-working labourers. They were given pitiful reward for their uninspiring work. In 1859, the author of *Realities of Paris Life* visited a master-sweep near the Clos Bruneau. He lived in a low-ceilinged loft. There was no window, but '. . . a hole in the tiles, which admits light, and with it, smoke and weather, for there is no glass and no shutter; cold air and rain avail themselves of it in winter, and heat, pestilence and vermin enter thereby in summer. Furniture there is none . . . In one corner are the contents of an *hotte*, in another a heap of hare-skins and old shoes, in wondrous and dire confusion; in the middle . . . stands a tumbledown iron stove, whose chimney crosses to the wall, where it finds an issue through the broken plaster. On the top of this inconvenient cooking-place, is a saucepan of gruel, or *soupe noire*, which the poor fellow is boiling for dinner.

'The first "room" is nearly filled up with a broad heap of straw – the sleeping-place of the whole family! They consist of our hungry-looking friend, his daughter, her husband, and two children, with three little sweeps who lodge with them. It is nearly twelve o'clock, and he is expecting them home to dinner . . .

'"Where are they now?"

'"To-day they are gone to Mass; it is a holiday." '[16]

If the working man earned a pittance, his wife earned even less; and in *Le Travail des femmes au XIXe siècle*, Leroy-Beaulieu left an eloquent record of the situation of working women in Paris.

'The first group to come to our notice is that of the young women who . . . are less concerned with making than with supply and sale. They give the merchandise the final touch of distinction; they present it to the customer, they decorate it, dress it, wrap it up, sometimes deliver it to people's houses; or else they keep the books and the

La Blanchisseuse, by Honoré Daumier.

accounts . . . In this category of working women, it is often the one who is modestly dressed, the one you meet in the simplest shops, who associates with the humblest public: it is often she who has the highest wages, the greatest comfort and the most assured future. It is a fact incontestably proved by the survey [of 1864] that the women employed by pork-butchers have higher wages and salaries than the elegant young women who wrap up and display the sweets at confectioners' with such taste; one also finds higher salaries for women working at vinegar-makers' or mustard-makers' than for those who sell cakes and ices with such distinction at well-known pâtissiers'. Indeed, one shudders at the thought that most of the young girls, who dress and speak like great ladies, do not earn more than 2 francs 50 a day, without the benefit of board and lodging, and that, among the 294 women stated to work at confectioners', the survey indicates only 12 who are paid 3 francs or more. This class . . . includes more than 10 or 12,000 women.

'The vast majority of women working in Parisian industry live by needlework . . . First of all, one must point out an *élite* of working women whose talent consists of taste and inventiveness rather than actual needlework. These do special tasks for women's milliners and tailors, and they earn as much as 5, 6, 8 and 10 francs a day. That is an extremely small minority, which does not represent one per cent of the women occupied by sewing in Paris . . . Sewing is the last resort of the woman with no support and no resources; and so every unhappy woman seizes this sheet-anchor, and manages, with great difficulty, despite her efforts, to keep herself above the gulf of poverty.'

A third class of working women in Paris was that of the women who did domestic work other than sewing: laundry, for example, or ironing. Seven-eighths of the laundresses earned 2 francs or 2 francs 50 a day; they often had soup, a glass of wine, or a glass of brandy, as well. Salaries were higher for those who worked for dyers and cleaners. Four-fifths of them earned 2 francs or more a day, and half of them earned 3 francs or more. This was one of the best-paid 'industries' in Paris. The fourth class of working women was concerned with luxury articles, and here the salaries 'reached their peak'. An ordinary working woman earned 2 francs 50 a day, a good one earned 3 francs or even 3 francs 50.

The final class which Leroy-Beaulieu distinguished was the class of '. . . women of all ages and all origins, some of them still children, others already old, some who have known prosperity, others who have known poverty since the cradle, all of them lacking resources, friends and wits, obliged by their incapacity to do all the easy, crude and ill-paid tasks . . . It is the category of the incapable, the declassed, the wretched, sometimes living on public assistance, sometimes on their unrewarding toil, sometimes on shame and vice: a vast legion which brings together thousands of creatures apparently occupied with different tasks, but condemned to the same destiny of material privations and moral trials. For such women the salaries are so low that it is hard to understand how they are enough for their subsistence.'[17]

The poverty of Paris, the underworld of the imperial city, was graphically recorded by

Alexandre Privat d'Anglemont. A dedicated Bohemian, he chose to live in destitution. He chose to spend his life preparing to write his survey *Paris inconnu*, and his private means seemed to him to be a barrier between himself and his subject. He spent his income, when it came, on feeding the starving poor of Paris; he mixed with pick-pockets and with rag-and-bone men. He spent his nights exploring Paris, regardless of his health. He died of consumption in 1859, at the age of thirty-nine. *Paris inconnu* was published two years later.

It is a bitter indictment of social injustice, a grim picture of the Paris which escaped the transformation of Haussmann, the benefits of legislation, and the philanthropy of those who believed in charity. It must be quoted, for it is as much a part of *la vie paris-ienne* as a gala ball at the Tuileries.

'The cloister of Saint-Jean de Latran stands opposite the Collège de France . . . It is a sink, a sewer, whatever you care to call it; but men are living there . . . Saint-Jean de Latran is a single house . . . with many staircases, and behind these are a series of virtual cesspools, sordid and ignoble, which are dignified by the name of yards . . . These hovels shelter the whole vagabond Bohemia of Paris: strolling musicians, street singers, sabre-swallowers, . . . acrobats, tooth-extractors and fire-eaters. Apart from this interesting class, one finds within these walls nearly all the little unknown trades which are carried on without licence; . . . in a word, all the vices and all the miseries.

'And so we saw people who spend their life cutting rabbit fur for felt hats, . . . and women who put wicks in night-lights . . . But the most curious thing we saw were two poor women who were living together in a little room which cost 40 francs a year. One was a waker-up, and the other kept an *estaminet des pieds-humides* . . . The task of the waker-up consists of calling the merchants and retail salesmen in Les Halles or the markets, who must be woken up in time for their work. The charge is five centimes a night, and generally the task begins at about midnight, and continues until four

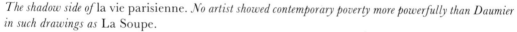

The shadow side of la vie parisienne. *No artist showed contemporary poverty more powerfully than Daumier in such drawings as* La Soupe.

Les Cris de Paris. *From* LEFT *to* RIGHT: *the pedlar, the porter from Les Halles, the coco-seller, and the rag-and-bone man.*

o'clock in the morning. Nearly all the people who work at night, the carriers and newspaper-folders, the market-porters, and a good many fruiterers, have their wakers-up. There are wakers-up who have up to thirty and forty clients; these are the millionaires of the profession.' The manageress of the *estaminet des pieds-humides* kept the humblest of workmen's cafés near Les Halles; the establishment consisted of a stove, a table, and a few chipped glasses.

Even such occupations as these did not mark the rock-bottom of society. Perhaps the lowest of the low was the old besotted ragpicker. 'No-one knew where he came from; he appeared one day in the neighbourhood, and he was drunk. No-one has seen him sober since that day. As soon as he has sold his basketful of rags and bones and broken glasses, he settles down in a corner with a bit of bread and a little brandy . . . By eight o'clock in the morning, he has rid himself of his night's harvest; and so he has ten hours ahead in which to get drunk . . . It is a declassed existence, a failure in his life which has led him to this besotted state. He drinks, he is always drinking, because he wants to forget, and his reason might not be strong enough to withstand the bitterness of his memories.'[18]

The misery of the poor in Paris was still more sharply recorded by the anarchist Jules Vallès. He had come from the Auvergne, as a young man, to try for the École normale, and in *Souvenirs d'un étudiant pauvre* he gave his account of the Bohemian world: a world which he did not see through Murger's eyes. In 1865, in *Les Réfractaires*, he again recorded the misery of Bohemia.

'Of course you may take a little recreation on Sunday . . .' La Bonne Bouteille, *by Daumier, shows a lighter moment in plebeian life.*

'*Le réfractaire de Paris*, the Parisian defaulter, pursues his way, in the face of laughter and derision . . . I have often seen valiant natures, generous spirits, noble hearts, wither and die because they have laughed, unseeing, in the face of real life, because they have *mocked* life, its demands and dangers! Life will make them perish, in revenge . . . I have seen people as good as we are, covering their hands with blood on a cemetery wall trying to go and sleep among the tombs. If someone had caught them by surprise, they would have thought that they had come to violate the graves, and cut rings off fingers.

'We need some or other shelter.'[19]

Poverty and resentment had already made Jules Vallès an unappeasable revolutionary. The *déclassés*, he wrote, 'must either settle down or take their revenge. And that is why so much absinthe flows down people's throats and so much blood on pavements. The *déclassés* become either drunkards or insurgents.' Vallès was a natural Communard. After 1871 he was exiled for his part in the Commune. He returned from exile to finish his masterpiece, the autobiographical trilogy *Joseph Vingtras*, in which he described his childhood, his struggle for a livelihood, and his later years of revolt. He dedicated the work 'to all those who have fed on Greek and Latin, and died of hunger.'[20]

5 La Vie de Bohème

One day in 1865, at the height of the Second Empire, Felix Whitehurst crossed the Seine, and ventured to explore the Left Bank. 'There is,' he wrote, 'Paris and Paris – one city and another . . . Yesterday I passed the river, and entered upon a Paris which existed before even the First Empire was a *fait accompli*. Paris of the days of old – Paris of beyond the Seine, of students, of cheap dining, dancing, dissipation – Paris of revolutionists, blouses, barricades, of patriots, police, domiciliary enquiries – in a word, Bohemia.'[1]

While the conventional and the prosperous lived on the Right Bank, the Left Bank, then as ever, was the home of Bohemia. But this Bohemia was already different from that which Murger had recorded in *Scènes de la vie de Bohème*. The world of Mimi and Musette, of joyous love among artists in their garrets, was part of the world of Louis-Philippe. It was not part of the world of Napoleon III. The Latin Quarter was not simply changing its appearance under the axes and spades of Baron Haussmann. It was also changing its way of life. Bohemian was a word in the current vocabulary of 1840: it had meant the artist or student, gay and carefree, idle and boisterous, the characters whom Murger had painted in bright, attractive colours. But, as Gabriel Guillemot wrote in 1868, in his survey *Le Bohème*, Murger's Bohemia, 'which one might call the Bohemia of legend, is well and truly dead . . . The climate is no longer favourable for that sort of fantasy.'[2] Murger's kind of Bohemian had long since lost his glamour; in 1868 men were measured by the gold they had in their pockets, there was no more indulgence for the poor. Poverty was not a vice, but it was a grave error.

The Second Empire Bohemians whom Guillemot described might, he said, be called 'the irregulars'. They included everyone who led a life of chance and rebelled against all discipline. They were a motley, unattractive regiment; and, when Guillemot had reviewed them, he drew some brutal conclusions. Bohemia, he said, was not the result of the social order, it was the result of nature.

'It is natural vice which makes the Bohemian.

'The Bohemian is the child of idleness and vanity.

Second Empire Bohemians: a detail from L'Atelier du peintre, *by Gustave Courbet, 1855.*

'As long as the idle and vain exist, there will be Bohemians.

'Look at them all!... They have education, strength and health and vigour.

'They could work and escape from this miserable position. They don't even think of doing so. My God! They're a thousand miles from thinking of it!... The most fortunate Bohemians soon die of exhaustion. Many of them cross the thin dividing line which separates them from the swindlers, and they fall into the hands of the police... Others end by finding employment in the depths of Parisian industry, some miserable work which saves them from hunger.

'But Bohemians very rarely reach an advanced age, or even maturity. The existences we have described are only possible for a short time. Infirmity has little pity on these irregular modes of life...'[3]

There was a certain justification for Guillemot's comments. *La vie de Bohème* was a pernicious mode of existence for the maladjusted and the ungifted, it was a way of life which could destroy the wholesome instincts of a man, the honourable elements in his character. It could help him to lose his love of family and country, his vital sense of responsibility. Maxime du Camp was to blame the disaster of 1870 on the generation of *petits crevés*: on the men-about-town who had wasted their youth and money on loose women. Perhaps he might also have blamed it on those who idled away their days round café tables, and spent their travesties of lives in attics and in brasseries, or watching passers-by on the boulevards. There were too many boulevardiers – one might call them Bohemians – who showed indifference to larger issues, and a cynical disregard of accepted standards.

Poets and artists of real distinction did not need to parade an ostentatious devotion to the Muse. But men of no distinction found literature and art a convenient pretext for idleness. They used genius, like the Emperor's clothes, to cover their nullity. Bohemia, as Murger knew, and as others repeated, should only be a stage in a man's existence. Bohemia was not a profession.

The Second Empire Bohemians were often found at Dinochau's, a modest little tavern in the quartier Bréda. It was a place to which the gossip-writers had given some or other special attraction, remembered Ernest Daudet, in his *Souvenirs de mon temps*. 'Why had people chosen this simple wine-shop in the first place?... No doubt because the food there was comparatively cheap. Then fashion had got hold of it, and people went there out of affectation... Local prostitutes, models and art students mingled there with more respectable customers. It was a real corner of Bohemia; and sometimes, in five minutes, you would make acquaintances there who were hard to acknowledge.'[4] 'A bourgeois, provincial dinner, greasy soup and boiled beef,' noted the Goncourts, of Dinochau's, in 1856. 'Always people without a name, always men of letters who should have made a name at their age and haven't.'[5] There was no suspicion of genius in most of those who frequented Dinochau's. Théodore Pelloquet wrote occasional monographs on artists, but he made his home in squalid cafés, and one was sure to find him there at any hour of the day or night. He died insane, presumably of syphilis, and his last words were a request for absinthe. Charles Bataille was also to die insane. He had had a promising start in life: he had come into a fortune, and he had been a not un-gifted poet. But he had lacked the character to make his career, he had spent his inheritance in taverns.

It was during the Second Empire that the brasseries began to compete with the cafés. They were soon patronised by writers and artists. The Brasserie Andler, in the rue Hautefeuille, was the headquarters of Courbet and Champfleury, and its regular clientele called it the Temple of Realism. The decoration was rustic: the wooden benches and tables were worn with use, there were stone slabs on the floor, and white-washed walls. Hams, and strings of sausages, hung from the beams on the ceiling. The clients emptied a good many tankards in the tobacco-laden atmosphere. The generation of Realists was followed by that of the Impressionists, as they were christened long afterwards; and the artists deserted the brasseries of the Left Bank for the cafés of Montmartre.

During the Second Empire the fame of Dinochau's and the Brasserie Andler was largely eclipsed by that of the Brasserie des Martyrs, not far from Notre-Dame-de-Lorette. More than one writer observed the ironic fitness of the name. Here, among the flaring gas-lamps, the mirrors and the gilt, in an atmosphere thick with conflicting smells of tobacco and sauerkraut, the Bohemians of Paris assembled: 'the weavers of rhymes, the poetasters still damp from the nest, the penniless philosophers indifferent to money, the hunters of pictures, the chasers of words, the roving artists of pen or brush, nearly all of them suffering more or less acutely from Panurge's disease: lack of money.'[6] There was Eugène Cressot, the poet, who, thanks to a little translation work, could manage to eat every other day. When one of his friends left him a small legacy, he was so unaccustomed to eating that he died of indigestion, after eating two meals within forty-eight hours. Such misery was not uncommon at the Brasserie: it was the home of the rejected and the desperate. 'A tavern and retreat for all great men without a name,' wrote the Goncourts, 'for all the men in lesser journalism. A heavy, boring, ignoble, gossipy atmosphere . . . Murger, their only man of standing, still has both feet inside – he talks to all these people, and he sits down with them as if he was in his spiritual home.'[7] There were in fact some Parnassians at the Brasserie – Glatigny, the Bohemian poet, among them. But some considered the Brasserie so low that they refused even to accept it as part of Paris. In 1857, when two of its customers reached the point of a duel, the superintendent of police observed: 'When you're insulted there, you must take a knife and kill the insulter. The police wouldn't interfere.'[8] A chronicler, writing of Paris in 1860, declared that even lorettes lost caste if they haunted the Brasserie des Martyrs.

It was the presence of the lorettes which kept the Prince of Poets, Leconte de Lisle, away from the Brasserie. He was conventional and high-minded, married and home-loving, and to him the place meant contamination. 'It was impossible,' wrote his biographer, 'to persuade Leconte de Lisle to frequent the Brasserie. He would not have found himself the only one of his rank, . . . but he had such a horror . . . of anything that suggested promiscuity, that he made no distinction between the friendly grisette and the exploiter of men. And, much more important, he would have suffered as from a profanation to have heard a single line of his poetry repeated by those lips which were easy to kiss.'[9]

He was not the only person to feel aversion. 'Whenever people talk of pleasures, of clandestine love, of ephemeral liaisons, ruined eldest sons, . . . one's imagination turns, irresistibly,' wrote Privat d'Anglemont, 'towards Notre-Dame-de-Lorette . . . As soon as you mention the name in the provinces, young girls avert their eyes, mothers cross themselves, and eligible young ladies look at you with displeasure. If you have the misfortune to say, in conversation: I was going to see a man I know in the rue Notre-Dame-de-Lorette, then you are lost . . .'[10]

Taverns and brasseries were not the only places in which to find Parisian Bohemia. If the boulevard was the parade-ground of the dandy, it was also the place where the world of fashion and Bohemia met. 'Bohemia swarms all along the boulevards, from the rue Montmartre to the rue de la Paix,' wrote Guillemot in 1868.

One of the saddest figures on the boulevards in the 1850s was Roger de Beauvoir. He had known the brilliant Romantic Bohemia of the Impasse du Doyenné and the Hôtel Pimodan. Now his life had outrun his fortune; his marriage had proved disastrous, and he had returned to a bachelor life. By about 1853 the exemplary dandy had become a down-at-heel Bohemian.

Outwardly he remained vivacious; and his social activity continued. 'What vitality!' cried Monselet. 'How he comes and goes! And he's always smiling. He spends his life greeting friends on the boulevards, . . . at Tortoni's and the Opéra. When he opens his mouth, he speaks in verse, and he only stops talking to drink champagne. But how gracefully he drinks it! Where does he find the time to write, this talker, this viveur, this lover of pictures, this traveller, litigant and duellist?'[11]

This ceaseless activity hid his unhappiness. In the late 1850s Gustave Claudin suffered from insomnia, and he used to wander down the boulevards, searching for people who would make a little of the night into day. And so he formed a small coterie with other noctambulists: Lambert Thiboust, the vaudeville-writer, Murger himself, and Nestor Roqueplan, the journalist, co-founder of *Le Figaro*. With this melancholy company was Roger de Beauvoir. They used to meet late at night and install themselves at the Maison d'Or or the Café des Variétés. They ate very little, but they talked abundantly. Roger used to eat fried eggs and compose impromptu songs, and, after two glasses of champagne, he began to tell incoherent stories. 'I have drunk 150,000 francs' worth of champagne, and written three hundred little poems, madrigals, epigrams and songs,' Roger said to Philibert Audebrand just before he died. Perhaps if he had resisted pleasure, shown more firmness of character, he would have taken a higher rank as a writer. He died in 1866, 'a mere wreck, . . . in a room almost destitute of furniture.'[12] He was virtually forgotten by Paris.

If men of letters lacked professional distinction, they redeemed themselves by being

LEFT *The 'Bohemian' poet Albert Glatigny;* CENTRE *the boulevardier Aurélien Scholl, and* RIGHT *Mme Sabatier and Baudelaire, a detail from* L'Atelier du peintre, *by Gustave Courbet, 1855*

picturesque. When Firmin Maillard recalled his memories of the boulevard, he conjured up a Bohemian vision of Aurélien Scholl sporting purple boots, and Nestor Roqueplan wearing a white flannel suit, with baggy trousers and red silk stockings and a small Spanish sombrero. Not everyone could afford such luxuries. Less prosperous Bohemians resorted to le père Porée, the secondhand-clothes man in the rue La Bruyère. He gave them suits on credit, and even slipped a few coins in the pockets. The money was not always repaid.

It was not surprising that when Guillemot published his survey *Le Bohème* in 1868, he included everyone who lived like parasites on society. Among them were the black-coated Bohemian, the professional cadger of meals, and the pillar-of-the-café, who operated at absinthe time, between five and six in the evening.[13]

Those who paused at the Café Tabourey, opposite the Odéon, would see a flamboyant and pathetic figure: the Bohemian Brummell, Barbey d'Aurevilly. An arrogant, posturing, ageing creature, he earned his living by writing; but his dandyism was known to many people who had never read a line of his work. 'His provocative hats, his cravats and cuffs, his frock-coats worn tight round the waist over a corset, and full in the skirt, his striped trousers, which he struck with his stick: all seemed to evoke some Romantic Franconi.'[14]

Yet it must be said, in fairness, that Bohemia knew its gifted men as well as its failures. Baudelaire occasionally went to Dinochau's, Courbet cut a revolutionary figure at the Brasserie des Martyrs; and the Brasserie was also the haunt of the poet and roving actor Albert Glatigny. Glatigny used to grow red with anger when he was described as a Bohemian. 'Bohemian!' he would shout. 'The cretins! The Bohemian doesn't work, the Bohemian always sits around in incurable indolence, the Bohemian has no idea what he will do tomorrow. But I am working all the time . . . I always know what I'll do next day. I'll be writing poetry. Me a Bohemian! None of those people know me.'

Despite his protestations, he underlines the difference between the natural Bohemian and the poseur. Here was a man who led a completely Bohemian existence, defying the demands of the social structure, accepting poverty, homelessness and continual physical hardship, and devoting himself to the two arts – acting and poetry – which he loved. There was no touch of the *cabotin* about Glatigny; he was no exhibitionist, he sought no audience except the audience of some provincial theatre, no public except the public who read his poetry. Glatigny led a Bohemian life from choice, and for himself alone.

There is one other cardinal difference between Glatigny and the large majority of Bohemians: Glatigny was a poet of distinction. His way of life was not a mere escape from maturity; it suited his character, and it informed his work. Glatigny's poems belong inescapably to the man and to the Bohemian way of life which he chose.[15]

Those who had the character to use their natural gifts, the luck and determination to succeed, could lead a life both Bohemian and elegant. One of the liveliest centres of Bohemian life was Doré's splendid house in the rue Saint-Dominique. Blanche Roosevelt, Doré's biographer, remembered: 'The house from basement to roof-tree realised the ideal of the residence of a wealthy gentleman with bohemian but artistic tastes. And yet it was palatial; the odour of its former ducal days still lingered about its apartments, blended with an atmosphere of such modern comfort, gaiety and unrestraint, that but to cross the threshold was to feel at once at home, and think of the number of great people, since the Regent's days, who had crossed that threshold. Their name was legion. I remember a few, and set them down here at random: – Rossini, Patti, Alboni, Nilsson, Théophile Gautier (father and son), . . . Alexandre Dumas (father and son) . . . ; Liszt, Pauline Viardot, . . . and Nadar, the "marvel", who has done everything and can do anything; Gounod, who sings as does nobody else in the world . . .

'Imagine that studio when it was filled with this delightful society; Madame Doré in a chair of state, receiving her guests . . . Madame Doré constantly wore her turban, and dressed in a sort of semi-Mauresque, semi-Andalusian fashion. M. Lacroix said of her that she always looked like an accomplished gipsy . . .

'Mme Doré's receptions were held on Sunday evenings, and were always preceded by dinner-parties which are reckoned nowadays among the historical events of Paris . . . It must not be assumed that these dinners resembled one another, except with regard to rich viands, fine wines, unlimited fun and abundance of celebrities, all of which were never lacking; for it was Doré's special study to devise some new entertainment or diversion for each dinner-party.'

Sometimes, perhaps, the diversions were those of a *collégien*. 'Once the red wine was decanted in carafes which were really Swiss musical-boxes. Doré was continually begging his guests to drink, and then, as soon as the flask was lifted, the music began to play.' But if some of Doré's guests drank claret, he himself drank nothing but champagne; and, on special occasions, 'Chevet brought an army of cooks and assistants to his aid, and the guests were treated to new dishes invented and prepared in honour of Gustave's latest illustrations.'[16]

One other *salon* must be mentioned, for it epitomised all that was best in Bohemia. This was the *salon* of Mme Sabatier, christened by Gautier *la Présidente*.[17] Apollonie Sabatier had been born in 1820, the illegitimate daughter of a sempstress and the Prefect of the Ardennes. Gifted with a remarkable voice, she would no doubt have become a concert singer had she not been discovered by a wealthy Belgian, Alfred Mosselman. He was impressed by her beauty, and set her up as his mistress at 4, rue Frochot, in the quartier Bréda: the quartier of the artist and the kept woman. Apollonie's beauty and goodness of heart, her understanding of artists, made her the friend of Flaubert and Berlioz, Meissonier (who painted her many times) and Gautier (who wrote her two of the poems in *Émaux et Camées*). She was, above all, the *Vénus blanche* of Baudelaire: the Muse and the Madonna who inspired a cycle of poems in *Les Fleurs du mal*. On Sunday evenings, in the rue Frochot, she drew a galaxy of famous men about her. As Gautier said, she was superior to other women, not just because she was more beautiful, but because she did not demand that men paid court to her. She allowed them to have the most serious and the most abstract conversations, she allowed them absolute freedom of speech. She contrived to show no special favour, but to favour all of them. And so it was that, after his great concert at the Exhibition of 1855, Berlioz chose to dine with la Présidente; and Gautier, returning from Russia on a Sunday evening, went at once, inevitably, to the rue Frochot, still in the exotic clothes in which he had braved the St Petersburg winter. In his memoirs of Gautier, Ernest Feydeau said that Gautier's wit shone most radiantly at the rue Frochot: there he felt himself in the 'sphere of benevolence' that every artist needs for the full flowering of his genius. No-one, continued Feydeau, 'could have any idea of the wit that sparkled round that table on Sunday evenings . . . I have not asked the opinion of everyone who used to come, but I think I can say that the happiest moments in all our lives were spent with la Présidente, and we owe this not only to the sterling, unfailing verve of Théophile Gautier, but to the sweet benevolence of that charming woman.'[18]

In time la Présidente became the mistress of Sir Richard Wallace, the founder of the Wallace Collection. Two days before the Siege of Paris began, he settled a handsome sum on her; and, after the Franco-Prussian War, she moved to the avenue de l'Impératrice, and decided to resume the Sunday dinners, to recreate the brilliance of the rue Frochot. But some conjunctions of the stars do not repeat themselves; some friends were dead, and some had drifted out of her existence. The dinners were pale reflections of the dinners in the quartier Bréda.

6 Hunting, Fishing, and Crikett

During the Second Empire, there was a remarkable understanding, a genuine *entente cordiale*, between England and France. This understanding was strengthened by the exchange of State visits between Queen Victoria and the Emperor, and, of course, by the allied victory in the Crimea. A British officer declared, just after the war, that 'history presents no example of two great nations passing so speedily and on grounds so reasonable and intelligible – on grounds, too, independent of political combinations – from coldness to confidence.'[1]

Some English observers were less enthusiastic. In his *Imperial Paris*, published in 1855, Blanchard Jerrold raised an eyebrow at traditional French arrogance: 'We are barbarians, to be raised from our vulgar debasement by the surpassing excellencies of French artists and French authors. Poetry is to arrive in London, presently, from Paris direct. This is the Parisian view of the consequences of our *entente excessivement cordiale* . . . The French have yet to discover that the poetic element dwells sometimes in London; that the English are establishing a notable school of art; that Britons can amuse themselves and do occasionally laugh; and that the soul of every son of Albion is not nailed, like a bad shilling, to his counter.'[2]

Yet perhaps Jerrold was wrong when he said that the verdicts of the English and the French on one another had not changed in the last fifty years. In 1855, many English visitors made their way to the Paris Exhibition, and lingered on under the three thousand gas-lamps of the Bal Mabille. Those who resolutely clung to their gastronomic habits visited His Lordship's Larder at 25, rue Royale, to comfort themselves, as the French guide suggested, with 'Scoth Ale, Barclay Perckins, Porter et Stouds, Wisky.'[3] Twelve years later, on the eve of the 1867 Exhibition, an English journalist noted with amusement: 'Among other curious indications of the coming season is a slight eruption of Anglomania. English signs begin to appear, and curious announcements . . . "Coffee and beer always ready, roast beef and plum pudding all day, and *stakes* from London every day and night." . . . One restaurant startles us with this horrible advertisement: "Real *live* turtle soup." '[4]

An early symbol of the entente cordiale: Un Anglais à Mabille, *by Gustave Doré.*

A banquet given by Le Figaro *at Peter's, 4 February 1864.*

Another startling sign of Anglomania was the behaviour of the young Duchesse de Persigny, whose husband had been Ambassador at the Court of St James's. She had developed such a passion for English customs that she affected to speak only English. Society called her Lady Persington.[5]

There were more serious indications of the English influence in Paris. 'We are *Englishing* ourselves more and more,' wrote a journalist in 1863. 'Women are beginning to wear leather belts, *à l'anglaise*, with steel trimmings; they have leather-coloured dresses, and dresses trimmed with leather. They have an Englishman, the famous Worth, as their *couturier*; they buy plaids and tweeds. In the meanwhile, men are not being cured of their whiskers *à l'anglaise*, their suits *à l'anglaise*, their bearing and jargon and carriages *à l'anglaise*. Those purveyors of Parisian elegance who are not called John are called John's or Peter's.'[6]

Among them was Peter's, the restaurant in the passage des Princes; it was simply a translation of the owner's name: Pierre Fraisse.

While fashion itself was dictated by Charles Frederick Worth, English nannies were already recognised for their sterling qualities, and the Prince Imperial was devotedly brought up by Miss Shaw; the Tascher de la Pagerie children had a governess from Yorkshire, Anna Bicknell.

One other English institution made a profound impression, and this was the club. In 1867, in *Les Plaisirs de Paris*, Alfred Delvau explained: 'England has her *club-houses*, France has her clubs, or *cercles*. Since when? Since the mania for imitating England overcame us. Once upon a time, we imposed our own customs on other people; today we allow our neighbours across the Channel to impose theirs. There is this difference between the English clubs and the French ones, that the former have exercised – and still exercise – a real influence on politics, on literature and the arts and everything in life, and that our own clubs exercise no influence on anything.'[7]

Club life was in fact a challenge to certain French traditions: to café life and *la vie du boulevard*, which had claimed the dandies, the men-about-town, and the prosperous intellectual élite. Club life was a challenge to the *salon*, and to the art of conversation. Some also saw it as a danger to family life: an ominous new attraction which would segregate men from society.

One of the Parisians most alarmed by the clubs was the middle-aged boulevardier, Gustave Claudin. In his *Paris*, which was published in 1867, Claudin maintained that Parisians, 'those modern Athenians, should alone set the tone . . . In future, we shall welcome foreigners, but we shall take special care to ask them to adopt our customs and habits, and not to impose their own upon us.'[8]

In the meanwhile, Claudin could only recognise that clubs were popular in Paris; and he blamed them for the decline in the quality of society. 'This custom, which came from England, has made disturbing progress here in the past few years. If these sorts of gatherings hold no danger for English society, it is not the same in Paris, where they have really broken what used to be called the home . . . The result is fatal.' And so Claudin struggled against progress. A few pages later, he declared that gaslight should be abandoned. 'It is,' he wrote, 'the absinthe of the eyes; it is, to put it briefly, the worthy counterpart of photography. Industry . . . should really find the means of bringing us back to the use of wax candles.'[9]

The most exclusive club in Paris in the Second Empire was l'Union, which accepted only diplomats and the highest aristocracy. 'Wealth does not give access to it,' wrote Charles Yriarte in 1864. 'Talent, even genius, . . . count as nothing, there. If Lord Byron had presented himself, he would have been admitted as a member of the Upper House.'[10]

L'Union had been founded in 1828 by the Duc de Guiche; he had lived for a long time in England, and he had been much impressed by the London clubs. They had provided advantages which were usually enjoyed only by those who were blessed with a large fortune: an extensive library, a fine cellar, sophisticated cooking, gaming tables, and pleasant conversation. He hoped that l'Union would provide the same amenities in Paris.

Every successive British Ambassador belonged to l'Union; and diplomats who frequented it found themselves spreading English habits and customs. In 1857, the club established itself in a handsome house in the boulevard des Capucines, which was furnished with English restraint and comfort. The cellar was famous, and members enjoyed, 'at a relatively moderate price,' wines which were unobtainable elsewhere. Gastronomes spoke with veneration of a transcendent Léoville and Clos-Vougeot. The diplomatic corps were found at l'Union (claimed Yriarte) in their entirety. There were five hundred permanent members, half of them foreign and half French, and two hundred and fifty honorary members. L'Union remained the club *par excellence*.

Socially speaking, it was like the golden barrier in the throne-room in the palace at Vienna, which only certain ambassadors could pass. The Jockey Club was 'like a chain which will finally bind together every class in our society.' The official name of the Jockey Club was Le Cercle d'encouragement pour l'amélioration des races de chevaux en France. As Yriarte explained: 'A fine name, a brilliant life, a taste for horses and for spending money ensure admission to the Jockey Club. It is always understood that the first essential qualification is the most perfect sense of honour.'[11] In 1864, when he published his survey, *Les Cercles de Paris*, there were still no representatives of the Bourse at the Jockey Club; but the most famous financiers belonged to it, and so did some of the most important industrialists. There was no limit to the number of members. Parisian solicitors used to say that membership of the Jockey Club meant another 200,000 francs in a dowry.

The club itself stood at the corner of the boulevard des Capucines and the rue Scribe; but inside it was remarkably English. Yriarte noted, admiringly: 'The dressing-rooms are upstairs; . . . there are eight of them, planned in the English style, equipped

Familiar to the man-about-town in Second Empire Paris: the Jockey Club, and RIGHT *the elegant figure of the Duc de Morny.*

with large white marble tables, and basins which attempt British proportions, and (an eloquent comment on the comfort at the club) two of these dressing-rooms are equipped with baths . . . I need not add that the pipes for hot and cold water, not to mention the electric bells, . . . are planned with all the care which the English show in this sort of installation.'[12] As for *le Betting-room*, it was hung with pictures of the Derby, and it was 'un coin de l'Angleterre'.[13]

The Jockey Club attracted the elegant, sporting aristocracy. Le Cercle agricole drew the legitimist aristocracy which had not rallied to the new régime: the aristocracy whose age and tastes set them somewhat outside the usual glittering circles of nobility. 'Everyone connected with the faubourg Saint-Germain who does not belong to the Union or the Jockey belongs,' explained Yriarte, 'to the Cercle agricole.' There were few diplomats or politicians at the Cercle agricole; most of its members lived in the country, devoting themselves to their châteaux and estates, and quietly lamenting the past. There seems to have been a slightly dated air about Le Cercle agricole, on the corner of the quai Voltaire and the rue de Beaune; but its table was distinguished, and Yriarte noted a revealing detail of club life: in 1858 the members spent 6,225 francs on cigars.[14]

L'Union artistique had been founded to bring together the nobility and the world of the arts. It did not have a purely social purpose. The literary committee organised readings of unpublished works, and recommended the publication of deserving writing. A second committee was concerned with the visual arts, and tried to arrange a permanent exhibition at the club. The music committee set out to organise weekly concerts, and to hear new compositions, and all musical celebrities passing through the capital. It was an ambitious programme, and Yriarte was well aware of the difficulties which were involved. 'Modern society,' he wrote, 'professes the most profound indifference for everything connected with the arts; we are the negation of artistic feeling, just as we are also the supreme personification of industrialism.'[15]

The industrialists had a club of their own: le Cercle des Chemins de Fer. Its existence was justified, so he wrote rather coldly, 'by the tendencies of the present generation'.[16] The club stood at the corner of the rue de la Michodière and the boulevard des Italiens. An anonymous English visitor, the author of *What's What in Paris*, dined there in 1867 with three friends. The dinner, he said, 'would have fed a convent. I was quite overwhelmed. Our smallest *entrée* was a calf's head! And this is the *haute cuisine bourgeoise*, the best native cookery.'[17]

It was also a comment on the bourgeois status of le Cercle des Chemins de Fer.

Parisian clubs owed much to English influence; so did Parisian sport. 'Men-about-town are now talking horses, racing and breeding,' Thomas Graindorge explained to his nephew in 1867. 'I advise you to try political economy, it will set you off in masculine society.'[18] That year, Gustave Claudin listed horse-racing among the new Parisian customs. 'It is,' he explained, 'from England that we have borrowed the passion for racing. Races have become an institution for us . . . The *Moniteur* [or official organ]

Racing at Longchamp, 1864, a detail from the painting by Édouard Manet.

of this institution is *Sport,* under its jurisdiction are the horse-breeders and the *sportsmen,* and the tribunes are the race-courses of Longchamp, Chantilly, Versailles and Baden, which correspond to Epsom and Newmarket.'[19] Alfred Delvau made the same point in *Les Plaisirs de Paris*: 'England had her horse-races, so we wanted to have ours. It is only strange that this Anglomania dates from the First Empire – a period when France did not exactly have good reasons to be Anglomaniac.'[20] It was not simply the fashion for racing which came from across the Channel. As the author of *Paris illustrée* pointed out, in 1858: 'In taking England as our model in the organisation of our races, we have borrowed not only most of her rules, but most of her traditional trappings. We have adopted official costumes for jockeys, . . . the different coloured caps and jackets.'[21] In 1864 Manet painted the races at Longchamp. The jockeys, in their multicoloured caps and jackets, are riding with headlong speed, the horses are thundering straight at the spectator. It is a brilliant impression of excitement.

The era of French racing triumphs had begun in 1856. 'Monarque was the prelude on the English race-course to the dazzling later triumphs of Potocki, Straddla, Brocoli, Dollar, Mandarin, Fille-de-l'Air, Mazeppa . . .'[22] The racecourse at Longchamp was opened in 1857. It was the versatile Duc de Morny, statesman, sportsman, social figure and amateur dramatist, who first thought of instituting a Grand Prix; and the City of Paris promised a prize of a hundred thousand francs for the race. In 1863 it was won by an English horse; but 1865 was the year of the immortal Gladiateur. On 30 May, that year, Henri Dabot recorded: 'The Jockey Club in the boulevard des Capucines is all illuminated tonight to celebrate the victory of a French horse at Epsom: Gladiateur, from the stables of the Comte de Lagrange.' A fortnight later, on

Un monsieur qui n'a pris que 198 leçons. — Milord. — Laisser-aller plein de grâce. — Le centaure Chiron, loge à pied et à cheval. — Clorinde et Tancrède, (rivière des Amazones).

Seen on the course at Longchamp: some sporting types depicted by Marcelin.

14 June, Dabot continued: 'Paris has gone quite mad with exultation; strangers are talking to one another in the street, which is a sign of a great event. And it is certainly a great event: Gladiateur, . . . which recently won the Derby at Epsom, has been victorious again in the Grand Prix de Paris.'[23] The following month, an enterprising publisher brought out 'the biography of no less illustrious a person than Gladiateur, accompanied by the history of the Comte de Lagrange's breeding stables.'[24] On 15 August, in the honours list for *la fête de l'Empereur*, the Comte de Lagrange was promoted Officier de la Légion-d'honneur. 'His Fille-de-l'Air and his Gladiateur,' wrote Dabot, with approval, 'have maintained the honour of French stables.'[25] The Prince Imperial's dining-room at the Tuileries was in time adorned by a painting of Gladiateur, the patriotic horse.

The racing season began on the first Sunday in March, sometimes on the last Sunday in February, at La Marche, a charming little park which was only a dozen kilometres from Paris, and five from Saint-Cloud. In the second fortnight of March, there were races at Vincennes; and about 15 April the spring meeting began in the Bois de Boulogne. This lasted until about 15 May, when it was followed by three days of racing at Chantilly. 'For some years,' wrote Henry de Conty in the mid-1860s, 'race-courses have been the meeting-place for the world of fashion in their sumptuous carriages. They are one of the pleasures most aristocratically enjoyed. People go there because they like it, because it's smart, and because they want to vie with one another's luxury and clothes.'[26] Maxime du Camp made much the same point in his survey of Paris. 'Whenever there are uniforms or clothes to be admired, the Parisian rushes there; he doesn't miss a review, and he goes to the races although he doesn't understand anything

'*Parisians were not inclined to swim* au naturel.' *A bathing scene during the Second Empire.*

about them. He is hardly interested in horses, but he goes there to copy *le tout Paris* . . . Serious intellectual pleasures leave him absolutely cold.'[27] On 2 June 1867, a Grand Prix of 100,000 francs was offered at Longchamp, half by the City of Paris, and half by the five great railway companies. The presence of the Emperor and Empress, the Czar and two Grand Dukes, and the Prince Royal of Prussia 'sanctified' racing.

The author of *Paris illustrée* had shown an equally snobbish attitude to sport. The youth of the day, so he maintained in 1858, took an interest in shooting, fencing and boxing. 'For some years, these forms of exercise have enjoyed great favour in high society . . . Lecour, our famous boxing master, . . . includes the finest names of the great world among his pupils.'[28] The Vicomte de Beaumont-Vassy wrote that 'hunting, fishing, and certain games like *crikett*, have become sports. Certain English fashions and customs, introduced at first as an affectation, are tending to become acclimatised here.'[29] Paris did indeed attempt to understand the mysteries of *crikett*. In *Paris for the English, 1867*, Blanchard Jerrold noted: 'Frequent Cricket Matches are announced for this year – on the grounds of the Paris Cricket Club, in the Bois de Boulogne.'[30] The Hon. Denis Bingham remembered playing there, 'and one day the Emperor and Empress came to witness the game.' But this form of sport, it must be said, never became acclimatised in Paris. The French, as Bingham added in his *Recollections of Paris*, 'have never taken to cricket. In the South a funny incident happened with some Englishmen, who were indulging in the national pastime. The mayor of the *commune*, unable to understand it, and suspecting something dangerous to the safety of the State, confiscated bats, balls and wickets, and sent them to Paris, asking for instructions.'[31]

Parisians on the Seine: LEFT *bathing at Bougival, and* RIGHT *two rowing enthusiasts dressed for action at Asnières.*

If Denis Bingham was amused by the French attitude to cricket, Felix Whitehurst smiled to see Parisians bathing. In the autumn of 1867, he found himself at Biarritz (it was often called the French Brighton). 'It is a droll scene,' wrote Whitehurst, 'that in front of the bathing-establishments . . . You pay 6d. for a suit of bathing-clothes and extra for towels. We will say that you are sitting quietly smoking a cigar outside the establishment, when before you pass two charming female figures in the very height of Paris costume, down even to the Alpenstock-handled parasol.' Ten minutes later, the same charming figures emerged from the establishment with their duckers.

'The party – male and female – is dressed in knickerbockers and a kind of *domino noir* . . . The two couples advance slowly, hand in hand, as if they were about to dance a minuet or gavotte. Gracefully – more or less – they meet each wave, to which they "set", and finally drop the lowest of curtseys, and are wetted from head to foot. When they are damp and sandy enough, they retire on their feet, or in old-fashioned sedan chairs, which are more suggestive of Bath than of bathing. Then the swells of the land, in every description of masquerade, run down into the swell of the sea, and divert themselves with performing fantastic dances to the vocal accompaniment of airs from the *Grande Duchesse*; and this is called bathing. Give me a boat and a swim *au naturel*!'[32]

Parisians were not inclined to swim *au naturel*. Zola recorded, in *La Curée*, how Renée and Maxime were obliged to go to a seaside resort for the sake of convention. They went there regretfully, dreaming of the boulevards as they sat, bored and irritable, on the beach; even their love-affair was strained by the exile. In their hotel room, Renée attempted to play *La Belle Hélène* on the piano; it sounded dismal. She consoled herself by wearing extravagant clothes. She 'could never make Maxime bathe. He was terribly afraid of the water, and turned quite pale when the waves reached his boots.'[33]

In Paris itself, Parisians swam for reasons which – as usual – seemed more social than athletic. The author of *Paris illustrée* observed, with benign satisfaction: 'The Imperial School of Swimming, on the quai d'Orsay, . . . is a perfect model of convenient arrangement, cleanliness, taste, and good manners. There the charm of the bathe is increased by a number of amenities which one would not find anywhere else: long open galleries, on whose carpeted floors the bather sets his foot as softly as on the moss in a forest; a huge divan, decorated in the Moorish style, which is kiosk and drawing-room together . . .

'You bathe, and drink, and smoke, and chat, and watch, and especially smoke. On an average, more than twelve hundred cigars are sold at the School of Swimming on a fine summer day; and cigars are the indispensable complement to the pleasure of the cold bathe. Thanks to this accessory, the cold bathe takes on the charm of the dreams and the nonchalance of the East.'[34]

Parisians never quite acquired the English love of messing about in boats; but those who did not move in the highest social circles were remarkably addicted to rowing.

'We are not such fanatics about boats as the English and the Americans,' Delvau admitted in 1867, 'but we have finally grown enthusiastic . . . We don't have a Yacht Club, but we have a Rowing Club. We don't go from Europe to America in a nutshell, but we have fresh water regattas and salt water regattas, at Le Havre and at Asnières, on rivers and on lakes. The taste for boating has developed remarkably in the last fifteen years; and what proves it is that an official list of pleasure boats recorded in the various maritime departments of France since the circular of 23 May 1862 gives a figure of 4,696 boats and craft manned by 5,776 amateurs, not to mention sailing boats, rowing boats and steam ships designed for the navigation of the river – there are more than 8,000 of these.'[35]

'The first regattas, like the first horse-races, begin with the spring,' wrote Édouard Gourdon. 'When the osier-beds enliven the banks of the islands between Asnières and Saint-Cloud with their tender green, the first oarsmen and their ladies appear in their boats once again. The joyful crowd, as agile as a flight of kingfishers, flash about the Seine, visit all its creeks and straits. This is the beginning . . .

'There have been many portraits of the Parisian oarsman, and I am not going to draw another. Wearing a woollen cap or an oilcloth hat, clad in a red jersey and thick woollen trousers, with a blue belt round his waist, the oarsman carries local colour to the point of fanaticism. He walks with the rolling gait of a sailor setting foot on land after six months at sea. To see him with his tarred apron, his resolute air, a boat-hook or an oar on his shoulder, you would think he was coming back from deep-sea fishing, or about to embark on it. Don't be deceived, he is coming back from Asnières, and not from Newfoundland; and, tomorrow, if you have to go to Paris on business, you stand a good chance of meeting the sea-dog in the boulevard des Italiens.'[36]

RIGHT At the race course, *a detail from the painting by Edgar Degas,* c. *1869.* OVERLEAF La Grenouillière, *by Claude Monet, 1869.*

One other sport may be mentioned. In 1855, when Michaux invented the pedal, cycling became a possibility, but as yet it could only be enjoyed by a few. It was, however, on a primitive velocipede, with iron-rimmed wheels, that Moore, an Englishman, won the first bicycle race ever organised, in 1869. That year Henri Dabot, the diarist of the Latin Quarter, reported that riders were trying out their machines in the Luxembourg Gardens.[37] That same year, Princess Mathilde gave the Prince Imperial a bicycle for his thirteenth birthday; and, at his birthday party at the Tuileries, elated by champagne, when he drank to the Emperor and Empress, the French army, the imperial navy and the Garde mobile, the Prince remembered 'Michaux, the inventor of the velocipede, and gave him an honourable mention'. The cumbrous imperial bicycle may be seen today in the Museo Napoleonico in Rome.[38]

The year 1869 was indeed a significant year in cycling history. On 7 November the first race was ridden on the roads of France. It was organised by *Le Vélocipède illustré*, the first cycling paper, which had recently been founded. Three hundred people had entered for the race, and a hundred actually started, an astonishing number for the period. The race, once again, was won by Moore, who covered the hundred and twenty-six kilometres in ten hours and forty minutes, that is to say at an average speed of some 12 kilometres an hour. It was a remarkable speed, when one considers the awkwardness of contemporary machines.

However, cycling still remained a plebeian sport; and it was only in about 1892, when pneumatic tyres were invented, and the Prince de Sagan boldly rode a bicycle in the Bois de Boulogne, that Parisians began to find it a sport which was socially acceptable.[39]

LEFT *La vie du boulevard: the scene outside Tortoni's, a detail from the lithograph by Eugène Guérard.*

CUISINE CLASSIQUE.

7 La Cuisine Classique

In 1888, when the journalist Philibert Audebrand set down his memories of the Second Empire, he recalled the early years of the régime as 'the golden age for eating. For want of other laurels,' he wrote, 'people cultivated the laurels of the kitchen . . . Then, if ever, was the time to quote the saying: "Great feasts have always heralded the fall of empires."'[1]

Audebrand was a born republican, and he was being politically wise after the event. But whether or not gastronomic pleasures were a sign of decadence, or political instability, Second Empire Paris delighted in food and drink; and if the gourmets were sometimes critical, the less discriminating were always able to indulge their appetites.

In 1864, Urbain Dubois and Émile Bernard published their monumental work *La Cuisine classique*. Dubois and Bernard were chefs to the King and Queen of Prussia, but no doubt their *pain de gibier à la gelée* and their *darne de saumon à la Tivoli* were served at the more pretentious tables in Paris, and the *nouveaux riches* in France admired such extravaganza as lyres and helmets moulded in nougat. 'My private table could not be anything like an anchorite's,' Baron Haussmann wrote, of his days at the Hôtel de Ville. 'My official table had to suggest that of Lucullus, if it was not to fall short of its mark.'[2] Perhaps – as in Victorian England – the food was rich and plentiful rather than delicate. Perhaps the Second Empire was an age for abundance and ostentation, rather than an age of refinement and experiment. One suspects that cooking – like some of the other arts – suffered from the vulgarisation of prosperity. But Brillat-Savarin, the author of the *Physiologie du goût*, and the ultimate arbiter of taste, had died in 1826; and if the restaurants of the 1850s and 1860s did not satisfy his formidable standards, they did at least give pleasure to the prosperous.

The restaurateurs were not unaware of their clients' wealth. It is said that a Russian nobleman, Count Teufelskine, once had breakfast at Bignon's, in the boulevard des Italiens. When the bill came, he read: 'Two peaches, 15 francs.' 'Peaches scarce, I presume?' he asked. 'No, sir,' explained the waiter, 'but Teufelskines are.'[3]

'Great feasts have always heralded the fall of empires.' The lavish gastronomic tastes of the age are suggested by this plate from La Cuisine classique, *1864.*

Of all the restaurants in Second Empire Paris, the one with the best claim to immortality was Magny's, at 3, rue Contrescarpe Dauphine; for there, on 22 November 1862, Sainte-Beuve and others organised the first of the *dîners Magny*: the dinners which, on alternate Mondays, gathered together some of the most celebrated figures in contemporary art and literature. Among them were Gavarni, the Goncourts, Gautier, Renan, Turgenev, Taine, and, on occasion, George Sand. An invitation to Magny's was a coveted intellectual distinction. Princess Mathilde, the Emperor's cousin, asked Sainte-Beuve if she might be invited. But she was politely discouraged. The presence of a princess, even if she was Notre Dame des Arts, might have restricted the conversation.[4]

Magny's was notable for its food as well as the conversation of its customers. In *Les Plaisirs de Paris*, in 1867, Alfred Delvau defined it as the Maison Dorée of the Latin Quarter. 'You sup there, and dine there, and lunch there,' he wrote, 'remarkably well, and, if I needed a proof, it would be the determination with which George Sand, the illustrious novelist, comes to lunch and dine there whenever she comes to Paris . . . Magny deserves this honour . . . Whatever you order there, you are sure to eat as you would like. But if you are inspired to ask for *pieds de mouton à la poulette*, you are perfectly certain of a banquet.'[5] Magny's had a small but excellent cellar; it boasted a Château Lafite 1847, and a Château Margaux 1848.

Those who appreciated good food, but lacked the intellectual qualifications for Magny's, might be found at Brébant's, in the boulevard Poissonnière; from about 1860 it became a meeting-place for *les turfistes*: the enthusiasts from Longchamp and Chantilly. They might also be found at Goyard's (better known as Aux Trois Frères Provençaux) in the Galerie Beaujolais in the Palais-Royal. It would, said Delvau, be a pleonasm to say that Aux Trois Frères Provençaux was first-class. 'Yet perhaps I might be bold enough to mention one of their gastronomic marvels. This is the famous cod with garlic. No-where else is it cooked as they cook it there.'[6] The banker Raphael Bischoffsheim chose less simple food when he entertained there.

'All the Press, all the dramatists, all the actresses and all the pretty women in fashion were invited to these banquets,' remembered Claudin. 'In the middle of winter there was a supper in the ground-floor room for a hundred and fifty. The room was brilliant with light and flowers. Champagne was flowing in torrents, and the table was cracking under the weight of turkeys stuffed with truffles, rare fish, asparagus, and hot-house peaches.'[7]

Near the Trois Frères Provençaux, also in the Palais-Royal, was another pre-eminent restaurant: Véfour's. Alfred Delvau declared that it was one of the glories of the place. Among the specialities there was 'a fine Rhenish carp, boned and stuffed, and surrounded by those soft roes and those thousand ingredients of which Véfour's know the secret.'[8] Henri de Villemessant, the journalist, was also an habitué of Ledoyen, in the Champs-Élysées. 'And let me tell those readers avid for an orgy of salmon that they should go at once to Ledoyen's . . . There, every evening, two waiters approach you. One of them carries a fish as big as a five-year-old child, from which he cuts you a

Les Nuits de la Maison Dorée: a glimpse of the famous restaurant, with a supper in progress.

large rosy slice; and the other bears a great silver urn from which he gives you several spoonfuls of a green sauce, the secret of which is unknown to other restaurateurs.'9

Another restaurant of distinction was Verdier *frères*, better known as the Maison Dorée, or the Maison d'Or, in the boulevard des Italiens. 'Do you want a succulent fillet steak, braised with tomatoes and stuffed mushrooms, browned on top, and rare inside, with a veritable gravy of truffles? If so,' wrote Villemessant, 'hurry off to the Maison Dorée, order it the day before, and take great care when you eat it not to be concerned about the price.'10 Roger Boutet de Monvel recorded that there were sixteen rooms of various sizes at the Maison d'Or, where gastronomes came to regale themselves with 'char, a rare and wonderful fish, king of the Alpine lakes and streams, or with fried liver of burbot, another little aquatic creature, equally delicious, and one of the most remarkable specialities of the place.'11 Among the most faithful customers of the Maison d'Or was Nestor Roqueplan, who was then director of the Opéra. Every evening, at half-past eight, unfailingly, he sat down at his table, facing the door. Roqueplan ate a good deal, and he drank even more, but he did both with discernment. In *Paris-Guide*, the massive guide for visitors to the 1867 Exhibition, Auguste Luchet discussed the great kitchens and cellars of the capital. He praised 'the restaurant de la Maison-Dorée. Some people even say la Maison d'Or, and they are right, if they are alluding to the solid qualities which distinguish it . . . M. Ernest Verdier, who runs it, with his brother Charles, has never allowed inferior food into his kitchen; and in any case the chef, Casimir, who is an artist, would not waste his talents on it. Those who have not eaten fish at the Maison Dorée do not know what fish is.'[12]

It was not given to everyone to eat at the Maison Dorée. In 1859 the Goncourts' servant saw a nun arrive with a handcart to collect the remains of the supper after a fancy-dress ball.[13] Others had to content themselves with a glimpse of the place in 1862, in *Les Nuits de la Maison Dorée*, a novel by the Vicomte Ponson du Terrail.

'A clock struck midnight in a private room at the Maison d'Or, where two men sat facing one another. They were both young and elegant, and beautifully mannered. They were both ideal prototypes of the *fils de famille*. One was called Raymond, and the other Maxime . . . They were sitting at a table which was laid for three. The pink prawns and the dish of piled-up crayfish were intact, the vintage Médoc had not been uncorked, and the champagne was waiting in a bucket of iced water . . .

'"Antonia won't come!" repeated Raymond for the third time.

'"My dear fellow," said Maxime, "are you mad tonight?"'[14]

Behind the scenes at the Café Riche: the kitchens after their rebuilding in 1865.

Antonia was not the only person to be elusive. Such was the prestige of the most famous restaurants that their proprietors scarcely deigned to make an appearance, unless their customer was a Royal Highness. 'I don't think I ever caught sight of M. Bignon in the restaurant which bore his name,' wrote Gaston Jollivet, in *Souvenirs de la vie de plaisir sous le Second Empire*. The sight of M. Bignon was an expensive privilege. A customer who arrived one night at eleven o'clock insisted on being served by M. Bignon in person. The master was duly roused from his bed, but he added to the bill: 'For personal service from M. Bignon, 1000 francs.'[15] More attractive, perhaps, was the sight of Henry, Bignon's maître-d'hôtel. He was 'completely spherical, always smiling, with protuberant eyes and good hungry lips. And the slow, caressing gesture with which he spread the sauce along a *barbue au vin rouge* or along a *filet Richelieu* made one so hungry that one could have eaten the maître-d'hôtel as well.'[16]

It was Bignon's elder brother who ran the Café Riche at 16, boulevard des Italiens. 'Bourgeois and men of letters,' wrote Alfred Delvau, 'bankers and men-about-town, actors and artists, all the Parisians who live with elegance, comfort and money, have haunted, haunt, or will haunt, the Café Riche . . . The wit and paradox which are consumed in this literary wine-shop would be enough to make the fortune of a good many poor men-of-letters, if there was anybody there except the well-to-do.' But the well-to-do, he suggested, should try the *sole aux crevettes* at the Café Riche. 'And don't let us forget the sauce, . . . which is simply the sauce of the Café Riche and the secret of its head cook.'[17] The Café Riche was always buzzing with activity, from eleven o'clock in the morning until well after midnight. Its customers included the chroniclers of the boulevard and the opposition journalists. They included Manet, who liked to sit on the terrace, watching the women stroll by, and admiring their mother-of-pearl complexions. They also included Offenbach, who settled himself every morning at his particular table. Even while he was eating his boiled egg and his cutlet, he would hum a tune, perhaps a new song which he was composing for Hortense Schneider. In the evening, nearly all the clientele of the Café Riche would appear in its white-and-gold salon. The café became the headquarters of the more conventional writers: among them were Edmond About, the novelist and journalist, and of course the Goncourts ('to think,' they wrote, 'that we don't know the name of the first pig who found a truffle!'). Later on, there came the inveterate noctambulists, among them Baudelaire, cold and correct.[18]

Yet for all the prestige of these restaurants, perhaps the most distinguished was the Café Anglais. In 1856, the closing of the Café de Paris made it the very zenith of fashion. It became the aristocratic restaurant *par excellence*, the cosmopolitan, festive meeting-place, the ultra-smart restaurant which was constantly being mentioned in gossip-columns, fashionable novels and end-of-year revues. Anyone with social or gastronomic pretentions felt obliged to go there immediately they arrived in Paris.

'It was generally agreed that the food was exquisite,' wrote Boutet de Monvel. 'It was incomparable, so much so indeed that Dugléré, the *chef de cuisine*, was one day christened by Rossini "the Mozart of French cooking".' The great feature of the place was the dinner in the cellar, that basic part of the building which was known throughout Europe for its vast and noble proportions, its comfortable furnishing, its fine regular passages sprinkled with sand. Two hundred thousand bottles filled its recesses, a small railway ran silently, bringing wine to each table, and, on festive evenings, countless bunches of grapes of different colours glowed under the vaults, along the pillars, in niches in the walls, making the cellars like some vast Bacchic grotto.'[19]

When Alfred Delvau came to write *Les Plaisirs de Paris* in 1867, he recommended the *écrevisses à la bordelaise* and the Château Lafite at the Café Anglais. Adolphe Dugléré, who had earned his tribute from Rossini, was considered to be the last great chef. Claudin recorded that he was paid the princely salary of 25,000 francs a year; and, in his *Mémoires d'un journaliste*, Henri de Villemessant spoke of Dugléré with veneration.

'M. Dugléré is known and envied by the maîtres-d'hôtel in all the other great restaurants, who ackowledge him as an incomparable master . . . When M. Dugléré goes out to supper, somewhere, . . . the chef is warned, in the depths of his kitchen, *that he is performing for the master.* Very often he is overcome by emotion, and he burns his steak or curdles his sauces. But, when he has cooked a successful dish, he receives the master's congratulations, and he is as proud as a soldier mentioned in dispatches.'[20]

The Café Anglais was a labyrinth of vestibules and corridors; it was really 'just a succession of *cabinets particuliers*, where, until sunrise, you could hear *La Femme à barbe* or *Le Pied qui remue* played on tinny pianos.'[21] *Cabinets particuliers*, explained Henry de Conty, '. . . are private, mysterious, isolated rooms, where you can dine *en famille* or in search of good fortune, far from the jealous and indiscreet glances of the public. These rooms are attached to all the big restaurants; they have a different entrance, a different staircase, a different bell, and different furniture; and so the meals there are expensive, and at times ridiculously dear. The wisest thing is to consult the menu in advance, and to regulate your expenses carefully.'[22]

One of the rooms at the Café Anglais was called the Marivaux; it was also known as *le cabinet des femmes du monde.* Society women used to reach it by a special staircase, which they hurried up for fear of being recognised. But of all these rooms there was only one in which you really needed to be seen, and to which only *le gratin* were admitted. This was room No. 16, *le Grand Seize.* There one might catch a glimpse of the young Duc de Gramont-Caderousse, the lover of Mme de Persigny and of Hortense Schneider (he was to die at the age of thirty-two). One might see the Prince of Orange (sometimes called Prince Citron), Russians like M. de Kougueleff – a millionaire twice over – Prince Galitzine and Prince Paskevitch. There were a few Orientals, including Mustapha Pasha, brother of the Viceroy of Egypt, and Khalil Bey, who lived in the Moorish palace in the avenue de Friedland and – like Gramont-Caderousse – was to die prematurely, after too much good living. There was Daniel Wilson (one day to be the scandalous son-in-law of President Grévy); there was Arsène Houssaye, the ubiquitous socialite. There were boulevardiers like Gustave Claudin and Aurélien Scholl, and Marcelin, the founder of that lively periodical *La Vie parisienne.* There were usually one or two celebrated *cocottes*: Blanche d'Antigny, or Léonide Leblanc.

The world of gallantry was so far from being despised at the Café Anglais that Dugléré created the succulent *pommes de terre Anna* (and a special apparatus to cook them) in honour of Anna Deslions, the courtesan, and mistress of Prince Napoleon.[23]

He also gave his own name to a sauce; but he may be better remembered by a menu which he planned at the zenith of the Second Empire. In 1867, when the Czar of Russia, the Czarevitch, the King of Prussia, and Bismarck had come to see the International Exhibition, they dined in *le Grand Seize* at the Café Anglais. Dugléré served them a banquet which, a century later, still remains a gastronomic classic.

Hors d'œuvre
Œufs de vanneau, poularde, caviar.
Potage tortue à la Charles VI.

Relevés
Carpe du Rhin à la Chambord.
Baron de mouton à l'anglaise.

Entrées
Filets de faisan à la Metternich.
Filets de poularde à la Mazarin.
Croustades à l'impératrice.
Filets de sterlet et crevettes Bagration.

Punch à la romaine et sorbets crème d'Alast.

Rôtis
Dindonneaux nouveaux. Ortolans.
Salade princesse. Romaine.

Entremets
Petits pois de Paris. Truffes en rocher. Petits
soufflés Lavallière. Bombe royale.

Dessert
Fraises, pêches, raisins, reines-Claude,
fromage de la Croix de Fer.

Vins
Madère retour de l'Inde. Château d'Yquem 1847.
Mouton Rothschild 1847. Château-Lafite 1848.
Romanée gelée 1858. Johannisberg Metternich 1837.
Tokaï 1824. Roederer et Pommery.

Eating en masse *became popular during the Second Empire. This lithograph shows the dining-room of the Grand Hôtel, in the boulevard des Capucines.*

Gustave Claudin added that 'the sovereigns and their suites much enjoyed themselves, and when they returned to their dominions they declared that Paris was the finest city in the world.'[24]

He himself had no doubt mellowed when, as an elderly man, he recorded this gastronomic poem in *Mes Souvenirs*. In 1867, the year of the International Exhibition, he had published a book on Paris, and considered Parisian food with disdain.

Claudin was a boulevardier of the most deplorable kind. Nothing existed for him beyond the boulevards; and it is hard to say which predominates in his book: his arrogance or his *esprit de clocher*. But he was also the victim of a bad digestion. 'I am,' he wrote, 'condemned by the particular nature of my stomach to abstain from eating and drinking. If I could take my meal in the form of a pill, I should be able to recruit my strength.' It was this dyspeptic critic who declared that 'restaurant-keepers are no longer artists. They have only one aim: to make a quick fortune . . . In Paris, you have the same meal everywhere . . . Chefs no longer have imagination.'

It was not only chefs and restaurant-keepers who lacked imagination. 'Now, more than ever, banquets are in fashion,' continued Claudin, 'but they are distressing in their simplicity . . . And princes and ambassadors are always served the same dinner.' In 1851, the Préfet de la Seine had given a dinner for the Lord Mayor of London. Claudin recorded the gigantic menu. This menu, he said, had since been repeated *ad nauseam* at official banquets, both in Paris and in the provinces. It would be found at ceremonies for a long time to come.[25]

Menus were not only monotonous at official banquets; they were also sadly familiar at the private dinner-parties given in Paris.

'Let me explain,' continued Claudin. 'Two or three restaurateurs have secured the monopoly of providing dinners, to order, in private houses. At 5 o'clock, the caterer's liveried servants come and take possession of the dining-room. The mistress of the house just provides the table . . . The table is laid, and the meal is served by the restaurant-keeper's men, in black suits and white ties. Fifteen minutes after the dessert, these employees remove the crockery and the linen, and sweep out the dining-room. There is no trace of upheaval in the apartment. The mistress of the house is delighted. From this point of view, the system has its advantages; but, thanks to this system, you eat the same food everywhere in Paris.'[26]

The catering trade was not the only innovation to rouse prejudice. New methods of cooking were fiercely debated. Conservative Parisians refused to cook by gas, and it was hard to overcome their antagonism. In 1856 Henri Dabot, a Parisian lawyer, recorded:

'They have just given a big dinner at the Hôtel du Louvre, and the dishes were pronounced to be excellent. There were dishes of every kind; they were admirably cooked, and they tasted delicious, and yet they had all been prepared on gas stoves, in the presence of well-known people who certified the fact. This dinner was given precisely to destroy the general prejudice against cooking by gas; people say it is very bad, they claim that the cooking is not really effective and that the meat has an after-taste of gas. This dinner at the Louvre seems to prove the opposite.'[27]

It also proved the attraction of the Grand Hôtel du Louvre, one of the largest and latest wonders of Paris. 'Everyone here wants to go and dine at the Grand Hôtel du Louvre,' Prosper Ménière had noted, the previous year. 'Yesterday the dining-room contained more than three hundred diners; this is only half what would be needed to fill it. You pay six francs a head. The service is magnificent, like the setting, and the admirers so numerous, although the thing is not finished, that you have to go and put your name down in the morning.'[28]

Eating *en masse* became a new fashion; and the 'popularising of prosperity' brought another innovation: the creation of popular restaurants. In 1858 the author of *Paris illustrée* recorded that 'the year 1854 saw the appearance of a new kind of restaurant which is a sort of intermediate between the restaurant and the table-d'hôte. It is an establishment where everyone pays the same price and eats the same dinner . . . *Le Dîner de Paris*, in the passage Jouffroy, only costs 3 francs 50 centimes, and yet you can have a nutritious and plentiful dinner there.'[29] Another innovation was the *bouillon* establishments. 'They are now found in every quarter of Paris,' wrote Henry de Conty, in the mid-1860s. 'They are really providential for people with small purses. We particularly recommend the bouillon *Duval*, in the rue Montesquieu, just near the Palais-Royal.'[30] In October 1864, Felix Whitehurst, the correspondent of the *Daily Telegraph*, ventured to try a 'people's dinner' there.

'We had,' he reported, 'excellent soup, which cost 2d; turbot, 5d; roast mutton, 3½d; salad, 2d; an omelette, worthy of Ude in his best days, 3½d; and Chablis at a franc a bottle . . . Our bill was 2s. a head; and it must be remembered that we had a *dîner de luxe*, and that you could dine extremely well for 1 fr. 10 centimes, having soup, meat, vegetables, and a pint of wine . . . The consumers are Government employees, officers on full or half pay, or *en retraite* . . . The cheapest dish on the carte is *bouillon*, which costs three halfpence; the highest is "bifteck", which is fivepence.'[31]

One is tempted to speculate on the identity of the fivepenny *bifteck*, for in 1865 there was a determined campaign to make horseflesh an acceptable meat. On 8 February, Anthony North Peat had recorded: 'The hippophagic, otherwise horseflesh, banquet came off yesterday, so I understand, at the Grand Hôtel, one hundred and thirty odd persons having taken tickets . . . Horse soup, horse boiled *aux choux*, horse *en bœuf à la mode*, horse roast, horse *pâté de foie* with truffles, were successively eaten and discussed.' On 1 July the following year, the same observer noted: 'The first butcher's shop for the sale of horseflesh will open on 9 July. The price of this meat will be about two-thirds cheaper than beef, and will, moreover, be sold without bone.' By the end of August, North Peat could report that 'horseflesh is proving a real boon to the poor.'[32]

Horsemeat might remain an economic necessity for the poorest classes in Paris; but there were other ways of eating cheaply. The author of *Paris illustrée* observed the soup and coffee vendors on the Pont Notre-Dame. 'You can have a basinful for a sou. That woman walking along the quais or down the boulevards of the quartier du Temple, pushing a dish-warmer or a portable stove, will sell you piping hot sausages, or fried potatoes in a white paper cornet, or fritters. Thanks to her, you can have a whole dinner: meat, vegetable, and dessert. It will cost you 5 or 6 sous.'[33]

The prosperous continued to eat in more conventional style. The eating habits of bourgeois Paris were recorded in 1871, by the author of *Life in Paris before the War and during the Siege*.

'Those who go to France with the old impression of "frogs and *soupe maigre*" will be surprised to find that all that has been said of the excellence and substantiality of a Scotch breakfast is rivalled, if not exceeded, by a French *déjeuner*. On entering the salle à manger you find a long table profusely covered with roasts, ragoûts, dressed fish, pastry, salads, fruits and sweetmeats, with all sorts of wines, while tea and coffee are handed round only to assist digestion. The French breakfast literally ends where the English one begins.

'The déjeuner à la fourchette, taken in the middle of the day, is among the most fashionable entertainments in Paris during the spring season . . .

'Dinner is not always the most substantial or luxurious meal, nor ordinarily that of etiquette . . .

'The supper is the grand meal, combining all that is brilliant in society and elegant in display.'[34]

There were exceptions to these rules. Albéric Second, the journalist, was invited to dinner by Dumas *père*, who prided himself on his prowess as a chef.

'What a success! What a triumph!' reported Second. 'A *dîner bourgeois*, such as princes do not taste every day! We started off with a cabbage soup, at which Dumas had laboured for two days; then followed fried smelts. To these succeeded roast pheasants, *écrevisses à la bordelaise*, and a salad of *mâches*, celery and beetroot . . . I watched Alexandre Dumas when the solemn moment of mixing the salad arrived, as I am not without pretentions to a certain strength in this department, so essential to every well organised repast. In the presence of the *chefs-d'œuvre*, which I saw seasoned before me, and which I tasted with a sensuality full of emotion and respect, it only remained for me to acknowledge my inferiority. I now confess it publicly. If Alexandre Dumas would open a restaurant near the Champ-de-Mars during the Exhibition of 1867, a restaurant, let it be understood, in which he was the cook, he would make 1,000,000 francs in six months.'[35]

The appetites of Dumas *père* and his fellow-Parisians demanded substantial supplies of food. In 1855 Blanchard Jerrold reported: 'French fowls lay eggs, for Paris alone, to the annual value of ten millions of francs.'[36] In 1865 the 1,700,000 inhabitants of Paris consumed 2,409,910 francs' worth of oysters; they drank 2,882,629 hectolitres of wine (a hectolitre being one hundred and seven pints).[37] But they were concerned with quality as much as quantity. 'What pleasure to savour an exquisite and authentic wine, long cherished, carefully borne in its little wicker basket; to gobble up the wing of some nice plump quail, to feel the juicy, melting pulp of a fish pâté rich with truffles in one's mouth! Many people,' wrote Taine, 'murmur to themselves that the cherubim and seraphim are less fortunate.'[38] Gourmets gazed in admiration at the windows of Chevet's, the fashionable grocers in the Galerie de Chartres at the Palais-Royal. 'Birds' nests from China, ortolans from Italy, truffles from Périgord, and *pâtés de foie gras* from Strasbourg, fascinated their gaze each time they passed its savoury precincts.'[39]

It was small wonder that epicures came from far and near to enjoy the pleasures of Paris. Felix Whitehurst observed that 'the Easter holidays of the House of Commons are the Saturnalia of the English residents in this glittering city by the Seine . . . I trust,' he added, 'that the elderly and respectable Member, whom I have chanced to meet night after night, and who is evidently taking a course of dinners, gadding about from the Maison Dorée to the Trois Frères, . . . will not be any the worse for his *studies* . . .' In April 1868, Whitehurst recorded the latest gastronomic fashion. 'There is now a large trade between Paris and Russia in game. The birds are packed in oats, put into wicker baskets, and arrive in Paris in five days.' Whitehurst grew lyrical when he recalled the truffles and champagne at the Tuileries; and, early in 1870, it was he who overheard an eloquent snatch of conversation at an Imperial ball. 'No soup, thank you; a little of that pâté à l'Isthmus de Suez, and truffle à la Harem. Thank you, a little pheasant au bois, a few truffles en serviette, – a little of that nice salad à la Paradis, a little pineapple, a few sweet cakes, two glasses of champagne and a café ice. Nothing more, thank you. I never eat supper.'[40]

8 Théâtres Divers

Theatre during the Second Empire ranged from the earnest to the flippant, and from the sober to the frivolous. 'The theatres, which have so big a place, one might almost say too big a place, in our lives, were all flourishing,' remembered Gustave Claudin.[1] Drama embraced both comedy and tragedy, and it satirised modern society with faithful attention to detail. Contemporary failings were often attacked by the dramatists of the École du bon sens, which reacted against the exaltation of Romantic drama and extolled the domestic virtues. One of the leaders of this movement was François Ponsard (1814–67). In *L'Honneur et l'argent* (1853) and *La Bourse* (1856), he satirised the contemporary worship of money. 'What is the use,' Gautier would ask, 'of heroes who did not speculate at the Bourse?'[2] In 1862, after years as a dramatic critic, Gautier went further: 'One of the things which the old theatre most likes to enlarge upon is the struggle between passion and duty . . . Our epoch is more pedestrian, and it creates a conflict between self-interest and the heart . . . As the religion of money is the only one today which has no unbelievers, it is usually a question of a substantial sum of money which can either be kept or returned . . . To give money away, when you would not have been brought to trial for keeping it, is the ultimate effort of modern heroism.'[3]

Purity, honesty, conscientiousness: these mid-Victorian virtues were all that the twentieth century may accredit to Ponsard; but one might feel more admiration for the work of Émile Augier (1820–89). Augier, another leader of the École du bon sens, wrote solid, well-constructed, conventional plays of bourgeois life and bourgeois morality. Among them were *Le Gendre de Monsieur Poirier* (1854), which he wrote in collaboration with Jules Sandeau; *Les Lionnes pauvres* (1858); *Les Effrontés* (1861), which satirised the Second Empire passion for speculation; and *Maître Guérin* (1865). Ernest Daudet said that Augier had written the three or four best dramatic comedies of the Second Empire. 'They also had the importance of a social work, but they showed a robust and healthy interpretation of life.'[4] In *Le Fils de Giboyer* (1862), Augier attacked contemporary efforts to mix religion and politics. His satire cut near the bone, and provoked fierce indignation, and this play was his greatest success.

The Tightrope-walker, *by Gustave Doré, 1869.*

Dumas *fils*, the natural son of the author of *Le Comte de Monte-Cristo*, had taken to literature to pay his debts. His novel *La Dame aux camélias*, inspired by the courtesan Marie Duplessis, had made him famous when it appeared in 1848; when it was dramatised in 1852 it was said to have brought the heart back to the stage. Arsène Houssaye said that Dumas *fils* had made Marie Duplessis 'a saint twice over in the calendar of hussies.'[5] Viel-Castel, the memoir-writer, the vigilant collector of contemporary scandal, declared that 'this play is shameful for the epoch which allows it, the government which tolerates it, the public which applauds it . . . *La Dame aux camélias* is in fact a full-scale public outrage.'[6]

However, thanks to Dumas *fils*, a new school of drama had triumphed. Arsène Houssaye suggested that it might be called the School of Truth. One of its exponents was Théodore Barrière. He considered that Dumas *fils*' rehabilitation of the courtesan was an offence against morality. He determined to give the public a true picture of the courtesan. *Les Filles de marbre*, which he wrote with Lambert Thiboust, was first performed on 17 May 1853. Its literary value was slight, but the courtesans came *en foule* to see themselves insulted, while the public eased its conscience by overthrowing yesterday's idols. After the play had run for a hundred and sixteen performances, the director shrewdly took it off, and re-introduced *La Dame aux camélias*.

It is probable that Dumas *fils* was impelled by Barrière's play to write *Le Demi-monde*. He coined the word to describe the world of the *déclassés*: the world which begins where the legal wife ends and finishes where the mistress begins. In the second act of the play, Olivier explains *le demi-monde* to Raymond. Go to Chevet's, he tells him, and you will see a basket of perfect peaches at twenty sous apiece. Beside it is another basket, where every peach has a tiny flaw, and costs only fifteen sous.

Alexandre Dumas fils, *and* RIGHT *a scene from his play* Le Demi-monde, *as performed in 1855.*

Olivier: Well, my dear fellow, here you are in the fifteen-sou basket. All the women round you have a fault in their past, a stain on their name; they press close to each other so that you see it as little as possible. They have the same origin as society women, they have the same appearance and prejudices, but they no longer belong to society. They form what we call *le demi-monde*; it is neither the aristocracy nor the bourgeoisie, but it floats on the ocean of Paris, and it summons, gathers in, and admits all those who fall or emigrate or escape from one of those two continents – as well as the chance victims of shipwrecks, who come from none knows where.

Raymond: Where does *le demi-monde* usually live?

Olivier: Nowhere in particular; but a Parisian will soon recognise it.

Raymond: How will he recognise it?

Olivier: By the absence of husbands.[7]

When Dumas' play was first performed in 1855, *le demi-monde* had already become the preoccupation of Paris. Gautier suggested 'that it might perhaps be time to leave those poor *Filles de marbre* in peace on their pedestals. For nearly three years they have almost entirely occupied the stage.' Dumas *fils* became one of the most successful dramatists of the Second Empire. He did not only triumph with *La Dame aux camélias* and *Le Demi-monde*. At the Théâtre du Gymnase, he won acclaim with *Diane de Lys*, *Les Idées de Madame Aubray*, *Le Père prodigue*, and *La Question d'argent*. In 1870 Gautier discussed his evolution.

'After the Romantic School and the École du bon sens, Dumas *fils* [he said] introduced a new form. It seems to me that this cycle of lively observation and psychic photography, in which the young author gained such splendid and well-earned success, is henceforth closed. Alexandre Dumas *fils* has examined life closely, he has observed well and truly. Now the observer is logically followed by the philosopher and the moralist. This modification is already felt in *L'Ami des femmes* and in *Les Idées de Madame Aubray* . . .

'Women displease him more than anything, and he does not disguise the fact in the preface to *L'Ami des femmes*, where he berates them so sharply. But he claims to correct the faults he points out. The human being is imperfect, but it is perfectible, and it can be brought back to the straight and narrow path . . . And Dumas *fils* seems to be going in this direction. In his new plays he will look for something besides pure entertainment. With a gift like his it will be a lofty and noble enterprise. He has too much wit to preach on stage, and the moral pill will be hidden in a sparkling envelope.'[8]

Dumas *fils* was followed by Victorien Sardou with *Monsieur Garat*, *Les Prés Saint-Gervais*, *Nos Intimes*, and *Les Ganaches*. 'M. Victorien Sardou,' decided Gautier, 'lacks the frank originality and literary value of Alexandre Dumas *fils*, but he has a prodigiously subtle mind. It is very sharp, very inquiring, very skilful, and astonishingly fertile in resources. M. Sardou possesses the dramatic gift to a high degree.'[9]

There was a constellation of stars to perform these plays. Among them were Provost,

Two popular actresses: the Brohan sisters, Augustine LEFT *and Madeleine.*

Régnier, Samson, Geoffroy, Bressant, Got and Delaunay. As for the farces, they had their own remarkable interpreters. The Variétés, the Vaudeville and the Palais-Royal were sparkling with verve and originality. Charles Deburau continued in the same path as his father, Gaspard, who had been the great mime of the century. The Second Empire delighted in Augustine Brohan, the brilliant soubrette of the Comédie-Française, and her younger sister Madeleine; they admired Mlle Plessis, Mlle Favart and Mlle Fix. The Second Empire also saw two of the greatest actresses of all time, and perhaps one may dwell on their careers. They illuminate the nineteenth-century theatre; they also symbolise the age of the *parvenu*, an age when ruthless dynamism so often brought extraordinary success.

Élisabeth-Rachel Félix, better known as Rachel, had been born in 1821, the daughter of an itinerant Jewish pedlar.[10] At the age of eleven, as she sang in the Paris streets, she had been discovered by the director of the École de musique sacrée. He had recommended her to a friend who ran a dramatic school, and in 1837, in a melodrama called *La Vendéenne*, Rachel had made her first public appearance. The following year

The supreme actress of the Second Empire: Rachel, from a photograph by Nadar, and RIGHT *as she appeared in her most famous rôle, as Racine's Phèdre.*

she appeared at the Théâtre-Français as Camille, in *Horace*; and Jules Janin, the critic, declared that she was 'the most astonishing, most marvellous little girl that this generation has seen on any stage . . . We must watch over her zealously, lovingly, paternally, this newcomer who will soon be the honour of the theatre.'

Rachel justified Janin's prediction. She resurrected classical tragedy; she conquered London, and earned the admiration of Queen Victoria, she went to Belgium and inspired Charlotte Brontë with the character of Vashti in *Villette*. She appeared as Phèdre (it was to be her greatest part); she made her début in the leading woman's part in French comedy, that of Célimène. She had a galaxy of lovers (in 1847, in London, she was said to be 'on the best of terms' with the future Napoleon III). In the summer of 1855 she gave six performances at the Théâtre-Français; they were her last before she embarked on a tour of America. And, since she was already suffering from the consumption which would kill her, these were her last performances on the first stage of France. On these last six 'almost supernatural' evenings, Janin observed a fever among the audience. 'She was irresistible, in these final struggles against the disease that was eating her alive, and, in the twinkling of an eye, in her fire, all ice had melted. She had hardly come on stage before she possessed the soul of her audience, entire.'[11] Gautier recorded her performance. 'The gentle Jean Racine would be astonished at the way in which Mlle Rachel plays Phèdre: that Phèdre whom the seventeenth century found an almost Christian heroine. What would his ghost have thought if it had huddled in a private box that evening, and seen that delirious passion, those sad spasms, that deathlike pallor, that dark gaze which suddenly flashed fire, that peplum crushed against the heart by a convulsive hand, that staggering gait, the drunken work of all the phials of Venus? Is that love, even incestuous love, as it was understood by the chaste poet of Louis XIV, the pupil and friend of Port-Royal-des-Champs? No, it is classical love, the love which seems like intoxication . . . With her wonderful instinct, Mlle Rachel understood her part like this . . . She gave a Greek and entirely new meaning to Racine's fine French tragedy . . .

'It was a brilliant evening. Phèdre almost vanished under an avalanche of bouquets, and it took two Greeks from Theseus' army, and no less, to clear the proscenium of flowers. And never had she performed with wilder or more furious passion. Like all true artists, Mlle Rachel increases in fire, in ardour and violence. Instead of growing cool, she becomes exalted; experience helps her to be freer, wider, more impetuous. What she once conveyed by intimation she now presents with a magisterial, flashing stroke.'[12]

Rachel died three years later, in 1858. She was thirty-six.

She had certainly been limited. When she attempted Dumas, Ponsard or even Hugo, she could not reach the spheres that she reached with Corneille and Racine. But Rachel was wise enough to recognise her limits; and when the critics urged her to move with the progress of drama, her answer was the comment she made on rejecting a modern play: 'Let the young man write me something Greek'. But if Rachel discouraged the art of her time, she offered instead the dream of an art greater than that which she interpreted. She had brought tragedy back with the toss of her peplum, the divine fire of her voice, and she bore it away in the fold of her robe; for she had not brought the resurrection of tragedy, but a personal triumph, a triumph as justified, as shining as any in the history of the theatre. 'I have had talent,' she once said, 'I could have had genius.' But the pedlar's daughter had been a genius.

In 1862, four years after Rachel had died, Sarah Bernhardt gave her first performance at the Théâtre-Français.[13] She was nearly eighteen: the illegitimate daughter of an ex-lawyer and a Parisian cocotte. She had been an unwanted child; and, on the eve of her fifteenth birthday, her future had been decided by her mother's current lover, the Duc de Morny. 'You know what to do with the child?' he said. 'Send her to the Conservatoire.' Perhaps he made the suggestion from genuine perception; perhaps he saw it as a way of ridding his mistress of an encumbrance. Whatever his motives, Sarah entered the Conservatoire; and he later saw that she entered the Comédie-Française. In 1862 she made her début in *Iphigénie*. She soon quarrelled – it was

Sarah Bernhardt. A photograph taken by Nadar soon after she had left the Conservatoire.

inevitable – with the Comédie-Française. In 1865 she signed a contract at the Odéon. She appeared as Anna Damby in Dumas' *Kean*, and already proved the spell of her voice. 'Her magic voice, her astonishing voice, moved the public,' said *Le Figaro*. 'She tamed them like a little Orpheus.'[14] In 1869 she suddenly became famous as the minstrel boy, Zanetto, in *Le Passant*. The play was the work of a young clerk at the Ministère de la Guerre, by the name of François Coppée.

Mlle Agar, Coppée's mistress, had recommended Sarah for the part of Zanetto; she herself played Silvia, the Venetian courtesan who sacrificed her love to save the boy from disillusion. *Le Passant* was first performed at the Odéon on 14 January 1869, and Gautier gave it pontifical praise. 'It is a long time since I have felt a more complete, more delightful emotion in the theatre . . . Mlle Agar, with her sculptural beauty, so played the part of Silvia that she exceeded the poet's ideal. Mlle Sarah Bernhardt is the most adorable Zanetto you could imagine, and it is really an act of virtue enough to pardon many sins to send her away.'[15] A few days later, at the request of Princess Mathilde, Gautier presented Coppée at the rue de Courcelles; and there, on 29 April, *Le Passant* was performed in the presence of Napoleon III. After this evening, Agar was received by the Emperor's command in the Comédie-Française, and Sarah's sovereign future was assured.

The following year, the Empire fell; but Sarah's career was to last for more than half a century. Rachel was her presiding genius, but their achievements were to be very different. Rachel had rarely succeeded in modern drama. Sarah played the plays of the nineteenth and twentieth centuries. Rachel was summed up in the word *tragédienne*, Sarah in the phrase *artiste dramatique*. Rachel had plunged deep, Sarah ranged wide over the theatre, thinking, too, of costume, décor, theatrical design, theatrical management. It is hard to say that one was greater than the other. And yet, in following the career of Rachel, one had the feeling of a dedicated spirit. But when an English critic observed that Sarah was a peerless institution, he came as close as anyone to the heart of the matter. Sarah's real achievement was the part of Sarah Bernhardt: her personal *mise en scène*.

The Second Empire, so fond of glitter and outward display, set much store by *mise en scène*, by elaborate presentation. Lavish production was a feature of the contemporary theatre; and, since the age saw the development of the *féerie*, one might take as typical a production of *Cinderella* in 1866. Gautier described it with admiration and weariness.

'Le Théâtre impérial du Châtelet has just produced *Cinderella*, a fairy-tale in 5 acts and 30 scenes. What! Thirty scenes for the modest enchantments of this childhood tale? . . . Thirty scenes, and no less. As you see, we are far from the antique simplicity of the good Perrault; we need something else to entertain the grown-up children of the nineteenth century . . .

'So, by way of analysis, let us quote the main décors: the Green Grotto, the Glowworms' Palace, the Golden Clouds, the Fiery Mountain, the Azure Lake . . . The Fiery Mountain is a wonderful sight. Gnomes are busy working under the incandescent rocks, bathed in a red light more vivid than rubies shot through by sunlight; then the waters gradually rise, the waves of the Azure Lake grow ever larger, and the great fire is extinguished by cool blue lights in which half-naked nymphs are swimming . . .

'The only criticism we can make of this fairy-tale is that it abuses brilliance; you can't look at it unless you're wearing tinted spectacles . . . Here and there one would be glad of a real décor, representing a pleasant view in its natural colours. It would be a relief from these splendours.'[16]

The subjects of Napoleon III were sometimes treated to even more spectacular entertainments. In this same summer of 1866, Blondin performed at Vincennes. He was hauled up to his tightrope by a pulley, remembered Gautier. 'He was dressed like a knight in the crusades, troubadour style . . . His legs were sheathed in glittering mesh, and sparkled in the light of the setting sun, and his helmet, with its two coloured plumes, reflected the sunlight as it struck him.' He held an enormous balancing-pole, and walked the tightrope with firm steps. Then he ran back along the rope to the changing-tent on the platform, and lay down on his back. 'He remained motionless, then he stood on his head on the rope, and stayed there for a few moments. Then he began to wave about like an aerial telegraph, transmitting its hieroglyphic signals . . . When he reached the platform, he performed his final feat. This consists of carrying his acolyte on his back. He had crossed Niagara Falls in the same way.'[17]

There is no more complete or vivid record of the Second Empire theatre, indeed of Second Empire entertainment, than the one which Gautier presents in his dramatic criticism. He had described Rachel as Phèdre and Sarah Bernhardt as Zanetto; he had pleaded Musset's cause to a public 'that takes no notice of thought or observation, poetry or style, and only sees in a drama a more or less skilful game of chess.' Just as he had supported Musset with vigour and discrimination, so, instinctively, he acclaimed Coppée and Banville. He welcomed the dramatic experiments of the new generation of poets. The stronger the poetry in an entertainment, the more eagerly he encouraged and defended it. And poetry, to Gautier, did not only mean a literary form, it often meant the primitive and simple, the entertainment furthest from reality. It embraced the pageants which appealed to the nobler instincts of the public and realised their dreams. Gautier found poetry in *la fête de l'Empereur*; that day, 15 August, was Napoleon's birthday, and, on the eve of the Second Empire, Napoleon III had decreed that it should be a national holiday.

'By some happy fortune, the weather was beautiful for *la fête de l'Empereur* [this in 1865] . . . The railways brought almost entire towns to take part in this birthday which is also the birthday of France. At six o'clock in the morning, salvoes were fired from the Invalides to announce the beginning of the festivities. Distributions of money were made in the Emperor's name to the families most in need in the twenty arrondissements of Paris. At one o'clock, a solemn mass was celebrated in the metropolitan church . . .

'But the real festival comes at night; when the sun has sunk below the horizon, and the sky has grown sufficiently dark, the illuminations light up. The Tuileries garden and the Champs-Élysées are afire, the one all spangled with coloured lights, the other all a-sparkle with gas-lamps. In the place de la Concorde the fountains, which are lit from below, shed their sheets of diamanté round the basins . . . Tricolour streamers are fluttering from Venetian masts, and obelisks in coloured lights, surmounted by eagles, adorn the terraces of the Tuileries . . . There is a ground-bass of cannonfire to this riot of light and noise; but now a splendid façade bursts into light. It is made of burning diamonds . . . In the centre, the great imperial N is traced in stars.'[18]

Poetry, in its widest sense, did not only include public festivals; it also included the pantomime, and no-one took more pleasure in these Punch-and-Judy shows than the dramatic critic on the Government paper.

'Down there, in the Champs-Élysées,' he wrote in *Le Moniteur universel*, 'under the cool shade of the great trees, there are four or five stalls in the Pompeian style . . . Whether the stream of carriages is flowing towards the Arc de Triomphe or rushing like a torrent towards the place de la Concorde, you will always see them peacefully sitting in front of the wooden actors: children, nurses, invalids, and a few philosophers who know the value of time well enough to waste it . . .

'As we write these lines, the truncheon blows are echoing on the wooden heads, Punch and Judy's speaker is whistling and stammering, the executioner is knotting the noose in which he will catch his own head, the cat is smartly boxing Punch's ears (for Punch has been excessively familiar), and, in a moment, when we have scribbled our signature at the end of this article, we shall see Punch's insatiable public back at its post again, indifferent to the carriages which cradle the Venuses of the bal Mabille and the Château-des-Fleurs in a froth of flounces, deaf to the music of the *cafés chantants*, not even listening to the brazen fanfare of the circus, but gazing, wide-eyed and open-mouthed, at the décor lit by two Argand lamps, or lanterns, which serves as a backdrop to the frolics of its dear marionettes.'[19]

A poet and an artist himself, Gautier deplored the inartistic nature of his compatriots. He regretted their inability to content themselves with the 'plastic forms of poetry: painting, music and dancing.'[20] Their demand for moral and meaning, their constant rationalism, made them unjust to such purely artistic entertainments as ballet. For such unfortunate rationalism he himself made amends. The critic who had stood at an easel in Rioult's studio enjoyed the ballet for its plastic qualities; he saw it, above all, as the realisation of a dream. 'It is the ideal made palpable,' wrote the author of *Giselle*. 'It is love translated into pictures, rhythmic grace, harmony condensed into figures, music carried from sound into sight. It is a wordless hymn to the rotation of the spheres and to the movement of the planets.'[21] Gautier's articles on ballet are some of his finest transpositions of art. The great Romantic ballerinas dance in and out of his reviews: individual, and visually convincing; through his eyes we may also see the ballet of imperial Paris.[22]

On 20 October 1858, Emma Livry made her début in *La Sylphide*. At the age of sixteen, she boldly appeared in a part which was indelibly stamped with the name

Two stars of the ballet: Emma Livry LEFT *as La Sylphide, and* RIGHT *Muravieva as Giselle.*

of its creator, Marie Taglioni. Her daring seemed to be justified. 'Assurance, neatness, precision,' wrote the critic Fiorentino, 'are only acquired after much practice and toil, but what cannot be learnt is the marvellous lightness and the natural distinction which she possesses.'

Emma Livry's future seemed assured. Marie Taglioni sent her a portrait of herself, inscribed: 'Make me forgotten; do not forget me'. In 1860, when the Emperor saw her dance in *Le Papillon*, he asked that the ballet should be repeated a few days later, so that he could see it a second time.

The gods had loved Emma Livry too well. In November 1862, during a rehearsal of *La Muette de Portici*, she stood too close to the wing-light, and her dress caught fire. She was incurably burned, and she died a few months afterwards.

'When you glimpsed her through her transparent veils,' wrote Théophile Gautier, 'she seemed a blithe spirit, an Elysian apparition . . . She had the same imponderable lightness, and when her silent flight crossed space you did not even hear the brush of air. In the ballet – alas, the only one which she created ! – she took the part of a butterfly, and it was no mere gallantry of choreography. She could imitate the fantastic and charming flight which alights on flowers and does not bend them.'[23]

The years of Emma Livry's brief career had also been the last years of Amalia Ferraris; she was the sole representative of the Italian school, and the highest paid dancer in Paris. Early in 1861, she created the title-rôle in *Graciosa*, a one-act ballet by Lucien Petipa. The music was written by Labarre and the scenario by a member of the Jockey Club. At the end of the ballet, the stage was covered with camellias, white lilac and Parma violets; most of them were thrown from the boxes occupied by the Jockey Club: a tribute to Ferraris and to their fellow member.

A few months later, Marie Petipa made her début in Paris. The illegitimate daughter of a St Petersburg millionaire, and the wife of the choreographer Marius Petipa, she was now in her vivacious prime. 'She is truly Russian,' wrote a critic. 'She does not aspire to the fine classical effects of the French style, or to the warm and powerful fantasy of Italy, or to a Spanish fury. She is a delightful caprice, ever floating between a heedless folly and a graceful melancholy, a strange mixture resulting from her Slav character.'

A few weeks after Emma Livry's tragic accident, when Ferraris' engagement was approaching its end, Émile Perrin had assumed the management of the Opéra. Within a month of his appointment, he offered a contract to the well-known Russian ballerina, Martha Nicolayevna Muravieva. Since she was only engaged for six months, it was important that she should appear in a ballet which she already knew. It was ten years since *Giselle* had last been given at the Opéra, but Perrin entrusted the revival to Lucien Petipa, who had created the rôle of Albrecht, and he spared no expense. New sets were commissioned from Despléchin, Cambon and Thierry; nearly a hundred and fifty people were to take part in the first act, including about ninety peasants and a hunting party of nearly forty courtiers, with horses. Fifty Wilis were to appear in the second act. The extravagance was typical of the Second Empire theatre, and the revival of *Giselle* was a predictable success. Théophile Gautier himself, the author of *Giselle*, was so delighted by the décor that he devoted his weekly article to the stage-designer's art.

In 1866 Adèle Grantzow, the daughter of a *maître de ballet* at Brunswick, made her début in Paris as Giselle. 'Mlle Grantzow,' wrote Gautier, 'is neither blonde nor blue-eyed like Carlotta. Her hair is black, her eyes the same colour, but her features are none the less charming, and they have an innocent, tender expression, such as the rôle demands . . . Not for a long time has a dancer been so warmly welcomed at the Opéra.'[24] The comment has its interest, for Gautier remained in love with Carlotta Grisi, who had been the first Giselle; in a letter to Carlotta, he wrote rather differently: 'I took Estelle [my daughter] to see *Giselle* danced by Mlle Grantzow. She who had not seen the true, the only, the incomparable Giselle, the Giselle with golden hair and violet eyes, was very happy with this one, in spite of her black hair and black eyes. For me, no-one will ever dance Giselle, but really Mlle Grantzow is the one who has so far vexed me least in the part which you made so charming, so tender, so touching, so poetic, and so impossible for the future.'[25]

146

The truth was, perhaps, that the Second Empire was not a remarkable age for ballet. Adèle Grantzow, Giuseppina Bozzacchi, Eugénie Fiocre, were not legendary figures like their Romantic predecessors. They lacked the distinction of Taglioni, Elssler, Grisi and Cerrito. During the last twelve years of the Second Empire, the Romantic ballet was in twilight. The career of Emma Livry, and the production of *Coppélia* in 1870, both glowed with the splendour of the setting sun. Only in the twentieth century, under the influence of the Russian ballet, would there be a renaissance of the art.

Ballet, in a sense, was ageless; but a new kind of show came into being in France in the Second Empire. The immense success of the Great Exhibition in London in 1851, the architectural triumph of the Crystal Palace, were followed, predictably, by an international exhibition in Paris. In March 1852, the future Emperor – then Prince-President – ordered that a permanent exhibition centre should be erected by the Champs-Élysées. Within a year he laid the foundation-stone of the Palais de l'Industrie. The building was one of the first in France to be constructed largely of iron. It was not aesthetically satisfying, but it was generally approved. However, when it was decided to hold an inaugural exhibition in the spring of 1855, it became clear that the building

L'Exposition universelle, 1855: the main entrance of the Palais de l'Industrie.

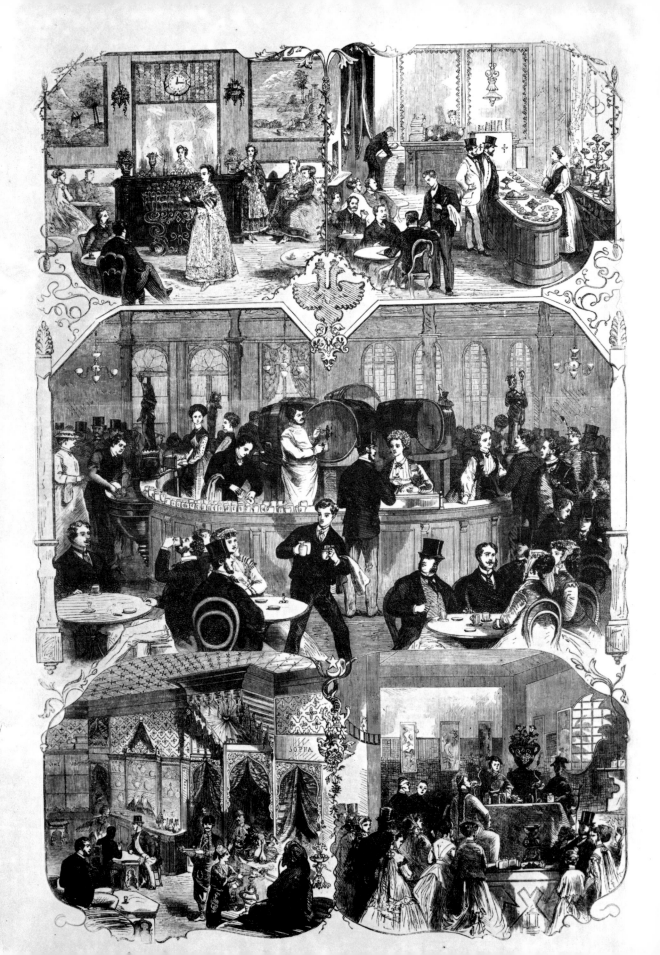

was too small. A long gallery had to be built on the quai de Billy to house all the machines. The fine arts were displayed in a large rotunda called the Panorama, near the Rond-Point of the Champs-Élysées. This was connected by a bridge to the quai de Billy, and the whole exhibition was linked together. Between the various buildings were gardens scattered with fountains, kiosks and pavilions. It all showed what has come to be called 'exhibition style'.

However, for the first time in France there was an international exhibition. Prince Napoleon presided over the organisation. For all his political turbulence, he was a man of wide interests and much intelligence. On his advice the Imperial Commission undertook to transport the foreign exhibits, free of charge, from the French frontier to Paris. Nine thousand five hundred French exhibitors took part, and ten thousand five hundred from abroad. With a liberality which was remarkable for the Second Empire, the Commission itself had been set up irrespective of political parties; and, in order to bring the Exhibition within reach of the people, the entrance fee was reduced to five sous on Sundays. The Emperor opened the Exhibition on 15 May 1855, and, before it closed on 15 November, he and the Empress made numerous visits. The Empress even had her special boudoir at the Palais de l'Industrie, where she entertained her guests.

It was not yet the age of great international fairs, dedicated to pleasure; in this respect, the Exhibition of 1855 is a long way from its successor of 1867. But it remained an exciting novelty, and it drew thousands of visitors. It also inaugurated the era of middle-class excursions to Paris.[26]

The International Exhibition of 1867 seems, in retrospect, the apotheosis of the Second Empire. It was held largely for political reasons. In 1866, Prussia had defeated Austria at the Battle of Sadowa. It was clear that Prussia intended to unite Germany under her; and it was clear that France would not tolerate the thought of Prussian supremacy on the Continent. Sooner or later there would be a conflict. But there was no French general to match von Moltke, there was no French statesman to match Bismarck; and, at the time of Sadowa, the French army was in no condition to undertake a campaign against Prussia. As an English observer wrote: 'Napoleon III has probably come to the conclusion that, in default of incessant victories, the Parisians' goodwill is largely dependent on his ability and efforts to provide them with magnificent public shows and Court pageants.'[27] This was one of the main reasons why he decided to hold an International Exhibition in Paris in 1867.

Early that year, Parisians learned details of the buildings which different nations were erecting on the Exhibition site in the Champ-de-Mars. England was presenting a Bible Society kiosk, a Protestant church, agricultural machines, a model farm and a school. Nothing could have shown more clearly the social and spiritual chasm which divided mid-Victorian England from Second Empire France. To Parisian eyes, the English exhibits must have seemed the most foreign of all. And yet there was no lack of the exotic. Morocco sent the tents of the Emperor and the Imperial Guard, Turkey erected a mosque and a Moslem sarcophagus, Japan showed a bamboo house, and

The international café life at the 1867 Exhibition.

Prussia's most impressive exhibit in 1867 was 'Krupp's Great Gun'. Paris remained lighthearted, and enamoured of Thérésa, the star of the café-concert.

China presented a café, two bazaars, and a porcelain pagoda in a garden. Prussia sent a fifty-ton Krupp gun and an equestrian statue of Frederick the Great. She had not changed her nature overnight.

On 1 April the Emperor opened the Exhibition. The Goncourts decided that France had finally turned American. Edmond Got, the actor, was hardly enthusiastic. 'The gallery of machinery is astounding, it makes you dizzy – all the machines are working, and it's certainly worth a visit. But what does it really mean? Except that in this fever the pulse of the future is beating. As for the rest, it isn't much more than a grandiose fair.'[28]

It was certainly a grandiose fair which Blanchard Jerrold described in *Paris for the English, 1867*.

'The English visitor will naturally open his inspection of the Exhibition with a stroll through the British Section. The British contributions to the Exhibition of 1867 occupy a wider space than those of any power, except those of France. The departments of industry in which we show the greatest advances are those of Art-manufacture. The English vestibule trophies consist of the triumphs of Minton, Copeland and Wedgwood, and our notable upholsterers; while over them are our leading stained-glass manu-facturers . . .

'The visitor's way now lies towards the central garden, through the American section, and those of Egypt, China, Morocco, Persia and Tunis, which are in its neigh-bourhood. The trophies, and groupings of strange products, are most comprehensive and picturesque. They consist of wool and corn; furs and antlers; Turkish food; horrible-looking bread; mineral waters; a Turkish fire-engine . . .'

The French Food Courts, as might be expected, were copiously stored; every wine district had its own exhibition and cellar. 'The Tunisian café is a great attraction. Moorish minstrels, a Moorish dame de comptoir, and solemn native waiters, occupy the visitor's attention while he drinks the thick coffee, served in little egg-cups. To the south of the Bey's palace are the gardens, tea-kiosk, and buildings of the Chinese and

Japanese; and, beyond, the gardens of Persia, the Egyptian temple, and the outdoor show from the Brazils. The Chinese tea-house and the Brazilian temple involve extra payment. They are French speculations.'[29]

Early in May, Ludovic Halévy, Offenbach's librettist, confessed: 'A day at the Exhibition seems a mere hour. I have already been to it six or seven times, and I've promised myself to pay it many more visits. How many things there are to see! . . . There are two miles or so of cafés and restaurants . . . You can eat and drink in every language . . . And the park round the palace, the houses from every land, the factories for glass-blowing and diamond-cutting, the bakery, the machine for making hats, and the machine for making shoes, and the machine for making soap . . . They make everything, these damned machines. I looked everywhere for the machines that turned out plays and novels. They are the only ones that are missing. They will be at the next Exhibition.'[30]

Most of the royalty of Europe arrived, that spring and summer, to visit the astounding Exhibition; and among them was the King of Prussia, accompanied by Count Bismarck. Von Moltke was also present; and Albert Vandam, the English chronicler,

Le Bal Bullier. A detail from a lithograph by Provost.

wrote in later years: 'The journey to France of Moltke and his royal master in 1867 was not a pleasure trip, but a downright military reconnaissance.' To the appraising eyes of von Moltke, it was clear that the French army, for all their glitter and panache, were pitifully unprepared for modern warfare.

The Exhibition closed on 3 November. A French journalist wrote: 'Thank goodness, the festivities are over. We are rid of all the abominable crowd. Paris will be Paris once again. We shall still have some good times, if Count Bismarck is willing.'[31]

Count Bismarck was not willing. Three years later, in 1870, he provoked the Franco-Prussian War.

Meanwhile, in the 1860s, Paris remained the capital of pleasure and the metropolis of entertainment. In 1865, another new craze burst upon the scene: Thérésa, the latest star of the café-concert. Even the Comtesse Tascher de la Pagerie was tempted to go and hear her.

'I asked myself,' she remembered, 'how this woman, sprung from the people, could draw the whole of Paris, earn their applause, and earn from five to six thousand francs a month ... I went to the Alcazar; it is a café-concert where men are allowed to smoke, and I can assure you that they took advantage of the permission ...

'We waited for Thérésa.

'She appeared, and she was greeted with thunderous applause.

'That evening she was well dressed, not at all *décolleté*, dressed like a respectable person.

'Her speciality is little songs, which are broad, with the most scurrilous double meanings; she sings them with the most perfect diction that you can imagine, and a full voice, with attitudes and gestures which are rather *canaille*, if you like, but genuinely graceful. She surprises you, she makes you laugh, she charms (that is the word), she carries you with her, and you have to applaud her like everyone else.'[32]

Princess Metternich did more than applaud: she learned Thérésa's songs, and sang them at Court with unqualified success.

The air of Paris was as vital as Thérésa's songs. Charles Augustus Cole, who produced *The Imperial Paris Guide*, struggled in vain with his Victorian instincts, and abandoned himself, at last, to a life of pleasure. 'To smoke a cigar on a summer evening, on a chair, before one of the cafés on the western boulevards, observing the full tide of life streaming past, is not,' he confessed, 'an unpleasant way of passing an hour or two. The scene witnessed there will not easily be forgot.'[33]

He was also ineluctably drawn to the open-air balls. 'Every male tourist,' so he explained, 'who wishes to form some idea of Parisian life, ought certainly to visit at least one of them.' He himself was slightly disapproving, but enthralled. 'Though they are frequented by and established for the benefit of the *demi-monde*, they are conducted with such propriety that even the most strait-laced old gentleman will not be able to find fault with the behaviour of the company he finds there, excepting always the fact of their *being* there.'

152

RIGHT *Four costumes by Alfred Albert for the 1870 production of* Coppélia. ABOVE LEFT *and* RIGHT *Franz and Dr Coppélius;* BELOW LEFT *and* RIGHT *L'Hymène and Paysanne.* OVERLEAF *Le Pré-Catalan au Bois de Boulogne. From a lithograph by Eugène Guérard.*

Coppelia
Ballet 3 tableaux.
St Léon

2.

Frantz
Mlle Fiocre.

Coppélia.
Ballet en 3 tableaux.

N° 1er

Coppélius.
Mr Dauty

Alf. Albert
1870

Alf. Albert
1870

Coppélia
Ballet 3 tableaux

3

L'Hymenée
Mlle Ribet

tulle illusion
blanc.

Alf Albert
1870

Coppélia
Ballet en 3 tableaux.

5

4 Paysannes
Sujets.

Alf Albert
1867

The Jardin Mabille, off the Champs-Élysées, was 'tastefully laid out and illuminated. The fashionable nights,' Cole explained, 'are Tuesday and Saturday, when the entrance is 3 fr.; Thursday and Sunday, the entrance is only 2 fr.'[34] Near the Jardin Mabille was the Château des Fleurs, where 'the gaslights in the midst of the plants and flowers frequently produced the most charming effects.' But what most attracted Cole were the Château Rouge, or Nouveau Tivoli, in the rue Neuve Clignancourt, and, above all, the Closerie des Lilas.

'To the attractions of music, dancing and fireworks these gardens [at the Château Rouge] add various other amusements . . . In none of these three balls, however, is the far-famed *grisette* to be found, known to every reader of a certain class of French novel . . . That typical creature can only be seen in full feather in the Quartier Latin, where the students live, and particularly at the Closerie des Lilas, near the Jardin du Luxembourg. There also a glimpse may occasionally be obtained of the cancan, a far more expressive than elegant way of dancing, which only the presence of the police can keep within the bounds of decency.'[35]

The open-air balls were not the only entertainments which Cole observed with Victorian eyes. He visited the gardens of the Palais-Royal, long since left behind by the tide of fashion. 'Here are hosts of white-aproned nurses, with that endless variety of caps and headdresses which the different departments of France afford; about them flutter gay Lotharios in baggy red trousers, not quite so smart and important as our guardsmen, yet with a something about them . . . But your real man of fashion is never seen at the Palais-Royal . . .; his open-air sphere of action in Paris is limited to the Boulevard, and the Bois de Boulogne.'[36]

Feeding the carp at Fontainebleau was a treat for the Second Empire child. There were many others for him in Paris. At Séraphin, in the boulevard Montmartre, there were shadow shows, children's plays and magic marionettes. At the Marionnettes lyriques, in the boulevard de Strasbourg, there were vaudevilles, fairy-plays and ballets. 'Apart from these two establishments,' wrote Henry de Conty, in his *Paris en Poche*, 'we recommend the following as rewards for good children: the Cirque Napoléon and the Cirque de l'Impératrice, the children's dances at the Pré-Catalan in the summer, the conjuring tricks of MM. Robert-Houdin and Manicardi, and – as inexpensive treats – the goat-carts in the Champs-Élysées, the aerial boats, and the merry-go-round.'[37]

A panorama of the Paris Exhibition of 1855. From a painting by Lami de Nozan.   157

9 Literature and the Press

Poetry in the Second Empire embraces the past, the present and the future. The four great poets of the Romantic movement were still alive when the Empire began. Alfred de Musset, it is true, had practically ceased to write by 1852, the year in which he was elected to the Académie-Française; but he lingered on for five more years, his health and character wrecked by his way of life, and he died at the age of forty-seven. Lamartine's political career had really ended with *Recueillements poétiques* in 1839; but he published his tale *Graziella* in book form in 1852, and his political writings and collected speeches in 1864–5. Troubled by financial hardship, he survived until 1869: a sad but impressive relic. For the last two years of his life he was given a government pension. Alfred de Vigny was another melancholy relic of the past. From 1853 he was living in Paris, with few outside interests except his duties as an Academician. He died in 1863; the following year, eleven of his poems were published as *Les Destinées*. They all revealed stoical resignation to earthly suffering, and to God, if God existed, as the ruthless Divinity of the Old Testament. In 1867 Vigny's *pensées*, daily jottings, and drafts of unfinished works were published as *Journal d'un poète*.

Over these demi-gods towers the inescapable figure of Victor Hugo. Incapable of Musset's wit or his elegance, of Lamartine's piety, or of Vigny's intellectual grasp, Hugo remains a gigantic figure in poetry. His most 'Romantic' poems had been published by 1840; and he had been disheartened by the failure of his poetic drama, *Les Burgraves*, in 1843. But literary success and the passing of years had developed his political ambitions. His articles in *L'Événement* had done much to facilitate Louis-Napoleon's entry upon the scene; and Hugo was disappointed when the Prince-President failed to offer him high office. After the coup-d'état of 2 December 1851, Hugo went into exile; and, after a period in Brussels, he settled in Jersey (1853) and finally Guernsey (1855). In 1854 Jules Janin, the critic, reported that Hugo was bored to death by exile. 'He is completely urban: he needs an audience and flatterers.'[1] Hugo refused to return to Paris some years later, when an amnesty would have made this possible, and he declared that he would wait until liberty had returned. He came

One of the greatest poets in French literature:
Baudelaire, photographed by Nadar.

159

LEFT *The apostle of Art for Art's Sake, Théophile Gautier in about 1856, and* RIGHT *the chief Romantic, Victor Hugo in 1868.*

back on the fall of the Empire, and explained, with his usual grandiloquence: 'I have returned with the Republic, in order to defend Paris, the capital of civilisation.'[2] He had not been unaware that exile enhanced his prestige; and he returned to find that a *légende Victor Hugo* had duly arisen.

Hugo was a prolific writer, and his years abroad had been productive; apart from novels, political writings, and criticism, he had published *Les Châtiments* (1853): a collection of political and invective verse. This was followed by *Les Contemplations* (1856); by the first books of *La Légende des Siècles*, a grandiose historical panorama (1859–83); and by *Chansons des rues et des bois* (1865).

While Hugo himself would continue to write, abundantly, until he died in 1885, the Romantic School which he had led and symbolised had spent its fire before the Second Empire came into being. It was, in time, to be followed by the Parnassian School of poets; but before the Parnassian era there were already signs of the new direction in poetry.

The great precursor of the Parnassians was Théophile Gautier, the apostle of Art for Art's Sake.[3] A born Romantic, and a famous and flamboyant figure at the *bataille d'Hernani* in 1830, Gautier had gradually come to profess a creed of his own. Though, at heart, he kept all his Romantic exuberance, his Romantic love of the historical and the exotic, his Romantic sensibility, he made a more personal contribution to French literature. In an increasingly uniform and materialistic world, Gautier insisted that art should be cultivated for its own sake. The achievement of formal beauty was the only purpose of art, and aesthetic value was all that counted. The phrase Art for Art's Sake became the rallying cry of Baudelaire, Banville and Flaubert, in their fight for liberty in art. It acquired the further meaning that beauty in a work of art was a matter of perfect expression and of the indissoluble unity of form and content. In the novel, the outcome of Art for Art's Sake was to be Realism, and a passionate devotion to style; in poetry, the creed of l'Art pour l'Art led to the impassive, descriptive verse of the Parnassians: among it Gautier's *Émaux et Camées*, which appeared in 1852. On this book his fame as a poet largely rests.

Émaux et Camées. The title is fair. The poems are chiselled and engraved by the most diligent craftsman. And, indeed, by the most conscious; for where another poet might have delighted in diversity of form, Gautier finds pleasure in writing nearly all the anthology in octosyllabic verse. And yet, if we persist in seeing the book as the triumph of an inspired technician, we shall miss its significance; for this restricted verse-form clothes widely different inspirations. *Émaux et Camées* is significant for its style; it also enlightens many moments of Gautier's life, many aspects of his writing, discloses a man both sensual and sensitive, lyrical and philosophic. And it reflects not only Gautier, but the sober-suited years of Louis-Philippe, and the iridescent years of the Second Empire. It recreates the Paris of a century ago. It may not do so with the ferocity and power of Baudelaire, but it does so quite as surely.

In 1857, five years after *Émaux et Camées* was published, there appeared a book of poems dedicated

> To the impeccable poet
> the perfect magician of French literature
> my most dear and most venerated master and friend,
> THÉOPHILE GAUTIER.

This book, which was offered to him with 'the deepest humility', was *Les Fleurs du mal*, by Charles Baudelaire.[4]

The poems were written at various dates, but their grouping and their emotions give them unity. The theme is the antagonism between *spleen* and *idéal*, between evil and good, by which man is torn. Baudelaire discards the criterion of idealised beauty, and he draws poetry from reality. He finds inspiration in the streets, in the hidden life of Paris, or in evil itself. He analyses his own nature, and he is haunted by a sense of damnation which drives him to revolt and blasphemy. But these cannot prevail against God, and he longs for death and the discovery of the Beyond.

In 1857, when *Les Fleurs du mal* appeared, Baudelaire was prosecuted and fined for offences against public morals. The prosecution was a blow not only to his finances but to his pride and his awareness of his genius. Yet if some of his contemporaries did him little justice, others already recognised his power. Hugo declared that Baudelaire had introduced *un frisson nouveau* into poetry. Verlaine, in 1865, at the age of twenty-one, sensed Baudelaire's true distinction.

161

'The profound originality of Charles Baudelaire is, to my mind, his powerful presentation of the essential modern man . . .: the physical man of today, as he has been made by the refinements of an excessive civilisation: modern man, with his sharpened, vibrant senses, his painfully subtle mind, his intellect steeped in tobacco, his blood burned up by alcohol . . . The future historian of our age should study *Les Fleurs du mal* with pious attention. It is the quintessence, the extreme concentration of a whole element of this century.'[5]

Gautier had already perceived the symbolic correspondences of colours, scents and sounds; but Baudelaire expressed this theory to perfection, and in doing so he was a precursor of modern poetry. He explored the musical powers of the French language, and he showed astonishing powers of evocation. Rimbaud was strongly influenced by Baudelaire; Verlaine was instinctively and profoundly in sympathy with him, as much of his own poetry bears witness. Baudelaire was a significant critic of literature, painting and music; he was one of the greatest poets of the Second Empire, and, indeed, in all French literature.

Gautier and Baudelaire do not belong, exclusively, to any school of poetry; but both of them had indicated the way in which French poetry would move. After 1860 there was a clear reaction against the poetry of the Romantics. The personal was replaced by the impersonal, the enthusiastic by the impassive, the inspired by the immaculately written. The theory of Art for Art's Sake, which Gautier had proclaimed, was carried a stage further by the Parnassians.

The Parnassians were a group of poets who represented the scientific and positivist spirit of the age. Parnassian poetry was objective, impersonal and restrained; it confined itself to descriptions of nature, remarkable for their static, pictorial quality. It often introduced an exotic element, or evoked an historic or archaeological past; it attempted to convey philosophical conceptions. It aimed at formal perfection. Technical liberties were rejected. Théodore de Banville, in his treatise on French poetry, wrote one chapter notable for brevity. '*Licences poétiques*. Il n'y en a pas.'

The Parnassians, in the 1860s, found their publisher in Alphonse Lemerre. It was he who, in 1866, issued the first eighteen instalments of *Le Parnasse contemporain*, the anthology from which they took their name. His little shop in the passage Choiseul became a meeting-place for the new generation of poets.

But the Mecca to which the Parnassians went in pilgrimage was a fourth-floor apartment in the boulevard des Invalides. There lived their unchallenged leader, Leconte de Lisle. In 1852 he had published his *Poèmes antiques*, and, ten years later, his *Poèmes barbares*. They are typical Parnassian poetry. In *Poèmes antiques* his inspiration is largely Greek or Indian; in *Poèmes barbares* the poems are inspired by Egyptian or Nordic mythology or biblical history, or they are pictures of exotic scenery and of jungle life. Both collections are typical of the formal perfection and the visual rather than emotive beauty which characterise Parnassian poetry. Subject and treatment are often dictated by the poet's own embittered and atheistic philosophy.

The master of the Parnassians, Leconte de Lisle LEFT *and his favourite disciple, José-Maria de Heredia.*

Leconte de Lisle had been forced by poverty to accept an imperial pension, but he still dominated his disciples by his poetic achievement, his lofty nature, and by the prestige of his years. He had been born on Réunion Island, in the Indian Ocean, in 1818, the son of a former surgeon in Napoleon's armies; his mother, who belonged to the island, was a cousin of the poet Parny. Leconte de Lisle had come to France as a youth of nineteen, and he had studied law, and since 1846 he had lived in Paris. The Revolution of 1848 had ruined his family and ended his private allowance, and for some years he had struggled to subsist on journalism, translations and private tuition; in the intervals of such prosaic work, he had devoted himself to poetry. His legal training and his financial stress combined to make him rigidly self-disciplined; and his character – like his poetic principles – remained severe. He was a dedicated poet, and, to his young disciples, a natural master.

Nearly thirty years after *Le Parnasse contemporain* had first appeared, François Coppée recalled the weekly visits to Leconte de Lisle as 'the finest hours of my youth'.

'Usually the Master himself would open the door to us, and his smile – which was readily sarcastic – became cordial and benevolent, when he was greeting poets. We hastened to greet Mme Leconte de Lisle. She was a charming young woman, and her husband, who was much older than she was, treated her with touching, paternal gentleness. At first our arrival crowded up the two small rooms, very modestly furnished, which were the only reception rooms he had. Soon the rooms were full of clouds, for we were allowed cigarettes; and it is through this cloud that I recall the poet's Olympian head, his balding and impressive skull, with its halo of long hair (already greying), his regular features, the sparkling eye behind his monocle, his proud and

163

disdainful mouth. And then we talked, and we only talked of what we all loved, of literature and poetry . . .

'But our great delight – it was all too rare – was when Leconte de Lisle himself agreed to recite some unpublished poems to us. I remember how we had "gooseflesh" with enthusiasm when he read his *Qaïn* . . . Leconte de Lisle was very interesting to watch when he was reciting his own poetry . . . His voice, rather dull, and almost trembling, gripped the very bowels of the listener. One felt a tremor run across that marmoreal face, which had suddenly grown tender. The eyes, especially, became terrifying. They grew hollow; and, under the trembling lids, the pupils rose, as if in ecstasy . . .'[6]

It was an awe-inspiring experience, and Coppée was not alone in feeling veneration. In 1884, in *La Légende du Parnasse contemporain*, Catulle Mendès would still write that Leconte de Lisle 'remains our poetic conscience in person . . . He condemns or absolves, and we submit.'[7]

The Master's favourite disciple was José-Maria de Heredia. Born in Cuba in 1842, the son of a Spanish father and a French mother, Heredia was educated in France, and from 1861 he lived in Paris. He studied law, and attended the École des Chartes, but he soon devoted himself to poetry, and he was one of the first Parnassians. His fame rests on the 118 sonnets of *Les Trophées*, which were published in book form in 1893, a year before his election to the Académie-Française. Heredia transfixes some fleeting image of beauty from antiquity or a less remote past. He creates an effect of sculptural perfection, and the sonnets remain the ultimate expression of the Parnassian ideals.

One of those who might be seen in Lemerre's back room, and in the salon of Leconte de Lisle, was the young Paul Verlaine.[8] He had been born in 1844, the only child of an army officer and a respectable, well-to-do mother, and he was now, in the late 1860s, a clerk at the Paris Hôtel de Ville. His bourgeois sinecure and his careful dress gave a false impression of the man: or, rather, they revealed only half the truth. For, throughout his life, Verlaine would be a double personality: a bourgeois and a bohemian, or – as his future wife would say – Prince Charming and the Beast. From his father's family he seems to have inherited his alcoholic tendencies; and already, when he was eighteen, these had been manifest. Alcohol would move him to outbursts of homicidal violence, it would in time help to destroy his poetic powers and his physical frame. Verlaine, well aware of his ugliness, was also bisexual. In 1870 he would marry a girl of seventeen; in 1871, a few weeks before the birth of their child, Rimbaud would burst into his life, break his impossible bourgeois marriage, and determine the course of his life and poetry. No other passion in Verlaine's life – which was a life of many passions – ever approached this relationship with Rimbaud: a relationship which was physically and spiritually complete.

His first book, *Poèmes saturniens*, was published in 1866; but, while he wrote his poetic essays in Parnassian style, as a form of literary discipline, he was already drawn,

The author of Madame Bovary*: Gustave Flaubert, painted by Eugène Giraud.*

instinctively, to poetry of quite another order. From Leconte de Lisle, Verlaine borrowed the heroes of classical mythology, the interest in Indian epic, and the ideal of impassivity; and, in his *Épilogue*, he insisted, with all the force of a convinced Parnassian, on the supreme importance of unremitting work and technical perfection. But it was not Leconte de Lisle who left the clearest imprint on this book: it was already Baudelaire. His influence may be seen in Verlaine's interest in modern Paris, but, above all, it is seen in mood. The most memorable *Poèmes saturniens* were, already, poems of mood. 'The more people read me,' Verlaine would write, a quarter-century later, 'the more they will be convinced that there is a sort of unity between my early works and those of my maturity.'

Verlaine had revealed his instinctive sympathy with Baudelaire, and he had begun to establish himself as a poet of mood. In his next book, *Fêtes galantes*, which appeared in 1869, he showed himself to be a poet of extraordinary technical accomplishment, a poet of exquisite sensibility. He re-created a distinctive world. Inspired by the paintings of the eighteenth century, Verlaine created a series of tiny verbal pictures, of miniature conversation-pieces. In the twenty-eight poems of *Fêtes galantes*, he caught and enshrined the world of Watteau, and the world of the *commedia dell'arte*. *Fêtes galantes* was, in many ways, an impersonal book, but it showed that the poet had come into possession of his powers.

Shortly before it was published, Verlaine had met Mathilde Mauté, the young girl whom he was to marry; and his sudden love for her inspired *La Bonne Chanson*. This new book (announced in the summer of 1870, just before the fall of the Second Empire), is a record of Verlaine's longing for domesticity. It marks a stage in his spiritual progress; and, in the poems where his love for Mathilde is generalised – notably in the poem remembered as 'L'heure exquise . . .' – he reveals himself as a poet of rarified happiness.

In the three books which he wrote during the Second Empire, Verlaine had shown his infinite power of creating mood and suggestion, of recording the poetry of dream. He had brought French poetry as close as it would ever come to music; he had already revealed his personal contribution to French literature.

One of the most remarkable features of the literature of nineteenth-century France is the versatility of its exponents. Victor Hugo, whose presence was felt in Second Empire poetry, also put his hand to the novel. In 1862 he published *Les Misérables*. This is the story of Jean Valjean. Once a kindly peasant, he has suffered years of imprisonment for a trivial offence, and he has been turned into a criminal. On his release from prison, Valjean has many adventures, but, for all his moments of bravery, affection and nobility, he finds it impossible to forget his past. *Les Misérables* is a complex and unsatisfactory novel, and it is made even more unwieldy by the insertion of long political or sociological dissertations. *Les Travailleurs de la mer* (1866) is set in Guernsey, where Hugo was living. A young girl, Déruchette, promises to marry the man who can salvage her father's steamboat. Gilliatt, a fisherman, is in love with her; he manages at

Émile Zola, painted by his friend Édouard Manet, 1868.

Two prolific novelists: LEFT *George Sand, in 1864, and* RIGHT *Alexandre Dumas* père, *in 1867.*

last to dislodge the wreck, only to find that she loves another man. He nobly helps her to marry his rival; and, as the couple set sail for England, he sits on a rock to watch their vessel pass, and allows the tide to engulf him. *L'Homme qui rit* (1869) attempts to give a picture of English society at the end of the seventeenth century; but Hugo's account is often unintentionally amusing, and – like *Les Misérables* – the novel is obscured by long digressions.

Théophile Gautier had earned renown as a novelist in 1836 – with his controversial *Mademoiselle de Maupin.* In 1863 he published *Le Capitaine Fracasse.* The captain himself is a *jeune premier* to delight the heart of Hugo or Dumas *père.* The heroine is the illegitimate daughter of a prince, the villain is Byronically seductive, the father greyhaired and noble. In this romance of a troupe of strolling players, every melodramatic décor re-appears. The plot is no more plausible than the characters. Yet if *Le Capitaine Fracasse* is not an outstanding work of fiction, it remains a tour de force, an example of the descriptive art.

Balzac, that huge Romantic figure, had died before the Second Empire began; but another giant was Dumas *père* (1802–70). He produced twenty-two volumes of *Mes Mémoires* (1852–5), and such latter-day novels as *La Comtesse de Charny* (1852–5), which dealt with the Revolutionary years. He also published tales of country life, including *Le Meneur de Loups* (1857). Even in his old age, Dumas *père* remained one of the prodigies of nineteenth-century French literature; his *Œuvres complètes* fill a hundred and three volumes. The works of George Sand (1804–76) fill one hundred and five, and some of these were written during the Second Empire. Among them were the four volumes of *Histoire de ma vie* (1854–5) and a number of novels, including *Le Marquis de Villemer* (1863).

But George Sand's novels belonged, now, to the past; from about 1850 French novelists had new preoccupations. They were not concerned with sentiment or with melodrama, but with questions of form, technique, and the function of the novel. Just as the Parnassians reacted against Romantic poetry, so the Realists and Naturalists showed a new conception of the novel. They were no longer interested in idealism; they reflected the positivist spirit of the age. They intended to document their novels, and to show real life.

Jules Husson, better known as Champfleury (1821–89) published one of the first studies of the movement: *Le Réalisme* (1857), and he became a leader of the movement as well as the author of some now more or less unreadable works of fiction. Ernest Feydeau (1821–73), had begun his career as a stockbroker, but in 1858 he published a novel which was considered one of the triumphs of Realism.

'As for Ernest Feydeau,' wrote Ernest Daudet, many years later, 'one must recall the scandalous success of his novel *Fanny*. It was his first work . . . He had a real gift for presentation; and the audacious situations, the novelty of the work, and, above all, its seductive, corrupting scent, heady with spices: these assured him a brilliant success. For some weeks, *Fanny* was in fashion, although the society women through whose hands it passed did not always confess that they had read it.'[9]

Among the later works of Feydeau was *Sylvie* (1859), the heroine of which was largely based on the courtesan Mme Sabatier (Feydeau had introduced himself to her *salon*); the hero, Anselme Schanfara, a Bohemian artist, is partly modelled on Baudelaire, whom Feydeau cordially disliked. The story is a footnote to the love which had inspired Baudelaire to write his poems to *la Vénus blanche* in *Les Fleurs du mal*.

Most of Prosper Mérimée's creative work was done before the advent of the Second Empire, though his *Carmen* appeared in *Nouvelles* in 1852; most of the work of Alphonse Daudet was published after the Empire had fallen. Gérard de Nerval, the Romantic poet, the translator of Goethe, published poems and tales in the early years of the régime: among them *Les Filles du Feu* (1854), a collection of tales which included his masterpiece *Sylvie*. In 1855, the year of his mysterious death, there appeared *Le Rêve et la Vie*: a collection of prose and poetry. The collection included *Aurélia*, the record of the phases of his mental derangement. It has earned him a place as a precursor of much of the 'hallucinatory' writing of modern times.

A highly popular novelist of the period was Octave Feuillet (1821–90), who is especially remembered for his sentimental *Roman d'un jeune homme pauvre* (1858). Eugène Fromentin (1820–76) gave up the law for art, and art for literature, and was most successful with his writing. His travel books, *Un Été dans le Sahara* (1857), and *Une Année dans le Sahel* (1859), were followed in 1863 by his most important work: *Dominique*, a novel of psychological analysis. It was an isolated precursor of the genre which developed some thirty years later. Fromentin then felt unable to satisfy his literary standards, and he returned to painting. 'One puts a good deal of one's own heart into one's first book,' wrote Jules Claretie. 'We find a smiling melancholy on every page of *Un Été dans le Sahara* and in that calm and gentle novel, *Dominique*. In the midst of the Yankee activity of our time, Fromentin was a dreamer who was rather bruised by the shocks of life, and very quickly consoled by fine visions.'[10]

One must also mention a writer in a very different category who established himself during the Second Empire. This was Jules Verne (1828–1905); he might be called the creator of science fiction. He was educated for the law, but his only real concern was writing, and in 1863, inspired, no doubt, by his friend the balloonist Nadar, he published his first success: *Cinq semaines en ballon*. The following year, he again showed his gift for popularising science – this time geology – in *Voyage au centre de la terre*. Two years later, in *Les Aventures du Capitaine Hatteras*, Verne turned to polar exploration. In 1870, he introduced the public to Captain Nemo and his submarine, the Nautilus, in *Vingt mille lieues sous la mer*.

All these writers have their place in the history of the novel or of popular fiction during the Second Empire; and from 1852 French novelists were faced by formidable rivals from abroad. Hachette, the publishers, brought out translations of English novels, and *La Petite Dorrit* and *Jane Eyre*, in their red paper covers, appeared in booksellers' windows alongside current French fiction.

During the last years of the reign, Émile Zola was collecting the documents on which he would base *Les Rougon-Macquart*: the series of twenty novels which would be 'the

Jules Verne, the pioneer of science fiction, photographed by his friend Nadar, and RIGHT *Prosper Mérimée.*

natural and social history of a family during the Second Empire'. The first volume, *La Fortune des Rougon*, was already written when the Empire fell. 'As an artist,' Zola explained, 'I needed the fall of the Bonapartes. I saw it inevitably at the end of the drama, but I did not dare to hope that it was so near. It came, and gave me the terrible and necessary conclusion for my work.'[11] The first volume of *Les Rougon-Macquart* appeared in 1871, and the last in 1893.

But Zola published few books during the imperial age. The novelist who towers over the Second Empire is unquestionably Gustave Flaubert.[12] Born in Rouen in 1821, a surgeon's son, he studied law in Paris, failed to pass his examinations, and turned to literature. He settled with his widowed mother at Croisset, near Rouen, and there he led a hermit's life, dominated by his writing. His standards were rigorous, and his first published novel, *Madame Bovary*, appeared in 1856 in the *Revue de Paris*, after years of dedicated toil. Flaubert was prosecuted for offences against public morals; but – more fortunate than Baudelaire – he was acquitted. *Madame Bovary* appeared in book form in 1857. It is set in Normandy, near Rouen. Emma Bovary, the heroine, is the wife of a country doctor, who cannot come to terms with real life. She tries to bring it closer to a romantic novel by taking lovers, but her love-affairs are predictable failures. She falls into debt, and, terrified that her husband will discover everything, she takes arsenic. Flaubert paints a devastating picture of a petty provincial town; he gives a magisterial likeness of the maladjusted woman, trying desperately to make reality resemble her dreams. As a study of provincial life, and of human nature, as an example of literary style, *Madame Bovary* is a masterpiece.

Flaubert followed it with *Salammbô* (1862), in which he gave full rein to the romantic side of his nature; but some critics considered that this novel of ancient Carthage was weakened by his archaeological detail. In 1869 he published *L'Éducation sentimentale*, which is sometimes held to be his finest work. Frédéric Moreau, the hero, is a law student in Paris. He is in love with Mme Arnoux, and this idealistic love is not weakened by his less platonic affairs. After nearly twenty years, Frédéric receives an unexpected visit from Mme Arnoux. She had guessed his love, and returned it. She leaves him with a lock of her hair, which has now turned white. *L'Éducation sentimentale* owes something to Flaubert's own idealistic love for Mme Schlésinger, the wife of a Paris editor, to whom he was devoted for most of his life. The political and social background is superbly painted, and the characters are drawn with rare skill. *Madame Bovary* and *L'Éducation sentimentale* set Flaubert in his place as one of the greatest novelists of all time.

Edmond de Goncourt (1822–96) and his brother Jules (1830–70) remain a phenomenon in French literature. They wrote in such sensitive collaboration that although death ended the partnership early they are seldom mentioned apart.

'I have never seen more perfect or more extraordinary harmony,' wrote Joseph Primoli in 1869. 'One wears the watch and the other carries the purse. When you talk to them separately, they both give you the same answers, without any prior consultation.

'I only once knew them to disagree, and that was when one of them had to be decorated. The elder brother wanted it to be the younger brother. He was the one, he said, who wrote most and showed the greatest wit. The younger brother wanted it to be the elder brother, saying that he had good sense and – that he was older. This consideration prevailed. They were then at Trouville (August 1867). Mother wrote to congratulate Edmond; when he answered, he signed the letter alone and ended it: "*Vos* très reconnaissants *Edmond* de Goncourt." '13

The Goncourts were unsuccessful dramatists, they were critics and champions of eighteenth-century French art, and the originators of the documentary novel. Their works are among the most quoted examples of Realism and Naturalism in nineteenth-century French fiction. *Germinie Lacerteux* (1864) is the history of a servant of their own, who had worked for them faithfully for years; they later learned that all the time she had been leading a life of debauchery. Blanchard Jerrold considered that 'a more scandalous libel on the working men of the French capital was never written ... Why,' he asked, 'did MM. de Goncourt write a maudlin preface to their memoirs of a drunken and immoral cook, and present the picture as one of French working-class life? The *peuple* will be very angry with them; the educated classes will turn from their pages with loathing. Germinie is not instructive, for she is not a type; she is a monster.'14 The principal character of *Madame Gervaisais* (1869), a study of religious mania, is drawn from one of the Goncourts' relatives; and, when the brothers were writing *Sœur Philomène* (1861), they visited the Hôpital de la Charité to study hospital life from the inside. *Charles Demailly* (1860) described a Bohemian world of men of letters. *Renée Mauperin* (1864) and *Manette Salomon* (1867) were novels of manners.

The Goncourts felt they were pursued by an unkind fate. Their first novel had appeared the morning after the coup-d'état of 1851, and it had naturally been doomed to failure. Their play *Henriette Maréchal*, produced in 1865 with support from Princess Mathilde, roused an anti-Government demonstration. The Goncourts took each mishap personally, and, when Jules died in 1870, Edmond called him a martyr to literature.

Edmond later presided over a literary *salon*, le Grenier des Goncourt; his name is perpetuated in the Académie Goncourt (he had left a sum of money to found it). But such achievements, and the novels he wrote single-handed, and his works on Japanese art, all pale before the immense Goncourt *Journal*.

He and his brother had begun to keep it in 1851, and, after Jules had died, Edmond continued it until his own death. Flaubert curtly dismissed the work. 'The Goncourt memoirs are no better than any of the others, even though they say that Edmond takes down the conversation on his left-hand cuff, under the table.'15 But, whatever Flaubert's *boutade*, the *Journal* is a mine of literary criticism, literary and artistic information and gossip; it is a social chronicle and a historical record. It is not often kind or generous, but it is witty, scandalous, shrewd, vivacious, and revealing. At times, as in the account of Paris during the Franco-Prussian War and the Commune, it is profoundly moving. Few celebrities of the Second Empire, or republican France, have escaped the

The closest collaborators in French literature: Edmond and Jules de Goncourt.

Goncourts' daily record. The twenty-two volumes of the *Journal* are essential to our knowledge of the age, and they remain the Goncourts' paramount contribution to literature.

The Second Empire saw a number of notable historians, but none of them showed active sympathy with the régime. Alexis de Tocqueville (1805–59) chose to live abroad after the coup-d'état of 1851; he abandoned his political career, and devoted himself to his writing. He believed that, far from being a complete break with the past, the French Revolution had shown the continuity of history. He planned to write a three-volume work to prove his contention, but *L'Ancien Régime* (1856) was the only part of it which he completed. Adolphe Thiers (1797–1877) was both a statesman and an historian. He had published the first of his two famous works, *Histoire de la Révolution française* between 1823 and 1827. In 1840 he went into opposition over the foreign policy of Louis-Philippe, and he retired to write his second masterpiece, *Histoire du consultat et de l'empire* (1845–62). After the last volume appeared, he returned to active politics as a republican and an anti-imperialist; he led the peace negotiations in 1871, and he was first President of the Third Republic.

Another historian and statesman was François Guizot (1787–1874). His political life had ended before the Second Empire began, and, when the régime came into being, he was in retirement in Normandy, devoting himself to the writing of history. The nine volumes of his *Mémoires pour servir à l'histoire de mon temps* appeared in 1858–68. *Histoire parlementaire de France* was published in 1863; and the last year of the Empire saw the first volume of his *Histoire de France racontée à mes petits-enfants*.

Louis Blanc (1811–82) was again a politician and an historian; after the February Revolution of 1848, he fled to England, where he completed his *Histoire de la Révolution française* (1847–62). It was written with a marked socialist bias, and it has now been largely superseded. In 1871 he returned to France and to left-wing politics.

Jules Michelet (1798–1874) was also an opponent of the Empire. His refusal to swear allegiance to the régime cost him his posts at the Archives and the Collège de France. He then lived in the country, and finished his eleven-volume history, *Renaissance et temps modernes* (1855–67).

Ernest Renan was, with Taine, the foremost representative of French thought in the later years of the Second Empire. Historian, Hebrew scholar, philologist and critic, he was born at Tréguier, in Brittany, in 1823. He was educated for the priesthood, and, from 1843, at the seminary of Saint-Sulpice in Paris. His study of the Semitic languages and of biblical texts led him to question the divine inspiration of the Bible and the fundamental doctrines of orthodox religion. He was unable to take his vows, he left Saint-Sulpice, and he established himself as a Semitic scholar. In 1862 he was appointed Professor of Hebrew at the Collège de France. His lectures were considered unorthodox, and suspended by Government order. His Chair was suppressed after the appearance of his *Vie de Jésus* in 1863, the first volume of his work *Les Origines du Christianisme*.

'It is in the name of constant experience,' wrote Renan, in his introduction, 'that we banish miracles from history. We do not say: "Miracles are impossible." We say: "Until now no miracles have been proved" . . . Until things change, we shall therefore maintain this principle of historical criticism: that a supernatural account cannot be accepted as such, that it always implies credulity or imposture, and that the historian's duty is to interpret it and to discover how much truth and how much falsehood it may conceal.

'These are the rules I have followed in writing this book. I have not only read the texts, I have also found a great source of illumination: I have seen the places where the events occurred . . . The striking agreement of text and places, the wonderful harmony of the evangelical ideal with the countryside which was its setting were to me a sort of revelation. I had a fifth Gospel before my eyes: torn, but still legible, and, from that moment, through the accounts of Matthew and Mark, . . . I saw a human figure live and move . . .'

It was an intellectual approach to Christianity. It was an approach which allowed disbelief, indeed depended on doubt. 'To write the history of a religion,' Renan continued, 'one must in the first place have believed in it. And, secondly, one must no longer believe in it absolutely, for absolute faith is incompatible with honest history. But love exists without belief. If one does not accept any of the forms which command the adoration of men, one does not renounce delight in the goodness and beauty which they contain.'[16]

Beneath Renan's lyrical picture of the carpenter's son in Galilee lay a rationalisation of the fundamental belief in the divinity of Christ. 'As for the sublime person,' he ended, 'who still presides, every day, over the destiny of the world, we may call him divine, not in the sense that Jesus absorbed all divinity, . . . but in the sense that Jesus is the individual who has made his fellow men take the greatest step towards the divine . . . Whatever the unexpected phenomena of the future may be, Jesus will not be surpassed. The worship of him will always be young; his legend will inspire endless tears; his sufferings will move the noblest hearts; every century will proclaim that among the sons of men none has been born who is greater than Jesus.'[17]

The words – like Darwin's theories in *The Origin of Species* – have lost their power today. But, at the end of the nineteenth century, Jules Troubat, who had been secretary to Sainte-Beuve, recalled that the *Vie de Jésus* had caused a schism in religious consciences.[18]

Renan himself, deprived of his Chair at the Collège de France, had remained undeterred by the tumult. In 1866 he published *Les Apôtres*, the second volume of *Les Origines du Christianisme*; in 1869 he published the third. In 1870, when the Empire had fallen, the Provisional Government reinstated him at the Collège de France. He became its head in 1883, the year in which the eighth and final volume of his great work appeared.

With the growth of the Press and the reading public during the nineteenth century, the professional critic came into being; and criticism at its best became a separate form of literature. Hippolyte Taine (1828–93) did much to mould the thought of the generation who reached maturity in about 1870. He emphasised the interdependence of the physical and psychological factors which influence human development; and he applied these principles to the study of literature, history and art. His theories owed much to positivism, and he expounded them at length in *De l'intelligence* (1870). In his famous introduction to the *Histoire de la littérature anglaise* (1863), Taine had already emphasised the importance, for historians and critics, of studying the physical and psychological factors which were responsible for cultural and social development. Taine's views made him the theorist of Naturalism, but they are far from representing the whole extent of his thought. There are passages in *De l'intelligence* which herald the exploration of the unconscious found in some of the masterpieces of modern fiction.

While Taine advanced the theories which were to influence criticism and creative work, the criticism which appeared in the Second Empire Press was dominated by two figures. Théophile Gautier was an artist and a poet, not a conventional journalist; and, for that reason, he gave journalism a new status and significance. He made it, at its best, a work of literary art. He had begun to write for *La Presse* in 1836, and for the next nineteen years he was its critic-in-chief. He reviewed the theatre, he discussed books, he considered the Salons and lesser exhibitions; in the intervals he described his travels, or topical events. In 1855 he left *La Presse* for *Le Moniteur universel*; in 1869 he joined the new government paper, *Le Journal officiel*. Gautier was not an intellectual; but his criticism offers a panorama of cultural life under the bourgeois monarchy and the Second Empire.

His friend and contemporary, Charles-Augustin Sainte-Beuve, was born at Boulogne in 1804. Educated in Paris, he was a medical student for years before he turned to literary journalism.

The first half of his career was devoted to literary criticism and the writing of poetry and his autobiographical novel, *Volupté*. For a brief spell he became professor at the University of Liége. The second half of his career began in 1849, when he returned to Paris and started to review for *Le Constitutionnel*. This was the beginning of the famous *Lundis*, the literary *causeries* which he contributed weekly to *Le Constitutionnel*, then to *Le Moniteur universel*, and finally to *Le Temps*, until his death in 1869. Sainte-Beuve believed – and it was a novel belief in his day – that criticism should be re-creative rather than dogmatic, that the critic should discuss the formative influences on an author's character. Sainte-Beuve was a born intellectual, and astoundingly well-read. His conversation delighted his contemporaries by its diversity and its critical power. His *Lundis* and his earlier *Portraits* remain an essential guide to French literature, especially that of the seventeenth century.

If journalism touched new heights with Gautier and Sainte-Beuve, it also suffered, during the Second Empire, from strict censorship. Unable to write freely about politics and religion, many journalists were forced to turn to trivia, and the gossip-writer came into his own.

'People have a taste for glass-houses,' noted Blanchard Jerrold in 1866. 'They expect to have their *salon* and dining-room, the dinner they give to their friends, their getting-up and their going to bed, duly set forth in a newspaper. A year or two ago, it was only at intervals that the private life of a known man or woman was served up for public amusement; but now M. de Villemessant appears to have given orders to his staff of writers [on *Le Figaro*] to set a glass front in the house of every notability in the French capital.'[19]

If the Press did not enjoy political freedom, it did at least expand in other ways. The popular Press had been established since *La Presse* was founded in 1836; specialist publications appeared, to cater for the artistic and the literary, for financiers, and for those who were addicted to sport, and the serial story was an established newspaper feature when the Second Empire began.

There were a number of distinguished editors in the Second Empire Press, but one of them stands head and shoulders above the rest, and dominates them by his years and diversity of achievements, by his personality, and by the influence which he exercised. He was the founder of the modern Press in France; he was also an exemplary figure of his time. One might consider Émile de Girardin in some detail, for he was a classic example of the triumphant *parvenu*.[20]

He had been born in 1806: the illegitimate son of Mme Dupuy, the wife of a counsellor at the Cour royale in Paris, and of General Comte Alexandre de Girardin. He

Émile de Girardin was renowned for his Press deals. In Daumier's cartoon RIGHT *the startled reader recognises Girardin (by his famous lock of hair) behind* La Liberté, *the paper bought by Girardin in 1866.*

never knew parental affection or a proper home. Throughout his adult life he sought to erase the stigma of his birth by material success and by the acquisition of power.

At the age of twenty, he tried to enlist in the hussars, but he was rejected because of his poor physique. It was then that, 'being unable to wield a sword, he took up a pen: that is to say the weapon par excellence of the nineteenth century.' The future Napoleon of the Press did not make his début in journalism. He wrote a book, *Émile*: the complaint of an illegitimate child against society. On the day he came of age, the author of *Émile* made a more open comment on his origins. He took the name of Émile de Girardin.

Like many of his contemporaries, Girardin determined to make his fortune by speculation. He had a flair for Press deals, and 'he took up the newspaper industry as he would have chosen mining if his taste had led him to metallurgy.' In 1828, he founded *Le Voleur*. It was a weekly selection of articles from the Press; and its title – which might be translated as *The Thief* – did not at all detract from its success. The following year, he launched *La Mode*. Gavarni published his first drawings in it.

The 1830 Revolution brought Louis-Philippe to the throne, and the bourgeois monarchy brought a new conception of society. New social strata had to be considered. As Girardin saw, there was a vast new reading public among the middle classes. He founded *Le Journal des connaissances utiles*, which cost 4 francs a year, and had a circulation of 130,000. He also founded the *Almanach de France*, which sold 1,300,000 copies; this was followed by a paper for elementary teachers, *Le Journal des Instituteurs primaires*. And, since the new public would need to buy books as well as periodicals, Girardin conceived the idea of a series of a hundred volumes which would contain the essentials of world literature. Girardin's idea of cheap editions of novels inspired several publishers later in the century.

In 1834, he became a member of the Chamber of Deputies; but political life was not enough for him. In 1836 he founded *La Presse*; and, thanks to innovations like features, serial stories, and, above all, a low price and a large circulation, he became one of the earliest Press magnates in the modern sense of the word. As an admirer was to write: when he sold *La Presse* at half the price of any other paper, 'he created a real revolution in journalism, a peaceful revolution which has benefited us all.'[21]

On 24 October 1848, Girardin was the first to suggest in print that Louis-Napoleon should stand for the Presidency of the Republic. He supported the candidature in no fewer than forty-eight articles; and such was his ardour that *Le Constitutionnel* and most of the provincial Press followed suit. On 10 December 1848 – partly due, no doubt, to Girardin's campaign – Louis-Napoleon was elected by an immense majority.

'Four days later, Girardin sent a memorandum to the new President. It contained a complete programme for the Government, beginning with a general amnesty and finishing with a simplified administration. This concentrated all the portfolios in three Ministries: the Ministry of Government, the Ministry of Receipts, and the Ministry of Expenditure. Girardin was offered the choice of being Prefect of Police or Director-General of Posts. He was urged most warmly to accept, but he repeatedly refused. On 20 December he was begged to accept the embassy in Naples. He again refused, and said he would never accept a post unless it allowed him to put his ideas into practice, and to prove their excellence.'[22]

Under the new régime, he saw the same blindness among politicians, the same abyss gaping open, the same mistakes being made. He was elected Deputy for the Bas-Rhin, and in the Chamber of Deputies he fought against the restrictive measures which were now imposed on the Press. In *La Presse* he attacked the measures with fervour. On 6 August 1851 he wrote: 'I do not reproach M. Louis-Napoleon Bonaparte for following a fatal policy. I reproach him for not showing himself *before* 10 December as he has shown himself *since* – or for not remaining *since then* what he was *before*. I am entitled to say that I have been deceived.' A few months later, Louis-Napoleon dissolved the National Assembly and assumed full powers.

Five years elapsed between the coup-d'état of 1851 and Girardin's departure from the editorial chair of *La Presse*. In those five years he showed no hostility in principle to the Empire; but, as an impenitent liberal, he disapproved of its actions. He was a close friend of the Emperor's cousin, Prince Napoleon; and nothing, wrote Arsène Houssaye, was stranger than to see them arguing at the Prince's dinner-table. Sometimes they used to go very far. 'Oh, what an almighty mess there would be, Monseigneur, if you came to power!' 'And yet, my dear Girardin, I shouldn't have you as my Prime Minister.' Girardin was also a friend of Princess Mathilde. For years he paid court to the Imperial Highness whose receptions at the rue de Courcelles were a social necessity for the ambitious. His letters to her reflected what he called 'respectful adoration'.[23]

All the while he continued to be one of the Grand Dukes of the Press. He had his châlet on the shores of Lake Enghien; and there, as a local guidebook explained: 'Every year, at the time of the regattas, the eminent publicist welcomes the élite of Paris society.' At Baden, the fashionable spa, Girardin made his appearance during the season.[24] In Paris, he entertained with grand-ducal splendour. Early in 1856 he gave a banquet in honour of Dickens; the author of *The Pickwick Papers* was dazzled.

Girardin's career in the Press remained as striking as ever. In 1866 he had bought *La Liberté*, which carried the first sports column in a French paper. At about the same time he founded *La Semaine financière*. But now, as the 1860s drew to an end, he became highly critical of the régime. In 1867 he was fined six thousand francs for his violent diatribes against it. Émile Ollivier, the chief minister of the Liberal Empire, was to write perceptively: 'He resented the fact that the Emperor had done with me what he had refused to do with him.' A portfolio might have appeased Girardin; but in 1869, when the Emperor discussed a new cabinet with Ollivier, he refused categorically to include him. Girardin was brilliant, but he did not inspire trust. In July 1870, he was made a Senator 'for services to journalism'. He never took his seat, for the War began.

10 Les Beaux-Arts

The history of painting during the Second Empire leads to a sad but inescapable conclusion. Generally speaking, mediocrity was in fashion; and artists of real distinction struggled to survive and to be true to themselves. Art suffered from the tyranny of the Salon jury, the rigid, academic beliefs of the hierarchy of the Beaux-Arts. It suffered from the inborn conservatism of the French public, and from the social changes of the time. An era of industrial progress, of *nouveaux riches* and *parvenus*, a superficial era which insisted on outward show, a philistine and thoughtless age which had little concern for fundamental values, was not an age for perceptive patrons of art. Ironically, it was the age of some of the greatest of French artists.

Two monumental figures were still active during the Second Empire. Perhaps they were accepted because they seemed to be survivals from another world. Jean-Auguste-Dominique Ingres was seventy-two when the Second Empire came into being, and, until his death at the age of eighty-seven, he remained the triumphant and uncontested leader in French art. In *Bain turc* (1862) and in *La Source*, the masterpieces of his old age, he proved that his genius for composition and drawing remained as perfect as it had ever been.

'If Ingres can arrange a Greek drapery to perfection,' wrote Théophile Gautier, 'he is no less skilful when he drapes a cashmere shawl, and he turns modern dress to wonderful account; his portraits of women attest the fact. Whatever his subject, Ingres brings to it a rigorous exactness and an extreme fidelity to form and to colour . . . When he paints a classical subject, he is like a poet who wants to write a Greek tragedy, and goes back to Aeschylus . . . In this sense he is Romantic – although to the general public any man who paints scenes from ancient history or mythology is Classical – and it is not surprising that he should have had many disciples among the new school.'[1]

One of the disciples of Ingres was Théodore Chassériau (1819–56); he, too, concentrated on linear expression, though perhaps he showed a more attractive sense of colour than his master. One might also mention Puvis de Chavannes, and Thomas Couture, who painted variations on classical themes. Gustave Moreau (1826–98) was

La Danse, *by Jean-Baptiste Carpeaux, 1869. This group, on the façade of Garnier's Opéra, symbolises the reckless gaiety of* la fête impériale.

later to keep a reflection of this *ingresque* purity, though it would be burdened by symbolism.

At the opposite pole of art stood Eugène Delacroix (1799–1863). The unchallenged leader of the Romantic School, he had brought a world of life and colour and passion into painting. Delacroix, wrote Gautier, 'had the merit of being stirred by the fevers of his time, and of representing its tormented ideal with singular poetry, power and intensity. He was inspired by Shakespeare, Goethe, Lord Byron and Walter Scott; but he was inspired freely, like a master who finds a work within the work, and remains the equal of those whom he translates.'[2] Delacroix, like Shakespeare, had been called a drunken savage; but, in time, he was asked to paint the throne room and the library of the Chamber of Deputies, and the cupola of the library of the Chamber of Peers. Early in his reign, advised by Nieuwerkerke, the Emperor commissioned the leading artists of the time and some of their pupils to decorate the salons at the Hôtel de Ville. Delacroix represented the Earth given Peace by Jupiter; round this central painting were eight caissons showing different deities, and there were twelve frieze-panels over doors and windows which showed the Labours of Hercules. In the Salon de l'Empereur was a ceiling by Ingres. All these paintings were destroyed when the Communards sacked the Hôtel de Ville in 1871.

The International Exhibition of 1855 was a triumph for Delacroix; his collected paintings were shown, and 'the most stubborn opponents of his glory could not resist this harmonious whole, brilliant and superb, this collection of compositions which were so diverse, so full of fire and genius.'[3] Yet, even now, in his fifties, Delacroix still found opposition. He was not elected to the Institut until 1858; and in 1859 he felt so insulted by the critics that he ceased to exhibit at the Salon.

Two unchallenged artists: Ingres LEFT *photographed in 1867, the year of his death, by Étienne Carjat, and* RIGHT *Eugène Delacroix.*

RIGHT L'Amateur d'estampes, *by Honoré Daumier.*

Some popular artists chose to steer a safe middle course: Dauzats, Marilhat and Tournemine, with their oriental inspiration, Jules Breton, Rosa Bonheur and Alexandre-Gabriel Decamps with their rustic scenes, and Alfred de Dreux with his elegant paintings of horses. As the middle classes grew richer and more influential, there arose a middle-class art. There was also a renaissance of religious painting; its most successful exponent was Hippolyte Flandrin (1809–64), who painted the apostles and martyrs in the churches of Saint-Germain-des-Prés and Saint-Vincent-de-Paul.

From the feeling for religion to the feeling for nature there was only a step. It was taken by Jean-Baptiste Corot. Born in 1796, he died in 1875, and he approached the world with the innocence of a child and the faith of a believer. It is said that Napoleon III, visiting the Salon, stopped in front of a picture of the dawn by Corot. 'I don't understand it at all,' he said. 'One would have to get up too early to catch this poetry.'[4] As Jules Claretie observed, 'it was precisely the *indiscernible*, the indistinct grace, the invisible, the intangible, the quality which seemed just a daub to the bourgeois, which was Corot's strength.'[5]

One would look in vain for Corot's freshness in some other landscape artists of the time, who bring us back to the fever, unease and dramatic visions of Romanticism: Narcisse-Virgile Diaz, with his luminous colours; Théodore Rousseau (1812–67), with the mighty nobility of his trees. In 1846, Rousseau had retired to the Forest of Fontainebleau: to Barbizon, where he gathered other artists round him. The Barbizon School shone throughout the Second Empire, and far beyond.

Its greatest figure, Jean-François Millet (1814–75), has been called a peasant of genius. He seemed to paint his peasant models in a single stroke, at one with the earth. He showed the toil of the fields with all the hieratic gestures which had been known for thousands of years. The age was not ready for Millet's work. He knew much poverty and suffering, and sometimes he was near starvation. In 1855, he painted *Un paysan greffant un arbre*. It was one of his finest pictures, but it would have stayed in his studio if Théodore Rousseau had not bought it for four thousand francs. He did so under a pseudonym, and it was a long time before Millet discovered his real benefactor. In 1856, Millet was rejected by the Salon, and in 1859 the Salon refused his picture of *Le Bûcheron et la Mort*. As for *L'Homme à la houe*, it reminded the public of Dumolard, a notorious murderer, who used to bury his victims in the fields. It happened that his trial was the sensation of the moment. The Second Empire preferred to see pretty, superficial pictures, and Millet was accused of forgetting the charm of the countryside. 'I have found much more in it than charm,' he wrote in 1863. 'I have found its infinite splendours.' He continued his poem of the fields, but not for public show. In 1870, he exhibited at the Salon for the last time.[6]

Political upheaval had brought a movement in the arts which Champfleury christened Realism. In literature, it was reflected in the novels of Feydeau and Flaubert, and, above all, in the novels of the Goncourts, with their rigorous insistence on factual record, their interest in bourgeois and working-class life. In painting, Realism was a

A controversial artist at work: a detail from L'Atelier du peintre, *by Gustave Courbet, 1855.*

theory of imitation, and a social theory of the rôle of art. While the artist's duty was to paint what he saw, the aim of art was to represent figures in everyday life, chiefly those of the working class. Realism fused these two separate purposes into one.

From time to time, French painting needs a transfusion of plebeian blood; and this it certainly received from Gustave Courbet (1819–77). Courbet's insistent, aggressive personality overflowed into his canvases. He lacked the intellect and culture of the great Romantics, he lacked the ability to compromise, and so much the better for art; but his principles could hardly have been further from those of Second Empire Paris, and, as people knew that his painting concealed subversive social theories, it became the fashion to revile it for its 'realism' and ugliness. Courbet came from Ornans in Franche-Comté, and there he found the subjects for his landscapes. Ornans also inspired one of his most controversial pictures: *L'Enterrement à Ornans* (1851). This, and his *Casseurs de pierre*, finally classified him.

In 1855, he tried to make his position clear: 'The title of Realist has been imposed on me, just as the title of Romantic was imposed on the men of 1830 . . . I have studied ancient and modern art without policy or prejudice . . . I wanted to know, so that I could achieve. I wanted to translate the customs, ideas, and appearance of my times, as I saw them. I wanted, in fact, to create living art.'[7]

This living art was not appreciated. In 1855, the jury of the International Exhibition rejected the most important works he submitted, and Courbet had a pavilion built, in which he showed forty canvases of his own. Critics continued to be hostile, or, at best, to profess their disappointment. Gautier, the apostle of Art for Art's Sake, recognised that he was powerfully gifted; he also felt that Courbet was pretentiously brutal. Courbet seemed to Gautier to reject the search for beauty, to deny the artist's heaven-sent purpose: indeed, he appeared to ignore beauty altogether, and to carry realism beyond its limits, indulging deliberately in ugliness. In Gautier's criticism of Courbet we see the concern which he would have spared a mediocre artist. In 1868, discussing *Aumône d'un mendiant à Ornans*, Gautier wrote:

'There is nothing more false, more strident, or more repugnant in appearance than this picture of such pretentious mediocrity. One might think that M. Courbet had completely lost his gift, and one might lament this misfortune, the greatest which can befall an artist, if there were not a reassuring picture called *Chevreuil chassé aux écoutes (printemps)* beside *Aumône d'un mendiant à Ornans*.'[8]

Courbet himself appears to have been indifferent to public opinion. He exhibited two fine seascapes in the Salon of 1870. The Minister for the Fine Arts had him awarded the Légion-d'honneur. Courbet refused the decoration. His refusal, so he said, was not a republican gesture (one may doubt this, from the future Communard), but he did not believe that the State could be a judge of painting.[9] Courbet saw large, he even saw rough, but his pictures already belong to modern art.

So do those of his fellow-Realist, Édouard Manet (1832–83). In an often academic world, Manet represented pure painting. In 1863 he and certain other artists attacked the jury which had refused their work for the Salon. Such was the debate in the Press

Millet's paintings of peasant life – among them La Lessiveuse – *were unappreciated by Second Empire Paris.* Le Déjeuner sur l'herbe, *by Manet, caused a sensation when it was shown in 1863.*

that the Emperor himself went to the Palais de l'Industrie, asked to see the rejected pictures, and ordered that they should be shown in a separate Salon. Henceforward, there must be not only a Salon des admis, but a Salon des refusés.

The result was an immensely controversial exhibition of the work of the new painters; and no canvas caused more controversy than Manet's *Le Déjeuner sur l'herbe*, in which a naked woman sat at a picnic beside two modern Parisians in frock-coats. The public thought the work indecent; the Realists defended themselves by quoting Giorgione's *Concert champêtre* at the Louvre. But Giorgione's concert was held in a half-mythological world, and Manet's *déjeuner* took place in a park which Parisians could visit every Sunday. Moreover – and this was the final touch of indecency – the woman in the foreground of his picture was not merely naked, she was undressed: her hat and dress were beside her on the grass.

Manet was accepted by the Salon the following year, and again in 1865, when his *Olympia* created a further scandal. It took two guards to protect it from indignant visitors. Gautier felt that Olympia, 'a paltry model stretched out on a sheet', only showed determination to attract attention at any price.[10] In 1867, both Manet and Courbet had their significant pictures rejected. They each erected a wooden pavilion in the avenue de l'Alma, and held a personal exhibition. In the eyes of posterity, these two pavilions seem a resounding affirmation of original vision and expression, and a symbol of liberation, in the face of academic tyranny.

The tyranny was nothing new. For a quarter of a century, the jury at the Salon had shown itself increasingly hostile to independent artists. Some artists had ceased to submit their work. Others had held exhibitions in their studios (for galleries, as we know them today, did not then exist). In 1867, at the height of the Second Empire, Realism was still fiercely attacked; and in 1868 Gautier wondered if middle-age had made him unable to understand the younger generation.

'The leader, the hero of Realism, is now M. Manet. He has frantic partisans and timid detractors . . . It is probable that the pictures of Courbet, Manet and *tutti quanti* have beauties which escape us old Romantics . . . Personally, we have made every possible effort to accustom ourselves to this painting, and, when we had the honour to be a member of the jury, we did not reject it. We tried to be fair to what we found repugnant, and this feeling must have been shared by many people to whom their studies, doctrines, work and tastes must have made such works unbearable.'[11] One of these people was Ernest Hébert, the director of the French School in Rome. 'I am glad to thank you for your article on Courbet, Manet and Monet,' he told Gautier. 'It is certainly time that a protest appeared against these gods of filth.'[12]

Claude-Oscar Monet, the third of Hébert's deities, had been born in 1840, the son of a grocer. In 1859, impressed by the works of Daubigny and Troyon at the Salon, he had begun to study art. He had soon met Pissarro, and at the Brasserie des Martyrs he had come to know Courbet and the Realists. In 1865 his pictures had been shown at the Salon, and enthusiastically received. He earned more success the following year with a portrait of his future wife. That summer he painted views of Paris from the Louvre and, at Ville-d'Avray, he painted his *Femmes au jardin*. Yet, like most of his contemporaries of real distinction, Monet had to struggle against poverty; before he left Ville-d'Avray, he slashed two hundred canvases in order to keep them from his creditors. In 1869 he was rejected by the Salon; and such was his destitution that he was forced to accept the help of Renoir. In 1870 he was again refused by the Salon; Daubigny resigned from the jury in protest.[13]

Eugène Boudin did not arouse violent protest or condemnation, but he had to fight against poverty and extraordinary indifference.[14] He was born at Honfleur in 1824. His father was the master of a small cargo boat, and, at the age of ten, Eugène sailed on it as a cabin-boy. The fascination of the sea never left him. In 1847 he decided to devote himself to painting; and in 1851 the Conseil municipal du Havre made him a grant so that he could study in Paris. In 1857, Boudin was back in the provinces, painting, and struggling against poverty; early in 1861 he determined to live in Paris. For the rest of his life, he lived in the capital during the winter, and hurried off, when winter ended, to Normandy, Brittany, Holland, or the South, so that he could keep his vision fresh.

In about 1863 Eugène Isabey suggested that Boudin might paint beach scenes at Trouville. As he pointed out, Society would welcome pictures of the Casino, the races and the regattas. Boudin took his advice. *La Plage de Trouville* was shown at the Salon in 1864. Boudin also painted the regattas at Trouville and the races at Deauville, and the opening of the casino at Deauville (with Mme de Metternich a conspicuous figure in the foreground). During the last years of the Second Empire, he recorded *le tout Paris* by the sea. Boudin had an exquisite gift for suggesting atmosphere: the sultry blue sky heavy over Deauville, or summer heat in mid-afternoon, with a stiff wind blowing, and a brilliant sea-shore light. He painted with love; and, writing from Paris one summer day in 1869, he confessed: 'I daren't think of the sundrenched beaches and the stormy skies, and of the joy of painting them in the sea breezes.'[15] Alas, the taste for his works was limited; and he was so bitterly discouraged that he relegated some of his canvases to a cupboard. They were not discovered for thirty years.

In the last years of the régime, Renoir, too, was struggling to establish himself. Born in 1841, he had studied painting in Gleyre's studio. In 1863 he had first exhibited at the Salon; in 1864 he had been obliged to show his work at the Salon des Refusés. The 1860s were difficult years for young artists. The Salon juries deprived them of their sole means of approaching the general public, few critics chose to notice them, and few buyers would invest in pictures by unknown artists who did not satisfy their taste for prettiness. At the Café Guerbois, near the Place de Clichy, Renoir often met the other painters of the Batignolles Group: Manet, Monet, Sisley, and Monet's friend Bazille, and occasionally, also, Cézanne, *l'éternel refusé*. There, too, was Degas, who had recently discovered his true *genre*: the multicoloured world of the grandstand, the jockeys, the stable-boys and trainers, the thoroughbred horses of Longchamp and Chantilly. The world of racing was to be followed, for Degas, by the world of ballet and the stage, and by the world of music. All these artists would listen to Camille Pissarro; and, at the Café Guerbois, 'the inefficiency of the Director of Fine Arts and the capricious judgment of the Salon juries were debated with the same eagerness . . . as the importance of the recent "discovery" of Japanese prints, the rôle of shadows or the use of bright colours.'[16] The Batignolles Group is recorded in *Un Atelier aux Batignolles*, by Fantin-Latour (1836–1904). In this painting, Manet sits at his easel, among his friends, including Monet, Renoir and Zola. This picture, which seemed to assure the future of Fantin-Latour, was shown in 1870, in the last Salon of the Second Empire.[17]

Great art was constantly discouraged during the régime, but secondary art was popular. Horace Vernet had died in 1863, but Adolphe Yvon had established himself as the illustrator of the imperial campaigns. 'There cannot be too many records of French glory,' wrote Blanchard Jerrold. 'Every battle, and every incident of battle of the First and Second Empires, are subjects dear to the pencil of every rising painter. There is a great market for them. The State buys acres of reflected glory. It glows from the walls of prefectures and sub-prefectures. It lights up provincial art-galleries, and makes – to put the dot on the *i* – a splendid advertisement for the Napoleon dynasty.'[18]

Decorative painting had been in decline during the First Empire and the Restoration; it had regained some of its brilliance with the July Monarchy. During the Second Empire, the imperial apartments, and those of wealthy private citizens, often called for painted walls and ceilings. Paul Baudry helped to decorate the new Opéra, and the *hôtel* of Mme de Païva, and Lefuel employed a number of artists to decorate the Empress's apartments in the Tuileries. Among them were Dubufe *fils*, the society portrait painter, and Chaplin, the portrait painter of English origin, who had been in favour in Paris since the beginning of the Empire.

And here we come to the artist who preserves the Second Empire on canvas as surely as Carpeaux does in bronze or marble. François-Xavier Winterhalter had been born in Baden in 1806; but, German as he was, he caught the elegance and spirit of *la fête impériale*. His picture of the Empress and her ladies-in-waiting was sometimes called *au rendez-vous des grisettes*, but it caught the tinsel charm of the subject. Winterhalter was to die three years after the Empire fell. But in his portraits of Napoleon III and Eugénie, of high society in the '50s and '60s, we can still see the Second Empire through a courtier's eyes.

There was nothing of the courtier in Constantin Guys.[19] Born in Flushing in 1805, the son of the Chief Commissioner of the French Navy, his childhood and adolescence remain obscure; but it is known that, as a young man, Guys went to England, where he earned his living partly as a tutor. In 1848, at last, he began his professional career. He joined *The Illustrated London News*, for which he later produced some of his best work as a war artist in the Crimea. After the Crimean campaign and a spell in the East, he took up his winter headquarters in Paris. He was to make frequent visits to England: he was drawn there for professional reasons, and he was an ardent admirer of all things English. But while he left some brilliant impressions of Victorian London, he achieved lasting fame with his impressions of high life and low life in Paris. His work has a general significance, but the variety and the truth of his observations made Guys the graphic historian of *la vie parisienne*.

For a creative artist, Guys was strangely bent on anonymity; and it was partly due to his own distaste for publicity that he did not receive proper recognition in his lifetime. But he was finely appreciated by one of his contemporaries: by Baudelaire, in *Le Peintre de la vie moderne*. This essay first appeared as a series of articles in *Le Figaro*; the first instalment was published on 26 November 1863. 'Two things are clear,' wrote Baudelaire, 'in M.G.'s execution. One is the application of memory: intense, evocative and resurrecting . . . , the other is a fire, an intoxication of the pencil which almost looks like madness. It is the fear of not going fast enough, of letting the phantom escape before its essence has been extracted and preserved.'[20]

Guys was a keen student of the pageantry of life; and no-one suggested, better than he did, the fairy-tale aspects of reality. His elegant carriages, with their small horses, recall the equipage of Cinderella; there is a touch of theatre about the splendid coats-of-arms on their panels, and about the liveries of the coachmen. No-one knew, better than Guys, how to sketch a simple coupé, with its smart black horses and military escort, bearing an emperor and empress on their way.

'In M.G.'s collection,' continued Baudelaire, 'one often meets the Emperor of the French. M.G. has reduced his face to an infallible sketch, without doing any damage to the likeness . . . One of these watercolours in particular has dazzled me with its magic quality. At the front of a box in the theatre, a box of heavy, princely splendour,

we see the Empress, calm and in repose; the Emperor is leaning forward slightly as if he wants to see the stage better; beneath them, two Cent-Gardes, erect, in military and almost hieratic immobility, receive the splashing brilliance of the footlights on their gorgeous uniforms.'[21]

Guys recorded the dandies of Paris: their outward frivolity, their assurance, their air of domination, their way of wearing a coat and guiding a horse, the calm strength of their attitudes. He recorded the *biches* and *cocottes*, the animal vitality of the prostitutes, the panache of the courtesans dressed overall like frigates at a naval review. More than once, Guys has been likened to Hokusai; and certainly he showed a truth and elegance of line, a sharpness of analysis, which recalled the Japanese artist. His ebullient prostitutes also seem, at moments, to anticipate the work of Toulouse-Lautrec.

Guys' life as an artist ended when, in 1885, he was run over by a carriage, and gravely injured. He lingered on in the Maison Dubois until his death in 1892.

One of the most famous lithographers and caricaturists of the century was still active during the Second Empire. Honoré Daumier had been born in Marseilles in 1808.[22] When he was a young man, his father had sent him to work with a *huissier*, and Daumier made his first acquaintance with the legal fraternity, whom he was to scourge in his lithographs and watercolours. But he was always bent on drawing; he did work for Parisian publishers, and he drew for *La Caricature*. In 1832, he was sentenced to six months' imprisonment for a virulent cartoon of Louis-Philippe. Daumier, undaunted, came out of prison to portray the political figures of his day. He remained independent of politics: he was, in time, to refuse the Légion-d'honneur from the Second Empire.

But he longed to express himself in painting, and, in about 1860, he abandoned caricature to devote himself to art. He was a noble painter of the human countenance, and he had a kind of grandeur which led Balzac to exclaim: 'There's some Michelangelo there!' But many years were to pass before justice was done to Daumier's painting, and in 1864 he was obliged to resume his post as a caricaturist. He produced many lithographs, but he found himself less and less able to draw, and finally he became blind. He died in 1879.

Sulpice-Guillaume Chevalier, four years older than Daumier, was better known by the pseudonym of Gavarni; a name he took from the Cirque de Gavarnie, a beauty-spot in the Pyrenees.[23] Born in Tarbes in 1804, he worked in a land surveyor's office before he came to Paris and established himself by his sketches of Parisian life. Gavarni drew students and grisettes, carnival costumes and women's clothes. A visit to London, where he observed the misery and vices of the poor, made his work more embittered in tone. He returned to Paris at the end of 1851, and undertook to provide a lithograph a day for a new paper. He kept his bargain for the three hundred and sixty-five days of its existence; and it was in this paper, *Paris*, that he published, under the general title of *Masques et Visages*, the series known as *Les Partageuses*, *Les Lorettes vieillies*, *Les Bohêmes*, *Les Anglais chez eux*, and *Propos de Thomas Vireloque*. In Vireloque, Gavarni condensed his misanthropy, his lassitude and his contempt. He died of consumption in 1866. The work of Daumier and Gavarni, wrote Baudelaire, had been called the complement of *La Comédie humaine*. 'Balzac himself, I am quite convinced, would have been inclined to agree.'[24]

Gustave Doré was born in Strasbourg, in 1832, the son of an engineer in the Département des Ponts et Chaussées.[25] As a boy, he became aware of his vocation for drawing, and in 1847, while his parents happened to be on a visit to Paris, he presented himself to Philipon, the founder and editor of the daily satirical journal, *Le Charivari*. Philipon was so impressed by his work that in 1848 he arranged with Doré's father that the boy should stay in Paris and work for him. Political caricature was a test of artistic stamina, and Doré gained useful experience, but four years later he began his true career when he illustrated four books by Paul Lacroix, better known as le Bibliophile Jacob.

In 1853 appeared his illustrated edition of Rabelais; the following year came his *Histoire dramatique, pittoresque et caricaturale de la Sainte-Russie*, with no less than five

RIGHT *The thoroughbred courtesan.* Fille au fond vert, *by Constantin Guys.* OVERLEAF *Le tout Paris by the sea. The Empress Eugénie on the beach at Trouville, from the painting by Eugène Boudin, 1864.*

hundred drawings. As Lacroix observed: 'He cast his inspirations before the public with such prodigality that half the world remained confounded with admiration, and the other half confounded with stupor.'

After his Russian caricatures, Doré turned to the Middle Ages. The *Contes drôlatiques* of Balzac and *Le Juif errant* marked the end of his beginnings. In the *Contes drôlatiques*, Doré matched the humour of Balzac by his own graphic laughter, and he presented the gusto of feudal times. In *Le Juif errant* he showed a strong Romantic influence – the influence of the generation then ending. There was a sombre Romanticism, too, in the lithograph inspired by the death of Gérard de Nerval. Doré matched the mysterious tragedy with a mysterious and haunting work.

He was tempted to turn to serious painting, but his lavish way of life in the rue Saint-Dominique (where he lived, devotedly, with his mother) forced him to continue his work as an illustrator. He was in constant demand, and he toiled on, day and night. During the years 1855 to 1860, Doré published only commercial work. He drew illustrations for *Le Journal pour tous*; he produced topical lithographs to exploit the interest in the Crimean and Italian victories. In 1861 he published his illustrated edition of Dante's *Inferno*. It is generally acknowledged to be his finest achievement.

It has a remarkably oppressive and consistent nightmare quality, an imaginative horror, a sense of claustrophobia, an other-world atmosphere which is unremittingly maintained.

'No artist could illustrate Dante better than M. Gustave Doré,' wrote Gautier. 'Apart from his gift for composition and drawing, he has that visionary eye of which the poet speaks – that eye which can disengage the secret and singular side of nature. He sees the curious, fantastic and mysterious aspect of things. His dizzying pencil casually creates those insensible deviations which give man the fearsomeness of the spectre, and trees a human appearance; it gives plants the disturbing bifurcations of mandragora, and it gives clouds those ambiguous, changing forms in which Polonius obligingly discovers, as Hamlet wishes, a camel, a weasel or a whale . . .

'What first strikes us in Gustave Doré's illustrations to Dante is the setting; it has no relation to our sublunar world. The artist has invented the climate of Hell, the subterranean mountains, the landscapes of the underworld, the brown atmosphere in which no sun has ever shone . . . He maintains this supernatural climate from one end of the book to the other with an incredible rigorous logic and likelihood of detail . . .

'It is all wonderfully dreamed and realised. M. Gustave Doré has a quality which is very rare in our French School: a school so sensible, so ingenious and so philosophic. He has imagination: that is to say the power of representing what does not exist in plausible form, and the gift of multiplying unseen or invisible things to infinity . . . As he goes on, his inspiration and talent seem to grow.'[26]

It was generous and splendidly imaginative criticism, and certainly, as Gautier said, Doré's talent grew. In 1862 came his illustrations to Baron Munchhausen, and soon afterwards his touching, romantic, sometimes sinister illustrations to the *Contes de Perrault*. In 1865 he enhanced Chateaubriand's *Atala* with his impressions of virgin

Femmes au jardin, by Claude Monet, 1867.

'He has invented the climate of Hell.' One of Gustave Doré's illustrations for Dante's Inferno.

forests, uncrossable mountains and limitless horizons. *Les Aventures de Don Quixote*, published the same year, showed his prodigious activity: he illustrated Cervantes' work with no less than three hundred and seventy compositions. In 1866 came Doré's illustrations to the Bible. That year, in London, there also appeared his edition of Milton's *Paradise Lost*. He planned to illustrate the complete works of Shakespeare; he was to illustrate *The Tempest*, but death prevented him from fulfilling his grandiose intention.

Doré had long been recognised in France (in 1864, he had overcome his legitimist sympathies and had been the Emperor's guest at Compiègne); in 1868 he arrived in England to find himself, so we are told, the hero of the season. That year he fulfilled an old wish, and illustrated the two remaining books of Dante's *Divine Comedy*. As the Second Empire drew to its close, his work was broadening. Doré the draughtsman and painter was followed by Doré the etcher. After 1871 he turned to sculpture.

He died in 1883, at the age of fifty-one. 'He was born a poet,' wrote a biographer. 'He was a painter, and he died a sculptor. On his way he had peopled the masterpieces of world literature with memorable pictures.'[27]

In the early years of the Second Empire, the sculptors of the previous age painfully prolonged their notoriety. Antoine-Auguste Préault worked on, a fully-fledged and middle-aged Romantic. Antoine-Louis Barye was fifty-six when the Empire was established; he rose above Romanticism, but he took Romanticism as his starting-point when he chose his models. Géricault and Delacroix had been inspired by animals, especially wild animals. In his *Tigre dévorant un gavial*, in his *Lion écrasant un serpent*, Barye had long ago set the academic lions to flight. He now confined himself to his

RIGHT *Gustave Doré, photographed by Nadar.*

little bronzes, but he had followers: the most important was Frémiet, the sculptor of the *Chevaux marins* on the fountain at the Observatory. Clésinger's *Bacchante se roulant sur les pampres* had created a scandal in 1848; he produced a *Combat de taureaux* in 1864 which was still Romantic in feeling and in movement. The ultimate authority in sculpture was Eugène Guillaume (1822–1905). He was a professorial figure, equipped with a solid classical culture, and in his work he re-created Roman beauty.

When Garnier launched his appeal to sculptors to decorate the Opéra, he found it difficult to discover a master of the first rank. It was Aimé Millet who sculpted *Apollon élevant son lyre d'or* at the top of the pediment, and it was Lequesne who sculpted the *Pégases* on the corners. As for the groups on the façade, Garnier asked Guillaume for *la Musique*, Jouffroy for *la Poésie lyrique*, and Perraud for *le Drame lyrique*. But he entrusted the last group, *la Danse*, to Jean-Baptiste Carpeaux, and this masterpiece alone symbolised the art of the Opéra.

Carpeaux had been born at Valenciennes in 1827, the son of a mason.[28] From his childhood, he understood the meaning of poverty. He had no formal education, he merely learned to read and write from the priests. He kept the customs and tastes of the working class like an ineffaceable imprint. Even when he was famous, he still enjoyed coarse bread and rough wine. When, in his thirties, he went to stay at Saint-Gratien, to work on his bust of Princess Mathilde, he used to go during the day 'and drink and gamble with the coachmen and the valets. She had . . . to ask him to stop.'[29] Carpeaux made amends for his lack of social attainments by the brilliance and nobility of his art.

As a child he had dreamed of being a sculptor. He had attended the École d'architecture in Valenciennes; then he had gone to Paris, where he had studied at the École royale et spéciale de dessin et de mathématiques. In 1854 he won the Prix de Rome, and, five years later, he made his name with his bronze figure, *Le Pêcheur à la coquille*. In 1862 he sculpted his imperial yet life-like bust of Princess Mathilde; it was shown at the Salon in 1863, with his imposing group *Ugolin*. In 1865 he was working fervently at his statue of the young Prince Imperial. He set all his hopes of glory on this statue, and the slight figure of the child with Nero, his dog, was undoubtedly one of Carpeaux's masterpieces. It was followed, in 1866, by the bas-relief, *Le Triomphe de Flore*, for the Pavillon de Flore at the Tuileries.

In the previous year he had been commissioned by Garnier to sculpt *La Danse*, for the main façade of the new Opéra. Carpeaux worked on the site for months, and on 27 July 1869 his group was at last revealed to the public. Some people found it a vulgar aphrodisiac, others found it delightfully voluptuous. 'The deuce!' said Henri Dabot. 'It grips you terribly.'[30] An anonymous spectator, moved by disgust, threw a bottle of ink on one of the dancers. Such was the controversy that Garnier nearly agreed to move the offending group inside the building. Soon afterwards came the fall of the Empire, and the affair was forgotten.

It was fortunate for posterity. No previous sculptor had charged inanimate matter with such a paroxysm of joy, such a passion for life. *La Danse* remains a perfect symbol of those feverish years, that rush to the abyss which posterity calls *la fête impériale*.

One other art remains to be mentioned: the new art of photography. It was an art which reached extraordinary heights in Imperial Paris. Two photographers dominated their profession. One was Étienne Carjat (1828–1908); the other was Félix Tournachon (1820–1910), better known by his pseudonym, Nadar.[31]

In an epoch which did not lack versatile and dynamic men, Nadar remained among the most remarkable. As an impoverished medical student, he had moved in the same circle as Henry Murger, the author of *Scènes de la vie de Bohème*; but he refused to waste his life in Bohemia. He earned celebrity as a journalist and a caricaturist; he astonished Paris by his exploits as a balloonist, in *le Géant*. Not content with this, he established himself as one of the great photographers of all time.

He had been led to photography by his work as a caricaturist; he had worked from photographs, to avoid asking his models to pose. The photographer's work demands a constant collaboration with his model. Nadar knew everyone in Paris; he also knew how to make them assume the attitude which suited them best.

Nadar launched himself as a photographer in 1853–4. He took his most famous portraits in his studio, at 113, rue Saint-Lazare, between 1854 and 1860; among them were photographs of Dumas *père*, Champfleury, Gautier, Banville, Baudelaire and Offenbach. Nadar attached much importance to photographic technique. He anticipated the cinema when he took fifty photographs of Chevreul, the chemist, in the course of a single conversation. He went down into the Catacombs – one of the wonders of Paris – and brought back the first photographs to be taken by artificial light. In 1858 he took the first known aerial photographs (they showed the avenue de l'Impératrice, in Paris), and he emphasised their importance in correcting cadastral surveys. During the Franco-Prussian War he commanded an observer corps in Paris which studied enemy movements from captive balloons. After the war, the Impressionists held their first exhibition in his studio.

In 1858 Nadar took the first known aerial photographs from his balloon. Among them was this view of the Arc de Triomphe and the Quartier de l'Étoile.

201

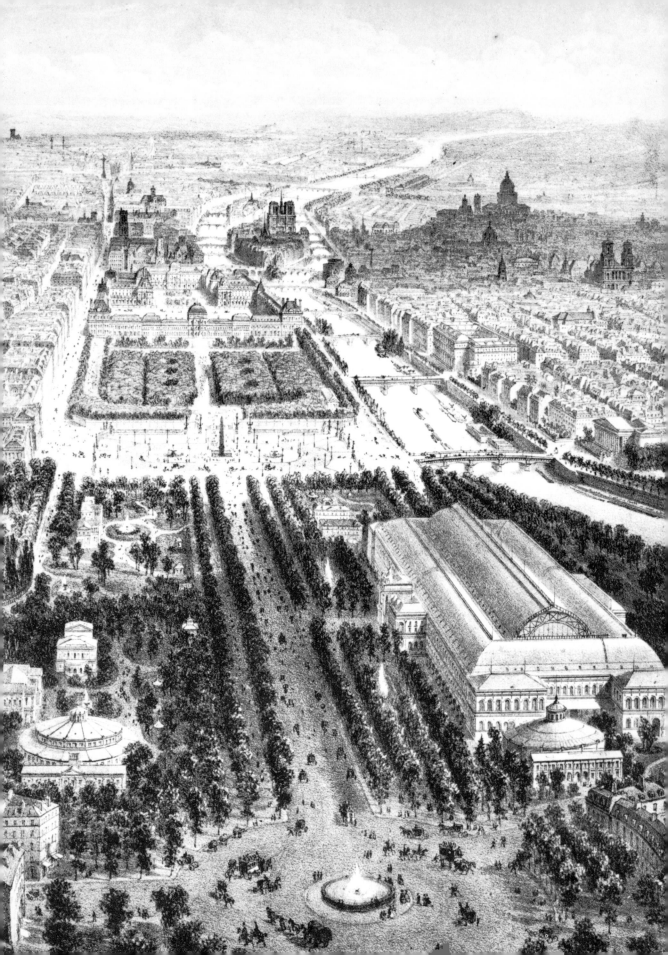

11 The Transformation of Paris

The capital into which the Emperor rode, triumphantly, on 2 December 1852, was a city which had grown, organically, over the centuries. It was a city in which the *flâneur* could still discover unexpected corners, forgotten streets and historical monuments. The impasse du Doyenné, that cul-de-sac of decaying, splendid mansions, in which Romantic Bohemia had dwelt, still stood within a few yards of the Tuileries; the rue de la Vieille-Lanterne, the sinister little passage in which Gérard de Nerval would meet his death, still existed on the site of the future Théâtre Sarah-Bernhardt. Paris was variegated, romantic, rich in architectural treasures. It was also deplorably unhygienic; it had grown awkward in an age when the railways were revolutionising travel, and bringing thousands of visitors to the capital. Hygiene and tourism made demands; so did the increase of commerce, the rise of a newly rich society which needed handsome residential quarters.

There were also serious political considerations. In the last quarter of a century, Paris had more than once witnessed revolution in the streets. In 1830, three days of fighting had preceded the abdication of Charles X; in 1848 there had been insurrection before the abdication of Louis-Philippe. It was clear to Napoleon III that Paris must be a city of straight, wide streets, in which troops could march abreast and, if necessary, fire ahead. The streets of Paris must be streets in which an ambush could not be prepared, in which barricades could not easily be erected and snipers could not readily conceal themselves.

To an Emperor who understood the meaning of coups-d'état, who was still unsure of his prestige, Paris had to be a city which made insurrection impossible. Above all, it had to be an imperial monument. Just as the Arc de Triomphe stood as a symbol of the First Empire, so Paris itself must symbolize the Second. To the Emperor's subjects, it must be a perpetual reminder of *la gloire française*; to posterity, it must be an inalienable sign that Napoleon III had confidence in his dynasty, and grandeur of conception. Only a *parvenu* or a man of vision would have needed to assert himself so splendidly. Napoleon III was both a man of vision and a *parvenu*.

Paris in 1860. On the right of the Champs-Élysées is the Palais de l'Industrie.
Beyond is the Tuileries; the central tower, the Pavillon de l'Horloge, and the
wing in which it stood, were to be destroyed by the Communards in 1871.

By some remarkable fortune, he found the man who was made to serve him. This was a man who believed implicitly in the authoritarian Empire. It was a man who accepted the Emperor's orders absolutely, who was ruthlessly exacting with his subordinates; it was a man of integrity, wide intelligence, and unremitting zeal, with an almost endless capacity for work. Georges-Eugène Haussmann was not an aesthete or an historian; but his physique, his manner, and his achievements showed that he was a giant.

He was a year younger than the Emperor. He had been born in Paris in 1809, the son of a civil servant. Educated at the Lycée Henri-Quatre and the Collège Bourbon, he had taken his *baccalauréat ès lettres*, entered the École de Droit, and taken a doctorate in law. In 1831 he had joined the prefectural corps as secretary-general to the prefecture at Vienne. He served as sous-préfet in several provincial towns before, in 1849, Louis-Napoleon – then President of the Republic – made him Préfet du Var. He later became Préfet de l'Yonne and, in 1851, Préfet de la Gironde. His years of provincial administration and his well-considered marriage were to stand him in good stead when, on 22 June 1853, he was appointed Préfet de la Seine.[1]

The title gave Haussmann the responsibilities of the daily administration of Paris. It also gave him the task of transforming the capital. Exactly a week after his appointment, he was received by Napoleon III – 'my Sovereign, my Master' – at Saint-Cloud. 'This *dreamer,*' remembered Haussmann, 'was not only the author of the plans which I carried out; he remained the faithful supporter of the executive agent whom he had chosen, from amongst all the Prefects of France, to make the interpreter of his thoughts: I dare not say, *his Second,* in Paris.' Even on that first visit, the Emperor showed Haussmann a map of the capital, 'on which I saw, traced by Himself, in blue, red, yellow and green, according to the degree of urgency, the various new routes which He proposed.'[2] And so began the monumental work of the Emperor's reign: the transformation of Paris.

As the Emperor shrewdly observed, the first problem to overcome was the conservatism of France: the stubborn attachment to routine which might well delay his plans. Haussmann must take advantage of the newness of the régime: he must produce quick, spectacular successes for the Empire. The Emperor's own ideas were simple: he wanted to free the great monuments of the past – the Louvre, the Hôtel de Ville, Notre Dame – from the clutter of buildings which surrounded them. He wanted to connect the new railway stations with the heart of the city. He wanted to make Paris a city of international importance, a city where foreigners would come for their pleasure, and trade would flourish. Haussmann himself approached his task in a spirit of dedication. 'If there is,' he wrote, 'a task before which all political passions should be stilled, to which patriotic thought should guide all men of goodwill, it is surely the vast enterprise which will make Paris a Capital worthy of France.'[3]

Haussmann worked unremittingly to satisfy his master. It is hard to say which were the Emperor's personal ideas, and which were those of Haussmann himself. The transformation of Paris was a common task, and into it, as into a melting-pot, went all the

One of the flowers that graced the Champs-Élysées. A hybrid fuchsia, from Alphand's Les Promenades de Paris.

plans of Haussmann's colleagues at the Hôtel de Ville. It was also a gigantic task. Every evening, the dossiers from his subordinates' offices were left on the desk of le Grand Préfet; and, during his seventeen years in office, except for some rare cases of *force majeure*, he never went to bed until his exacting task was done.

His financial needs were immense. The Emperor would not raise the money by imposing taxes which might make his plans unpopular; and Haussmann was obliged to accept this condition. But Haussmann also realised – it was a bold conception for the time – that the prosperity which the vast new works would bring would itself create the resources to repay the money which was needed. Soon after his appointment, he presented his budget to the Conseil municipal. He argued it point by point, won his case, and was given a substantial surplus budget to finance his first building operations. 'From that moment,' he was to write, later, 'I felt that I was firmly in the saddle.'[4] Haussmann had no doubt who ruled the Hôtel de Ville; but whenever someone expressed their admiration for the transformation of Paris, le Grand Préfet was careful to emphasise: 'It was the Emperor who planned it all. I have simply been his collaborator.'[5]

He wanted to finish the large-scale works which had been begun, with all possible speed. Among them were the boulevard de Strasbourg, which was opened on 16 December 1853, and the rue de Rivoli, which would allow him to clear great areas of slums and to link west and east between the Louvre and the Hôtel de Ville. There was also the building of Les Halles, the central market in Paris. Haussmann had put Victor Baltard in charge of the architecture for the City of Paris; Baltard had conceived Les Halles in noble, massive freestone, and only designed them in iron against his will, after a sketch by Napoleon III.

'I developed this sketch in a freehand drawing,' Haussmann remembered, 'and gave him the plan and the general elevation of this very modern building, conceived by my August Master, as it is seen today. Yes, the Préfet de la Seine under the Empire was both an administrator and an artist; enamoured of all great things; easily seduced by the harmony of mighty wholes; delighted by that poetry of order and balance which makes us marvel at the spectacle of the firmament; passionately fond of Beauty, that excellent, artistic form of Good . . .'[6]

As for the new works which had been decided by the Emperor and Haussmann, during their almost daily conversations, Haussmann did not wait for them to be financed. He asked one of his road-surveyors to draw up a plan of Paris.

During his years in London, Napoleon III had been profoundly impressed by the parks and open spaces in the capital. He had determined to give Paris some equivalent to Hyde Park. By a decree of 2 June 1852, the Bois de Boulogne had been ceded to the City of Paris. The City had undertaken to pay for its supervision and maintenance, and, within four years, to spend up to two million francs on improvements. By 1854, the transformation of the Bois was almost complete.

'Do you remember the Bois de Boulogne before 1852?' asked Victor Fournel, in

A monument to the Second Empire: Garnier's Opéra, with the ceiling painted by Paul Baudry.

Le Grand Préfet : Baron Haussmann, who created modern Paris.

Paris nouveau et Paris futur. 'It was a real forest . . . It was intolerable. At the gates of Paris, and on the most aristocratic side of the city! Whatever next? Luckily, this scandalous disorder was cleared up. The engineers took it over. Today, in 1865, the Bois de Boulogne is properly decimated, and . . . it is the triumph of elegant nature.'[7] Not nature, perhaps. 'Apart from the ground and the trees, everything,' added Fournel, 'is artificial in the Bois de Boulogne . . . All that is missing is a mechanical duck.'[8]

Fortunately there was no need for mechanical birds and animals. Le Jardin zoologique d'acclimatation, in the Bois de Boulogne, had been founded in 1860, in order to breed and acclimatize the animal and vegetable species which had recently been introduced into France. In his *Paris en Poche*, Henry de Conty advised the visitor to see the hot-houses, the Silkworm Rotunda, the great Aviary, the Poulerie and the Aquarium. Théophile Gautier was one of the earliest visitors; and in 1861 he described the aquarium in an article which Sainte-Beuve considered a minor masterpiece.

'You cross a simple little vestibule, and find yourself, as you do at the Diorama, in a wide corridor plunged into shadow. You glance instinctively at a series of pictures which are lit up by the light of a blue grotto, and magical in their effect. Nothing like them has ever presented itself to the human eye: it is the world as it is seen by the Nereids and the Sirens . . . Fourteen cavities or chambers have been made in the thickness of the wall . . . There is a bed of sand on the bottom of each fish-pond; and stones and fragments of rock, partly covered with aquatic plants, form . . . seascapes and

208

A châlet in the new Bois de Boulogne. From a painting by Pierre-Justin Ouvrie.

caverns of the most chimerical and picturesque strangeness . . . After a few minutes, the illusion is complete. You lose your sense of proportion. You think you are seeing the mountains and valleys of an unknown country, or, rather, of a new planet.'[9]

'The Bois de Boulogne and its lawns are always green,' explained Gustave Claudin, the incurable boulevardier. 'The sun is forbidden to burn them . . . I prefer this artificial beauty to the repulsive realities of our fields and woods.'[10] Even in winter, the Bois de Boulogne had its attraction.

'The ladies' hands are in their muffs,' wrote Édouard Gourdon, 'the men's faces are in their mufflers, the servants are wearing heavy coats over their liveries, the horses have covers over their harness, and the greyhounds are wearing overcoats.

'Scatter this crowd along the shores of the lake, on the paths and nearby roads. Sprinkle the skaters in their hundreds over the vast expanse of ice, and give some of them the agility and grace of swallows skimming a pool. Send out light, swift sledges with beautiful women in them, and fine gentlemen to push them. Stick frost on the trees, spread a grey sky over everything, with a dull, unshining copper sun, and you will have before your eyes one of the strange pictures which you sometimes see in the Bois in the coldest season of the year.'[11]

But it was in the splendour of summer that the Bois de Boulogne came into its own. It was in the June of 1861 that the Paris correspondent of *The Athenaeum* admired it: 'There is a new châlet on the island in the lake to which gondolas, gay with coloured lamps, float the fine evening through . . . How superlatively happy must the *Blouse* be with the acres of emerald green; the endless paths deeply shaded; the music and the incessant movement of this great wood and park, that is within the reach of every Parisian! It was a dusty, ragged place when Louis-Philippe was king, and you reached it by a poor and shabby lane. Now you approach it by a Rotten Row flanked by palaces.'[12]

The same journalist gave a vivid vignette of this Rotten Row in that distant imperial summer. 'The Champs-Élysées, that only two years ago were covered with a loose dusty gravel, are now one vast show of rare flowers. Gigantic lilies, geraniums of every colour, fuchsias of prodigious proportions are not too costly to enliven the morning walk of the high-capped *bonnes*, the lounging *pion-pions*, and the countless *gamins*, who crowd that vast space between the Place de la Concorde and the Rond-Point.'[13]

To Édouard Gourdon, in his book *Le Bois de Boulogne*, which appeared in 1861, the Champs-Élysées was only the ante-room of the Bois. There had, he wrote, to be a transition before one entered the earthly paradise.[14]

When the Emperor decided to turn the Bois de Boulogne into an English park, he entrusted the work to M. Varé, a landscape gardener. Varé had once worked at Saint-Leu for the Emperor's father, the King of Holland. He proved to be unequal to his new task. 'The almost illiterate gardener,' as Baron Haussmann called him, was later relieved of his post.

But, whoever was placed in charge, '. . . it did not prevent His Majesty, on more than one occasion, from picking up his pencil and altering the projects, or from going to the Bois every day, and in every weather, to see the effect of the work, and to assure himself that it was being quickly carried out. The Empress was also very interested in the work, and,' wrote Édouard Gourdon, 'I remember seeing an early plan on which the rivers and other parts of the park had been painted green, in watercolour, by the august consort of the Emperor. As you see, it was a rather exalted collaboration, and the work which was to ensue could not fail to be remarkably beautiful.'[15]

The Vicomte de Beaumont-Vassy, a member of the Conseil d'État, once found himself alone for a moment in the Emperor's study. The floor was covered with large maps marked by multicoloured pins; he recognised the different paths and the two new lakes which had been planned for the Bois de Boulogne.[16] Dr Evans, the Emperor's American dentist, remembered that, when the improvements were being made in the Bois de Boulogne, the Emperor often came early in the morning, '. . . not simply to see what the engineers had accomplished, but to superintend and direct, or, as an American might say, "to boss the job". I have been with him there myself, with M. Alphand, the chief engineer, when, having proposed some change, the Emperor has taken a hammer from a workman and planted a number of pickets with his own hands, to mark the line that in his opinion should be followed. He seemed to take great pleasure in indulging his taste for this kind of work.'[17]

The re-planning of the Bois de Boulogne had in fact been the work of several people, and among the most important was Haussmann's colleague, Jean-Charles-Adolphe Alphand.[18] Alphand had been born at Grenoble in 1817. A pupil of the École polytechnique, he had left in 1837 to become an engineer in the Départment des Ponts et Chaussées, and in 1839 he had been sent to Bordeaux. In 1854, Haussmann had summoned him to Paris, to be his chief engineer. Alphand was entrusted with the embellishments of the City of Paris, then with the lighting, the public highways and traffic control. The transformation of the Bois de Boulogne was the most spectacular work with which he was concerned, but he was also largely responsible for the public gardens in Paris, and the planning of the new squares, and it was to him that the city owed its hothouses and nurseries. He was to plan the fortifications during the Siege of Paris. Under the Third Republic, he was to be director of works for Paris; he continued the task which Haussmann had begun in such spectacular style.

No one who glanced through Alphand's two folio volumes, *Promenades à Paris*, could have remained in any doubt of the cost and labour involved in re-designing the Bois de Boulogne. Alphand described how the first important work had begun in 1853, and how the two lakes had been excavated, and the roads planned round them. He recalled how the huge artesian well had been sunk at Passy to feed the cascades in the lakes, and how sandstone had proved so expensive that artificial rocks had been made out of rubble. This was coated with cement and finally touched up with brushes. The invention had satisfied both the economists and – strangely enough – those who wanted 'to come closer to nature'. There must have been some need for economy, for the plantations in the Bois had alone demanded 420,080 trees or shrubs. The total cost was 634,900 francs, an average cost of 1 fr. 51 centimes for each tree.

Alphand's monumental volumes do not simply record such facts and figures; they are a handsome and detailed summary of landscape-gardening and town-planning in Second Empire Paris. They show the buffet in the Pré-Catalan, with the passing cyclist on his primitive bicycle; they show the skaters disporting themselves at night in the Bois. They show the architects' designs for kiosks, bandstands and pavilions, the landscape gardeners' designs for plantations. They show not only the designs for the Bois de Boulogne, but a thousand details of Haussmann's Paris: the wrought-iron railings for the square Montholon and the square de la Trinité – for squares were opened everywhere in Paris – the wildly ornate street lamps, the urinals, the sewers, the park benches, the fountains, and, above all, the opulent Second Empire shrubs and flowers: the begonias, canna lilies, petunias and fuchsias, the verbena and the pelargonium. The second volume of this survey appeared years after the Empire had fallen; but the work remains imperial in style.

Haussmann's task included not only the provision of flowers and trees, but the provision of a modern sewage system. Le Service des Eaux et des Égouts, as it was grandly called, was entrusted to Eugène Belgrand, as Engineer-in-Chief. Haussmann later declared that this service gave Belgrand 'the chance to make the Network of Paris

Sewers his finest and most incontestable claim to glory.'[19] The language may seem excessive, but certainly the sewers became one of the wonders of modern Paris. Late in 1866, *La Presse* reported that Princess Mathilde and Princess Clotilde, with a distinguished escort, 'had gone down the steps which led from the place de la Madeleine to the main sewer, and travelled down it as far as the steps which led to the precinct of the church of Notre-Dame-de-Lorette. Their Imperial Highnesses then got into a carriage and drove to the place du Châtelet, to go down again to the main sewer and follow it, by boat, as far as Asnières.'[20]

Haussmann also had to give Paris an adequate water supply. In the year 1852, recorded Dr Evans, '. . . the city was not able to distribute more than 105,000 cubic metres of water per day, while under the Empire the waterworks were so improved that, in the year 1869, 538,000 cubic metres were furnished daily. But this was not all. As late as the year 1866 the water used by the inhabitants of Paris, even for domestic purposes, was taken almost entirely from the Seine and the river Marne. It was impossible to preserve it from pollution, and consequently typhoid was endemic in the city, and the death-rate was high . . . The Emperor took up the subject of supplying Paris with drinking water from uncontaminated sources. For this special purpose work was begun in 1864, and the aqueduct of the Dhuis was completed in 1866, at a cost of 18,000,000 francs; it was 131 kilometres in length, and brought into the city 25,000 cubic metres of water daily.'[21]

One of the wonders of Paris: the sewers. A photograph taken by Nadar, using artificial light, 1861.

In December 1854 Haussmann presented the Conseil municipal with his plan for an underground city, in which all the common services of Paris would be concentrated. Above ground, the transformation continued. In March 1855, a new law decreed the completion of the rue de Rivoli, the central boulevard (the boulevard Sébastopol, on the right bank), and the opening of a boulevard between the place de l'Hôtel de Ville and the Châtelet (the future avenue Victoria). The law authorised the City of Paris to borrow sixty million francs. The completion of the rue de Rivoli brought the demolition of the fontaine du Diable, the hôtel d'Angivillier, the hôtel de Montbazon and the tour Bichat. But Haussmann's engineers had no time for history. 'M. le Baron Haussmann was King of Paris,' wrote Arsène Houssaye. 'He opened up avenues with no concern for men or monuments. He simply gave the explanation: "For the public good."'[22] And yet perhaps this tyranny sometimes hid uncertainty. 'Very few people,' wrote Haussmann, later, 'know how much patience, circumspection and diplomacy I needed, under an apparent trust in my powers, . . . to reach my goal. Life has taught me that, if you are to be good with impunity, you need to have a quite different reputation.'[23]

One contemporary who watched him sadly was Henri Dabot, a lawyer at the Paris Court of Appeal. Dabot lived in the Latin Quarter, and he kept a diary which reflects the point-of-view of the ordinary man. 'The fine front of the old church of Saint-Benoît has been demolished to make way for the rue des Écoles,' so Dabot wrote in July 1854. 'Paris is becoming cleaner and brighter, but poetry is leaving her as fast as its wings can carry it.' In 1859 a heavy-hearted Dabot recorded the widespread demolitions in the Latin Quarter. 'My heart is stricken by all this destruction,' he confessed in his diary. 'Progress is not made without anguish.'[24]

Haussmann's progress was inexorable. As the new year, 1860, began, the suburbs of Paris were officially annexed to the city, and came under the Prefect's administration. The capital – which had been divided into twelve arrondissements – was divided, now, into twenty. It became a fashion for every Parisian, 'even the gout-ridden and the paralysed,' to make the eight-league tour round the new metropolis.[25]

When Dr Henry Evans came to reflect on the Emperor's transformation of Paris, he gave an astonishing list of his achievements.

'It was Napoleon III who connected the Louvre with the Tuileries, who built the churches of Saint-Augustin, La Trinité, Sainte-Clotilde, Saint-Joseph, Saint-Ambroise, Saint-Eugène, Notre-Dame-des-Champs, Saint Pierre de Mont Rouge, and many others . . .; it was he who erected or restored the splendid edifices of the new Palais de Justice, the Tribunal de Commerce, the Hôtel Dieu, the Grand Opéra, the Halles Centrales, and the Temple; . . . it was he who built the great bridges over the Seine . . .; it was he who surrounded the parks and the gardens with their gilded railings and erected their great entrance gates, and who adorned the French capital with fountains and statues, and a hundred other ornamental structures.

'On account of the interest which the Emperor took in the arts and sciences, the

The transformation of Paris: a corner of the boulevard des Italiens, showing the new Théâtre du Vaudeville, 1868.

collections of the Louvre were quadrupled; the so-called Campana Galleries were purchased; the "Union Centrale des Beaux-Arts appliqués à l'industrie" was founded; the Musée d'Artillerie received rich additions; in the old Palais of Saint-Germain the well-known archaeological museum was created; the Musée de Cluny and the Tour Saint-Jacques were restored; the Hôtel Carnavalet was changed into a museum for a collection of the antiquities of the city of Paris; the Imperial library received some very valuable additions; and the Bibliothèque Sainte-Geneviève was thrown open to the public.

'In fact, the city of Paris, as it appears to the visitor today [in 1905], was created by Napoleon III.'[26]

The transformation of Paris, which was to be the most lasting monument to the Emperor, was not always welcomed by his contemporaries.

'Why not admit it?' asked Édouard Gourdon in 1861. 'This transformation of Paris, so universally approved, has had its critics. Its adversaries have been all those who feel less admiration for the future than regret for the past. The feeling which moves them is certainly one which deserves respect. You grow attached to the things which you have seen for a long time, and especially to those among which you have always lived. It seems that there is some mysterious relationship between them and ourselves, and that no-one can touch them without somehow touching us . . . For us, Parisians of another age, bees born in another hive, we are in modern Paris rather like foreigners in a spa: we take deep breaths of the fresh air we are given; we look, with wonderment

No. 8, Rue de Valois du Roule: a first-class hôtel privé.

and satisfaction, at the new streets, the houses they are building, the palaces which they are adorning; we understand that, in all this sunlight, we ought to feel well; we realise that what has been done has been done with great intelligence, and that, without any doubt, it is useful. But we don't go further than that; we are not moved. In short, we enjoy it all without being attached to anything, just as if this city were not our own, and as if, tomorrow, we were to pack our bags and move on.'[27]

Édouard Gourdon's melancholy was shared by Benjamin Gastineau, the author of *Sottises et scandales du temps présent*. 'The old, artistic, historic and political Paris has been demolished,' he lamented in 1863. 'They have driven through great avenues, opened huge arteries to let troops of soldiers pass abreast, to make room for a whole motley, floating, hurried, busy, frightened population of one or two hundred thousand provincials and foreigners, thrown up every day by the railway stations.' Gastineau regretted the deliberate destruction of history, the impersonality of the new city, the loss of the Parisian spirit.[28] Two years later, Victor Fournel, the erudite historian of Paris, declared that medieval Paris was a Shakespearean drama, and modern Paris was an epic poem revised by a grammarian. To Fournel, the new buildings were not so much houses as six-storey trunks.

'Parisian apartments combine extreme expensiveness with extreme inconvenience. You don't live there, you perch there, you camp there between heaven and earth, submitted to all the servitudes imposed by the proprietor, the concierge and the neighbours . . . Do you believe that all this has no effect on the anxious character, the nervous irritability which make the Parisians the most volatile and capricious people on earth?

. . . I am convinced that the English *home,* so peaceful and so comfortable, so isolated from all the tumults in the world outside, plays a great part in the prosperous political and social history of the English nation.'[29]

In 1867, in *Les Odeurs de Paris,* Louis Veuillot considered the new city with the same pessimism and apprehension. 'The buildings in the new Paris owe something to every style; the whole does not lack a certain unity, because all these styles are boring, and boring in the most boring way of all, that is to say the definite and regular. *Into line, dress! Eyes front!* It seems as if the Amphion of the city is a corporal . . . A quantity of sumptuous, pompous, colossal things are being built, and they are boring. There are also a quantity of very ugly things; they are boring, too . . . The inhabitants of the finished Paris will be bored as no-one on earth has ever been bored before. There is nothing that cannot be feared from a nation which is bored.'[30]

Alas, there was no hope of averting Haussmann's embellishments of Paris. 'There is,' wrote Fournel, 'an infallible man in the world, and it isn't the Pope, or the Great Lama. There is an all-powerful man in France, and it isn't the Emperor . . . The omnipotence of M. le Préfet is absolute, without restriction, without limits in the field in which it is exercised. He has power of life and death over the city. He is Paris. M. Haussmann . . . symbolises the ideal and the apogee of centralisation.'[31]

The Parisians of the Second Empire did not only regret the wholesale destruction of the past; they deplored the effect on their everyday lives.

'Everyone is complaining about the high rents,' wrote Dabot, late in 1863, 'and they are blaming the Prefect of the Seine, M. le Baron Haussmann, who has made premises scarce by demolishing a mass of houses. M. Haussmann maintains that he does not deserve this reproach; and, in a memorandum recently presented to the departmental commission, he says it is true that he has demolished 12, 240 houses in the department of the Seine, but he has rebuilt 61, 217. What the cunning baron does not say is that the apartments in his new houses are too expensive for the workers, the clerks and the petits bourgeois, who no longer know where to live.'[32]

Even foreign observers were disturbed by the speed and ruthlessness with which the Baron continued his huge task. Felix Whitehurst, the Paris correspondent of the *Daily Telegraph,* lamented in March 1865:

'We are, you know, knocking down old Paris and building new Boulevards. When you go out, you leave your key with the *concierge* and your compliments for M. Haussmann, and "if he does not particularly wish to pull down your house to-day, perhaps he will kindly leave it standing till to-morrow." . . . "All this over-building is a mistake," observed a man of the world. "You pull down poor men's houses, and build rich men's mansions. You rear a great palace, and the cobbler who dwelt on the spot before is forced to go into the suburbs, at increased rent and at a loss of his business. Nobody gains anything; the landlord is ruined, because he cannot find tenants; and the former tenants are ruined, because they cannot find landlords." . . . They are employing the surplus population in pulling down their own houses and building up dearer

ABOVE LEFT *Building the new boulevard du Prince Eugène (now the boulevard Voltaire), from an engraving by Thorigny, 1857.* BELOW *The demolition of old Paris. In the background the new Opéra emerges.*

217

residences; this may continue without mischief for months, but it can hardly continue for years.'[33]

A few months later, the correspondent returned to the subject. 'The Budget has again attracted the public attention to the Haussmannisation of Paris. "If they pull down any more streets," said the poor mother of a family yesterday, "we shall have to live in tents; and I do so hate a roving life." Yet new orders are coming out every day. Man in cocked hat calls and leaves paper (this is Monday); on Wednesday he returns,... and not only gives you notice to quit, but fixes the day and the hour; and as the last box leaves the tenement one workman pulls down the door ... You pass by on the Saturday, and all is a blank ... The first effect of this pantomimic transformation is that a quantity of nomadic tribes in search of new houses encumber the streets of this city.'[34]

'The fronts of the new buildings are both very ornamental and airy,' added the author of *Life in Paris before the War and during the Siege*, 'they also have plenty of sunshine, but in their rears they look into narrow courts, where the sun is never seen to throw his rays, and no free current of air is ever felt to blow; all is gloom and stagnation in this insalubrious atmosphere, for health has never been taken into account in making these extensive changes. All this mason and trowel work has been done to give labour to the people, and to clothe Paris in a fine Sunday suit; looking to the beautiful and forgetting the useful.'[35]

Some had made fortunes out of Haussmann's rebuilding of Paris. Victor Fournel declared, in 1865, that there was a new industry: that of the man who speculated on his expropriation.

'There are people who specialise in buying, building and establishing a commercial house in a district which they consider should soon disappear. It isn't hard to find the district: you simply have an *embarras de choix*. This has become a sort of speculation, but one which is safer than the others. People talk of a coffee-house keeper who has already been demolished three times, thanks to careful calculations. He has progressed from one indemnity to another until he recently managed to build an enormous and marvellous café – which he also hopes to see demolished before he dies. And then he will retire, and he will go and build a country house in some distant Arcadia where *l'utilité pratique* is unknown.'[36]

Some Parisians were understandably grateful to le Grand Préfet; but Haussmann's ruthless dictatorship had naturally made him enemies, and for some years he had been attacked in the Corps législatif. In 1868 Jules Ferry, the politician, published an open letter to the Commission of the Corps législatif who were considering the proposed new loan for the City of Paris. In this pamphlet, *Comptes fantastiques d'Haussmann*, Ferry made some acid comments on the new city.

'We recognise that they have made the new Paris into the finest hostelry on earth, and the parasites of both worlds find nothing like it ... Personally we think it ugly, but we agree that M. le Préfet's bad taste has as its accomplice the bad taste of the architects and of a considerable portion of the modern public . . .

'As for the old Paris, the Paris of Voltaire, of Diderot and Desmoulins, the Paris of 1830 and 1848, we weep for it with all the tears that come to our eyes, as we see . . . the triumphant vulgarity, the terrible materialism that we are to bequeath to our heirs.'

Ferry discussed Haussmann's financial accounts, and concluded that he should be dismissed.[37] Haussmann was not only attacked in print, and in the Corps législatif, he was even attacked in the Cabinet. The Emperor was attached to him, and he constantly defended him. More than once Haussmann had offered his resignation, but the Emperor had always refused to accept it. In 1870, the coming of the Ollivier Government brought some significant changes of office, and the Emperor asked Haussmann to resign. This time le Grand Préfet refused to offer his resignation. 'A man like me,' he answered, 'does not give in his resignation, nor does he cling to power. He is either kept or dismissed.' On 6 January 1870 a decree was published in *Le Journal officiel*, naming M. Henri Chevreau as Préfet de la Seine, 'in the place of M. le Baron Haussmann, who has been relieved of his functions'.[38] As *The Times* observed next day, in its leading article: 'The demolition of the great Paris demolisher has at last been accomplished.'[39]

Ludovic Halévy, Offenbach's librettist, wrote in his diary: 'It is an important event . . . Paris is a marvel, and M. Haussmann has done in fifteen years what would not have been done in a century. But for the moment that is enough. There will be a twentieth century. Let us leave a little work for it to do.'[40]

Perhaps one should leave the last word to Haussmann. In 1889, two years before his death, he wrote: 'From 1853 to 1870 I was the devoted instrument of that great and difficult work, the Transformation of Paris; and I remain the responsible author, in a country where everything is personified . . . I owe it to the Emperor's kindness (which was always great to me), . . . to see my name inscribed, by an imperial decree, . . . on the plaques of the boulevard Haussmann; and I cannot forget that every Head of State, resisting every vote from the republican Conseil municipal, has kept it there until the present day.'[41]

Hôtels privés *in Haussmann's Paris. From contemporary designs.*

Architecture Privée au XIXme Scle

Nouvelles Maison

Sous Napoléon III

Publié par Mr César Daly

De Paris

Volume 1.

Exemple A.2 Pl. 8.

au 10e. d'exécution

Sauvageot sculp.t

HÔTEL PRIVÉ

Deuxième Classe ___ N.º 4 ___ Rue de la Victoire ___ Cheminée-Calorifère en Stuc

12 Le Style Napoléon III

In 1867, at the height of the Second Empire, Louis Veuillot made a sad observation. 'They have rebuilt Paris, and they have almost rebuilt France, and no architect has revealed himself.'[1] The observation was all too true. Art seems to have lacked a model, a dominant inspiration. 'We are living on the capital we inherited from our fathers,' said a connoisseur some years after the Empire. And he added: 'Architecture has not found a definite formula in the nineteenth century.'[2]

In a secondary genre, however, building in iron, a new form of architecture had appeared. The use of iron increased a good deal at this period, because of the new combinations to which it lent itself. The Gare de l'Est, the work of Duquesnay, deserves to be remembered, and so do the Bibliothèque Sainte-Geneviève and the central market of Paris, Les Halles. The Second Empire was undoubtedly more favourable to architecture than the bourgeois monarchy had been. Private houses, or *hôtels privés*, sprang up round the parc Monceau, at the Cours-la-Reine, along the avenues du Bois, d'Iéna, and de l'Alma; they answered the *nouveau riche* demand for comfort and well-being, they fulfilled the desire to create an appearance.

Paris itself was growing vast, and so was the scale of individual buildings in the capital; but, as we have seen, the new apartment buildings were frequently inadequate behind their palatial façades.

'The new palaces,' wrote Victor Fournel, 'are whited sepulchres, made of old plaster and chips of stone, shaken from top to bottom by every wind. They are divided vertically and horizontally into thin slices, in each of which a Parisian household is stifling for want of air, light and space . . . The air which the administration has given back to the city by widening the streets is more than taken away by the landlords as they cut down the apartments. They certainly have to. Space is being eaten away by the width and multiplicity of the new streets.'[3]

Some of the new buildings in Paris were more convenient. In 1855, Dr Prosper Ménière noted that the Grand Hôtel du Louvre was not yet finished, but '. . . nearly all the apartments are booked. There are rooms at 2 francs a day, at 3 francs, etc. It will be a

A stucco chimneypiece for an hôtel privé. *An illustration from a survey of domestic architecture by César Daly, a government architect.*

marvel, and the small hotels will be much to be pitied. This hotel has cost more than 10 million to build and furnish. The staff have cork-soled shoes, you don't hear a sound, the bells are replaced by an electric apparatus with the help of which you can ask for what you want, from each apartment. It is all like a sort of enchanted palace. There will be a machine by the main staircase, designed to carry residents from the ground floor to any floor they choose.'[4]

Hotels, private houses and apartment blocks seemed to spring up overnight. As for public buildings, never had so many been erected. Haussmann needed monumental vistas for his straight new boulevards, and, when he did not find them, he created them. In the precincts of the old city, he demolished 19,722 houses, and he built 43,777; in the old suburbs, he demolished 4,682 and he built 30,820. The total cost of this transformation was two thousand five hundred and fifty-three million francs. Le Grand Préfet had a general staff of architects exclusively concerned with the new Paris: Baltard, Hittorff, Duc, Ballet, Gilbert and Bailly.[5]

Stations, theatres, churches, *mairies* and barracks all rose up with astonishing rapidity. But if Paris changed before one's eyes, it did not always grow more beautiful. Architecture lacked decision. It seemed to live on eclecticism or on compromise. People wanted to act grandly in accordance with the Emperor's ideas. In general, they acted pompously. There were academic exercises in religious building. Sainte-Clotilde, by Gau and Ballu (1846–56), was built in the Gothic style; Saint-Augustin, by Baltard (1860), in the Roman style; La Trinité, by Ballu (1863), in the Renaissance style. Non-ecclesiastical buildings showed little inspiration. Among them were the Palais de l'Industrie, by Barrault, the tribunal de Commerce, by Bailly (1860), and the two theatres in the place du Châtelet, by Davioud (1861).[6]

The architectural ideas of the previous age were hardly modified in the Second Empire, and they took the place of a new attitude. This was because the Second Empire almost exclusively employed the architects of the bourgeois monarchy. The newcomers, like Vaudoyer, Mauguin, and Lefuel, were their pupils.

In 1867, Eugène Rouyer, the architect, published Lefuel's designs for the Empress's private apartments at the Tuileries. He did so in a somewhat defensive manner.

'We need not point out the original style of all the decoration. We are not afraid to say "original" . . . If the style of the private apartments is not entirely new, that is because man is no more capable than Nature of creating something out of nothing . . . Posterity will certainly see, in the architectural works of our epoch, what we hesitate to recognise as the style of Napoleon III. Our age has been reproached for not finding a character of its own in the art of architecture, for constantly reproducing and copying the past. And yet, if we consider our great and widely different monuments as a whole, these vast boulevards lined with magnificent trees, we must recognise that they all show a style peculiar to our age. The active and generous impulse which the Empire has given to the various branches of art, the character of grandeur which it has stamped on architecture, will certainly be, in the eyes of posterity, one of the claims to glory of Napoleon III.'[7]

222   ABOVE *The* salle à manger *of Princess Mathilde in the rue de Courcelles. From the painting by Charles Giraud, 1854.* BELOW '*The true* salon *of the nineteenth century.' The* salon *of Princess Mathilde in the rue de Courcelles. From the painting by Charles Giraud, 1859.*

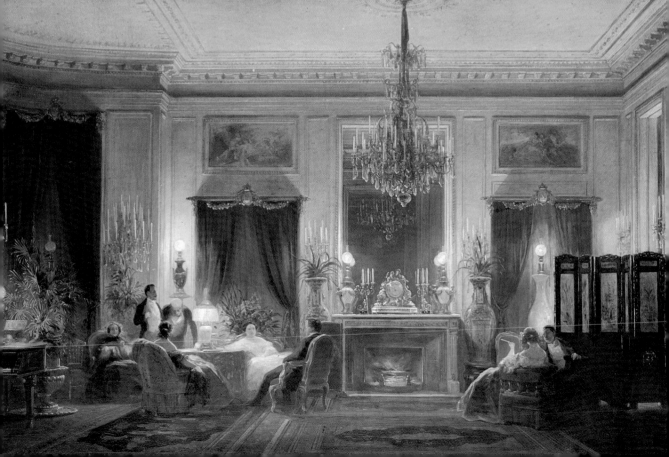

The same point had been made by Haussmann himself. 'The renovation of Paris will certainly not be among the least of the glories of the reign.'[8]

Haussmann had made the comment in 1864, in a letter to César Daly, a government architect. Daly had dedicated a massive work to him: *L'Architecture privée au dix-neuvième siècle, sous Napoléon III*. This survey of the new houses in Paris makes an illuminating study. The buildings are divided into *hôtels privés* (first, second and third classes), apartment houses, *maisons à loyer* (again of three classes), and *villas suburbaines* (again three classes). The elevations and the details, inside and out, show a lack of taste which is almost grotesque. The *hôtels privés*, of every class, present façades of pompous grandeur, a wealth of caryatids and ornate ironwork. Their interiors are heavy with statuary and marble, carved fireplaces and over-painted vestibules. The first-class suburban villa at Pierrefonds, even the third-class villa at Neuilly, are unbelievably pretentious. Daly no doubt intended his work as a tribute to the age; it shows, with almost humorous clarity, the *nouveaux riches* tastes of the Second Empire. This, one feels, is the era of the *bourgeois gentilhomme*: an era which depends on outward show, which admires the grandiose and has lost sight of artistic distinction.

'Architecture has fallen into utter degradation,' wrote Delacroix in 1860. 'It no longer knows where it is; it wants to do something new, and there are no new men. Oddity has taken the place of this novelty which is so sought after . . . Architects are not inventing, they are copying the Gothic.'[9]

French architecture and interior decoration during the Second Empire were indeed a catalogue of past manners and exotic styles. In or near the Champs-Élysées were the Roman palace of Émile de Girardin, the Gothic castle of the Marquis de Quinsonas, the Tunisian château of Jules de Lesseps, the amazing pink *hôtel* of the Duke of Brunswick, and the Renaissance *hôtel* of Mme de Païva. But one of the most remarkable buildings in Second Empire Paris remained the Palais Pompéien, in the avenue Montaigne. This had been built in 1860 for Prince Napoléon. It was built complete with atrium, impluvium, trichinium, tablinum, and xystos, or garden. The work proclaimed the current interest in archaeology (partly inspired by the excavations at Pompeii): indeed it is said to have inspired the neo-Greek cult. The Palais Pompéien also emphasised that, artistically speaking, the Second Empire was an age of pastiche.

'All modern French architects,' lamented Gustave Claudin, 'spell out and vaguely dream of a style which one would be tempted to call the neo-Greco-Gothico-Pompadour-Pompeian.'[10] And yet, to his mind, the art of architecture was not really lost. It was waiting for the completion of the last stretch of railway. When the engineers had no more railway tracks to build, they would, said Claudin, 'unite their efforts with those of the architects, and from their union will emerge the architectural style of the nineteenth century.' And Claudin underlined the point. 'I still maintain that, when this age has emerged from the fever of speculation, when it has halted the advance of *Americanism*, this inspiration which has made us what we are will move men's spirits once again and force them to engender something new.'[11]

Le style Napoléon III. *This* surtout, *in rock crystal and gilded bronze, was made for the Emperor by Froment-Meurice in 1864.*

LEFT *Charles Garnier, from the bust by Carpeaux, and* RIGHT *Eugène-Emmanuel Viollet-le-Duc.*

There were in fact two architects who imposed themselves on the Second Empire: Viollet-le-Duc and Charles Garnier.

Eugène-Emmanuel Viollet-le-Duc had been born in Paris in 1814; and, from his youth, his vocation had been clear. As a young man he had travelled around Italy, Spain and Portugal, Germany and France, sketching and analysing their architecture. His labours were to result in his *Dictionnaire raisonné de l'architecture française*. His abilities and his social connections (not least the friendship of Princess Mathilde) brought him to the notice of the Emperor. He had helped to decorate Notre-Dame for the imperial wedding; he became a favourite Court architect, and the Emperor commissioned him to restore the medieval castle of Pierrefonds, near Compiègne. Massillon Rouvet, who was his secretary during the Siege of Paris, found it hard to say whether Viollet-le-Duc had been more successful in his designs, or in his restorations; but, at the end of the century, he paid him a considered and illuminating tribute.

'The restorations are greatly admired, but there are too many for me to quote them all. However, let me note the first one he carried out: the church at Vézelay. He made his début there with prodigious assurance, and he was brilliantly successful. Then came Notre-Dame-de-Paris, where the countless problems might have occupied an architect for a lifetime. Viollet-le-Duc restored it with a felicity and vigour which astonished his contemporaries. Pierrefonds was a shapeless mass of ruins, sticking out of the brushwood; it was divined, and re-discovered, and it rose again from the levelled earth which had covered its walls. The ramparts of Carcassonne, and Avignon; the

ABOVE LEFT *a detail of the interior of Pierrefonds, the medieval castle restored by Viollet-le-Duc, and* BELOW *a wall of le Salon Bleu at the Tuileries, designed by Lefuel, the Emperor's architect.*

227

cathedral at Rheims, the queen of French cathedrals, the cathedrals of Saint-Denis, Saint-Cernin at Toulouse, of Clermont-Ferrand, and a score of other works were carried out at the same time by him alone. For he alone made his drawings, his designs and details, his portfolios of paintings. There were no offices full of draughtsmen.

'For every monument he was building, he spent several days drawing what the work demanded; every sculptor received his drawing, clear in every detail, and every decorator had his model. Once the explanations had been given and understood, Viollet-le-Duc turned to something else.

'When he got home, he sketched out the framework of his publications, his wonderful compositions for goldsmiths and silversmiths, like the altar for the cathedral at Clermont-Ferrand; he wrote his lively, clear and attractive works; he made his tours as inspector-general of diocesan buildings, and his reports to the commission for historical monuments. And, for ten years, he prepared and gave his courses of composition at the École nationale de dessin. Viollet-le-Duc was not content to be an architect and an artist, he was a lecturer, a distinguished publicist, and a populariser whose works were a pleasure to read.'[12]

He exercised a lively influence on the art of his time. In 1836, there were only three factories for stained glass, apart from Sèvres. In 1849 there were forty, and in 1863 one hundred and fifty. This increase was due to the increase in religious buildings and the restorations carried out by Viollet-le-Duc and his *diocésains*.[13]

Viollet-le-Duc was an archaeologist and a theorist rather than a builder. He did not give the measure of his talent in any great modern building. Charles Garnier, who was born in Paris in 1825, had a mind which was constantly in ferment, an imagination ceaselessly awake.[14] His ambition was to create a masterpiece, to accumulate in the Opéra, which Haussmann had commissioned him to build, all the materials and techniques of the past and present. He opened a large workshop in Paris, like those which had been opened for royal buildings in the days of the Valois; and here, under his direction, architects and sculptors, artists and decorators worked together. By the summer of 1868, Felix Whitehurst could report that 'the outer works of the Grand Opéra are now advancing with rapid strides; and the vast half-finished structure has a very odd effect today, as it stands in the centre of the new Place de l'Opéra.'[15]

The stage of Garnier's Opéra was claimed to be the largest in the world (twenty-two yards deep and seventeen yards wide); the lighting demanded eight thousand five hundred gas-jets, at a daily cost of one thousand three hundred francs. The building was both modern and curiously conservative. As Germain Bapst observed, years later, Garnier was convinced 'that no detail in the construction could have an effect on the acoustics.' It was not an opinion shared by Duvert and Charpentier, when they came to rebuild the Opéra-Comique. They already understood that a room 'gains or loses sonority according to the way in which its curves are disposed.'[16]

One cannot praise every feature of Garnier's Opéra – that 'universe of gilded shapes'. It is brilliant, vulgar, gay, monstrous and imposing. But no monument in Paris is more opulent than the Opéra, or more representative of an age.

Garnier's Opéra: a cross-section drawn by M. A. Deroy, 1875.

It represented the love of show, the superficial splendour of the time; it also reflected the extreme materialism of Second Empire society. Claudin was not the only critic to feel that Americanism had stifled the aesthetic sense of the nation. Delacroix considered that France was becoming all too American. 'They're talking of selling the Champs-Élysées to speculators!' he had noted in 1854. 'It's the Palais de l'Industrie which has created the fashion. When we're a little more American, they'll sell the Tuileries Gardens, too, as unbuilt-on land which serves no useful purpose.'[17]

Delacroix did not only deplore the commercialisation of the time; he lamented the decline of artistic standards. The undoubted decline in architecture, in interior decoration and fashion – indeed, in most of the visual arts – owed much to the coming of the industrial age. In his book on Paris, Claudin sadly enlarged on the subject. 'Thanks to the progress of the age, nearly everyone can eat white bread, and meat, and wear warm clothes in winter . . . This democratisation of prosperity has also replaced real luxury by false luxury. You find tinsel everywhere.'[18]

Once there had been an age of quality; work had been done for the discriminating élite. Now it was the age of quantity. Many French industrialists had brought home methods and machines from England. Napoleon III, who had lived in England, was imbued with social ideas; he wanted to spread the advantages of prosperity. But while new methods of production generated public wealth, they did not favour industrial art. Faced with the new powers of steam, gas and machinery, manufacturers were almost intoxicated. They forgot that they must not only adapt an object to use, but that they

229

must make it beautiful. Machines themselves do not create ugliness. They simply need to be given good designs, adapted to their possibilities. Industrialists failed to understand this essential truth. They lacked invention and taste, they lacked artistic enterprise. They simply reproduced the masterpieces of the past.

Théophile Gautier had surveyed the scene with the optimism of the idealist. 'Will our century have its own style?' he had asked in 1858. And he had answered his own question. 'We have reached the limits of a world which is ending, . . . but it is ending only to begin again, more brilliant and more radiant than ever. Who can foresee the forms that will be needed to-morrow by the new inventions, the prodigious discoveries of science, promptly put into use by industry?'[19] Unfortunately, industry and taste did not come together. There had been technical progress in the textile industry; but, to Claudin, there was the same difference between the curtains at Versailles and the modern fabrics woven at Lyons as there was between the paper of an Elzevir edition and a ten-sou book. As for modern furniture, it was desperately mediocre. 'For more than fifty years,' wrote Claudin, 'bad taste has filled our apartments with banal and clumsy beds, chairs, tables, cupboards and desks . . . Every rich or discriminating person who aspires to a little luxury is obliged to go back to the eighteenth century and to have it abjectly copied.'[20] Ernest Daudet, recalling the late 1850s, said that a new industry had come into being: that of reproduction furniture. There were, of course, a good many frauds.[21]

In the first years of the Second Empire, the art of furniture was struggling in uncertainty. Here, as elsewhere, the creative spirit seemed to be dead. It was an epoch which had lost its style and found itself in search of a form.

Queen Victoria's drawing-room at Saint-Cloud, 1855. A detail from a watercolour by Fortuné de Fournier.

At first the cabinet-makers thought that they had found it in the Renaissance. Michel Liénard (1810–70) turned to sixteenth-century prints, to the details of the façades of royal châteaux, to the furniture of the period. It was an academic Renaissance which inspired his furniture and his interior decoration, but it left its mark on furniture from 1840 to 1870 and even beyond.

In 1866, a massive publication appeared in tribute to him: *Spécimens de la décoration et de l'ornementation au XIXe siècle, par Liénard*. 'What are our new artistic theories?' enquired the publisher. 'And what formulas have been invented by the modern age in the rich field of industrial art?' He answered the question with a selection from Liénard's work. It was, he said, 'marked with an original imprint. This is not so much the imprint of the artist's personal talent, as the seal of the present century.'[22] The designs bear the seal of the Second Empire, and they do so all too clearly. Liénard presents a design for a terracotta vase, *genre réalisme*, a vase which swarms with gasping terracotta fish; he presents a state bed in the style of Louis XIV, with lamps on either side which recall the clustered onion-lamps outside the Théâtre-Français. He presents carved wooden trophies in the style of Louis XVI, a frieze for wallpaper in the neo-Greek manner. There is a wealth of pastiche, a riot of elaborate, conflicting and superfluous detail. There is no one design which reflects inventive thought, simplicity or elegance.

Such was the fashion for the Henri II style that – at least in the dining-room and study – it held out against the fashion for rococo, which invaded the salon and the bedroom from 1850. The rococo is the real furnishing style of the Second Empire. It reached its peak in about 1860; it still existed in the first years of the Third Republic. It was a homogeneous style, and perfectly adapted to everyday life.[23]

Sofas, easy-chairs and têtes-à-têtes reproduced the eighteenth-century models more or less faithfully. But the manufacturers added models of their own invention, like 'boulle' chairs inlaid with mother-of-pearl. The *confortable*, or easy-chair, triumphed in spite of its critics. The *crapaud* was low, with a very arched back, and its seat slightly raised in front. The *pouf* was a fat footstool, the *borne* was a circular sofa with a support in the middle. They all had fringes or furbelows to hide their ungainly feet. Upholstered in velvet. in figured silk, in sumptuous cloth, this furniture was in harmony with the crinoline. No one could call it elegant, but it was comfortable.

The Empress, who imposed her own preferences in furniture, was not concerned with comfort. Carried away by her cult for Marie-Antoinette, she surrounded herself with relics of Versailles or the Trianon; she asked her cabinet-makers for imitations. Georges Grohé provided the best of them. His reproductions were in all the imperial palaces, and he worked for the Corps législatif and the Ministère d'État. Thanks to him, the Louis XVI-Impératrice entered every elegant home in Paris.

And so the furniture of the Second Empire ended, as it had begun, in pastiche and copy, and this was a confession of failure. It was also, perhaps, a comment on Second Empire Paris. This conception of furniture pleased a *nouveau riche* society which was enamoured of luxury and comfort, and anxious, above all, to create effect.

Examples of Second Empire taste: LEFT *a corner-piece commissioned by Napoleon III in 1869;* CENTRE *a divan-jardinière at Saint-Cloud, and* RIGHT *the Prince Imperial's cradle, designed by the architect Baltard.*

Interior decoration, like furniture, showed the lack of invention of the age. Prince Napoleon had commissioned Charles Rossigneux, the interior designer, to make some Roman-style furniture for his Palais Pompéien. The interior decoration of the palace was inspired (if that is the word) by the same archaeological spirit. The walls were painted in plain colours, in the antique style, and decorated with architectural motifs and foliage by Chauvin. The only ornament in the dining-room were the arabesques; and, in the salon, Gérôme, the neo-classical artist, had put the final touch to a work which clearly bore his mark. Prince Napoleon also asked Rossigneux to reconstitute a Pompeian table-centre from exhibits at the Pompeian Museum at Naples. This *surtout*, the work of the goldsmith Charles Christofle, was flanked, at dinner-parties, by statuettes of the Muses Melpomene and Thalia, to which the sculptor Barre, with typical Second Empire vulgarity, had given the features of Rachel (once the Prince's mistress) and the actress Mme Arnould-Plessy.

Prince Napoleon had also commissioned Jules Diéterle to design a dessert service. Diéterle was famous for his stage designs, and he was sometime artistic director of the porcelain factory at Sèvres; his design was executed by Christofle. Plon-Plon enjoyed the company of artists, and he wanted to create an artistic movement, which his cousin seemed unable to sustain. But despite his enthusiasm, and despite the work of artists and archaeologists, the neo-Pompeian and neo-Greek did not prove to be a durable fashion.[24]

Since the Revolution of 1848, the art of the goldsmith and silversmith had become much more industrialised. The material of their work was vulgarised so that every bourgeois might preside over an impressive table. Charles Christofle (1805–63) used the electroplating processes which had been invented by Elkington in England, and acquired for France by the Comte de Ruolz-Montchal. This pseudo-silver allowed the bourgeoisie to make lavish use of silver plate. As Claretie recorded in 1867: 'Plated metal has taken the place of bronze, just as silver plate has deposed silver. This explains the apparent luxury you see everywhere.'[25] Napoleon III commissioned Christofle to make a service of twelve hundred pieces, in *ruolz*, for the Tuileries. The task kept his workroom busy for three years.

The industrialists of the time thought only of producing the model which would bring them most reward; Christofle concentrated on artistic quality. The history of his work is that of the goldsmiths' work of the Second Empire. To modern eyes, his work is extravagant; but, to the Second Empire, good design and opulence were synonymous. The word simplicity was unknown to the architect Baltard, who designed the Prince Imperial's cradle. It was unknown to the Fannière brothers when they designed 'La Trirème': the Emperor's offering to de Lesseps at the opening of the Suez Canal.[26] Whether one looks at tea-tables or mantelpieces, wallpapers or bathroom fittings, there is the same flamboyance, the same disregard for line and colour.

One notable record of the taste of the Second Empire was the imperial train presented to the Emperor and Empress by the Compagnie du Chemin de fer d'Orléans. The six carriages were built in five months under the supervision of M. Polonceau, the company's chief engineer. Viollet-le-Duc designed the decorations.

The outside of the four main carriages was painted in garnet red and ultramarine, set off with little columns, bands and cornices in gilded bronze; some of the panels bore the imperial arms and the Emperor's cipher. The *wagon d'honneur* was surmounted by an imperial crown, supported by eagles, also in gilded bronze, and lanterns hung at each of the four corners. The *wagon d'honneur* was hung inside with bright green damask silk; and the furniture, of heavily carved rosewood, was upholstered in the same material. On the ceiling were a series of star-shaped caissons with gilt mouldings, enclosing patterns of imperial crowns and ciphers, and sprigs of laurel, and surrounded by wreaths of roses. The imperial bedroom was hung with garnet velvet up to the ogees, and with bright blue velvet above; there were door curtains of the same material, lined with white gros de Naples and fringed with gold. The beds were made of carved ebony. All four coaches were thickly carpeted, and lit by lamps of gilded bronze.

Their Imperial Majesties first travelled in their train in June 1856, when they went to Bayonne. 'MM. les Administrateurs accompanied Their Majesties, and M. Polonceau drove the train. Their Majesties the Emperor and Empress deigned to express their great satisfaction.'[27] Yet perhaps there was some truth in Gustave Claudin's observation: the nineteenth century produced no artists because it had created the railways.[28]

13 The World of M. Worth

When, in 1898, Octave Uzanne wrote his massive study, *Fashion in Paris*, he made his opinion clear. 'With the Second Empire we reach the most hideous period in female dress that has ever vexed the artistic eye.'[1]

Alas, there was much evidence to support Uzanne's opinion. Women's fashions, like architecture and interior decoration, like the eating habits of the time, reflected an inescapable social fact: the Second Empire was an age of opulence rather than taste. The industrial era had come, with its factories, its mass-production, and, above all, its creation of a new moneyed class. The *nouveaux riches* were more intent on quantity than quality; they were anxious to display their wealth. They were encouraged by the Court of the Tuileries, which showed its *parvenu* nature by its reckless insistence on splendour; and never had a Court displayed such frivolity and extravagance. At Court, and in society, and in the *demi-monde*, there was an extraordinary disregard of real values, a feverish need to be amused, a desperate search for novelty and excitement. Fashion reflected this vulgar, prosperous and febrile world.

'*Cocottes* and *cocodettes* together inaugurated a reign of ugliness, of huckstering, of moral corruption, and vulgarity. Never, all through the century,' wrote Uzanne, 'were beauty, and grace, and elegance so openly defied . . . Anyone who will glance at the pictures and engravings of that period, will note the frightful crinolines that swell every woman into a prop for yards of unnecessary stuff, the wide and ugly half sleeves, the high boots brought in by that senseless admiration for the calf of the human leg which affected a whole generation of Frenchwomen, the wild-looking heads of hair, on which tiny velvet caps, or bonnets with flying strings, were perched, without a chance of covering them, the hideousness of the materials in vogue, the screaming vulgarity of the colours.'[2]

Cockchafer brown and sun yellow were among the smartest colours at the beginning of the Second Empire. But the colours which were favoured during the régime were – like so much about it – strangely crude. 'How,' asked Uzanne, 'can such overwhelming violets, such cruel pinks, such glaring greens, such shabby cockchafer browns, such dirty greys, such blinding yellows, ever have left the dyer's hands? But all these cheap oleograph tints were received with acclamation, and reds of every kind, *solferino, marengo, sang de boeuf*, and so forth, enough to drive all the bulls in Andalusia into madness, were constantly invented, and greedily purchased.'[3] Colours reflected the politics of the Second Empire: the Emperor's marriage to the daughter of the Count and Countess of Teba (later Montijo) started a vogue for a tint called Teba. The victories of the Italian campaign inspired the colours magenta and solferino; the Chinese expedition of 1860 suggested the colours Shang-Haï and Pékin. In 1867, Amédée Achard reported: 'It is a whirlwind of . . . cherry-red and purple, water-green and emerald green, azure blue and Sèvres blue. Ribbons flutter, jet is streaming, taffeta is shivering. The great battle of the dresses is beginning.'[4] Giafferri, in his study of women's fashions, maintained that emerald was the jewel and the colour of the Second Empire.[5]

During the first years of the reign, fashions did not differ much from those of 1850. Skirts grew even fuller. 'Bodies were made *à la vierge, à la Pompadour*, and *à la Watteau* – these last trimmed in a very graceful manner with lace, flowers, velvet, ribbons, ruches and butterfly bows.'[6] Court etiquette had restored embroidery to its old importance on civic dress and military uniform, and Defontaine, in his study of dignitaries' uniforms, says that 'there was no decree to establish the uniforms of the Imperial Household, and the functionaries who composed it were free to have their uniforms embroidered more or less thickly – *according to their passion for splendour*.'[7] Women's dresses also made abundant use of embroidery, but again quantity mattered more than quality. Lace, however, had never been more in favour than it was between 1830 and 1860, and black lace was particularly fashionable.

'For full dress, many ladies wore pink or blue watered-silk gowns, with basques trimmed with fringes, lace, or white feathers. Waists had grown a little shorter, but, on the whole, feminine costume was still elegant enough. The bonnets, small velvet caps, or straw hats, were in excellent keeping with the general effect of the dress, which was neither overfull nor overtrimmed. The tendency was to a gradual return, either to the fashions of the Consulate, or to the paniers of Louis XVI's time, when, during the second period of Napoleon III's reign, to the great astonishment of French ladies, . . . the hideous crinoline made its appearance.'[8]

It was in fact in 1853 that the crinoline began to be accepted, and it became more or less obligatory; the simplest taffeta dress needed no fewer than seventeen yards of material. The capture of the Malakoff in the Crimean War inspired the invention of a vast skirt called a malakoff. Presumably the name was meant to suggest that the wearer defended her approaches as fiercely as the Russians had defended their fortress. But this clearly defined determination did not prevent surprises. 'More than one malakoff was,' we learn, 'damaged, if not captured.'[9]

At Court, the problems were multiplied, for a skirt had to be long as well as wide. At Tuileries receptions, it was almost a necessity to wear a train four yards long. A woman could hardly get into her carriage when she went to the palace, and her husband

LEFT *The Empress Eugénie, who was introduced to the fashion-designer Worth by the Princess Metternich,* RIGHT *'the best-dressed monkey in Paris'.*

had to sit on the box outside. More than one woman must have followed the example of the Duchesse de Dino: in the days of Louis-Philippe, she had knelt on the carriage floor, with her dress ballooning on the seats.

Giafferri said that the crinoline was a stigma on the age; Octave Uzanne described it as a 'diseased fashion'. The most eloquent comment came from the Queen of Madagascar, to whom the Empress sent two crinolines, the creation of Worth. 'The Queen of Madagascar sent for the French Ambassador who had brought them, in order to thank him. When he arrived, he found Her Majesty waiting under a tree, barefooted, but attired in the magnificent red velvet, while above her in the tree hung a crinoline, as a red cashmere canopy.'[10]

The crinoline reached its largest proportions in about 1859, and lasted for another eight years. In 1867 it was shortened, under the influence of Worth, and in 1868 it disappeared. That year, in a manual of good behaviour, the Comtesse Dash suggested that the best way to be elegant was to show 'the skilful simplicity which would crush

MODES.

NOUVEAUTÉS pour COLS de la FABRIQUE du PHÉNIX.

Seule Maison ayant obtenu la Mention honorable à l'Exposition de Londres.

two million francs' worth of diamonds . . . Redeem your fortune by your simplicity,'
so she advised. 'Do not show the ostentation of parvenues . . . Do you think that your
splendour is worth the sigh of some poor creature who will never know it?'[11] But few
of *le tout Paris* adopted this *code du savoir-vivre*. If the crinoline had disappeared, the
demi-crinoline became the rage; dresses were still worn over small hoops, and they
were still a mass of draperies, ruchings and trimmings. These were the fashions which
the Empress was obliged to accept, and she did not create any others. Eugénie imposed
no distinctive style of her own.

At the time of the Imperial wedding (1853), the fashionable couturiers were Palmyre
and Mlle Vignon. Palmyre made the twenty ball and evening dresses for Eugénie's
trousseau, and Mlle Vignon made the thirty-two dressing-gowns and day dresses. But,
ironically enough, it was an Englishman who dictated Paris fashion during the Second
Empire.

Charles Frederick Worth had been born in 1826, at Bourne, in Lincolnshire.[12]
His father was a solicitor who had gambled away his money, and, at the age of eleven,
young Worth had been obliged to leave school and to earn his living. His charm and
poise and gift of conversation in later years would hardly have suggested that he had
been practically self-taught.

At the age of thirteen, he found himself a cashier in a London firm; he later worked
in several shops, including Swan & Edgar's, in Piccadilly. He spent his leisure in
museums and art galleries, and, before he was twenty, he left for Paris. He could not

238

speak a word of French, and he had a hundred and seventeen francs in his pocket. He went to work at Gagelin's, a silk mercer's in the rue de Richelieu, and there he began to revolutionise fashion. At Gagelin's he met the young *demoiselle de magasin* (the word mannequin was not then in current use) who became his wife. He designed his first dresses for her; and they were so successful that he was allowed to prepare a few model dresses and cloaks. Gagelin's soon let him install a dressmaking department, and foreign buyers came to inspect his creations and place their orders. During the reign of Louis-Philippe, Worth severed his connection with Gagelin, and set up his home and his shop on the first floor of No. 7, rue de la Paix. Someone later said that the street owed him such a debt that he, and not Napoleon, should have had his statue on top of the Colonne Vendôme.

Worth revolutionised not only the fashion in clothes, but the materials of which the clothes were made, and the processes by which the materials were manufactured. He tried to improve the quality of the fabrics themselves, to revive old materials and create new ones. As his son observed: in 1858 the only available satin was 'a kind of lustrine used to line candy boxes and cover buttons . . . The only materials in current use were faille, moire, velvet, grosgrain, terry velvet, and taffeta.'[13] Worth was also concerned in developing new trimmings, or *passementerie*, and in resurrecting old patterns in lace and embroidery. 'My father,' remembered Jean-Philippe Worth, 'first took up the cause of *passementerie* when he created escalloped and pleated flounces, ruches, roulletes, to add variety to his early Gagelin models. One of the first trimmings he used was jet . . . It held its decorative own for fifty years.'

Worth did not only give new life to the *passementerie* industry. 'Lace, which soon became one of the strong competitors of jet, at first received the same cold reception . . . However, my father persuaded certain of his customers . . . to permit him to use their priceless heirlooms, and the result . . . vanquished all opposition. When the supply of real lace ran out, as it soon did, he brought imitation lace . . . to the rescue. And again through my father's efforts was another industry, that of lace making, resuscitated and made prosperous.'[14]

The reign of Louis-Philippe had not been remarkable for the splendour of its fashions; but the Second Empire brought with it many official receptions, where only the most magnificent dresses were admissible. The Second Empire brought with it Princess Mathilde, Princess Metternich, and the ladies of the Tuileries. In 1859 the Empress bought her first Worth dress. With some persuasion from her husband (for she thought the material was like a curtain) she bought a dress of Lyons brocade. It was beige, and the flower design which was woven in the fabric had been taken from a rare Chinese shawl. Thanks to this imperial gesture, Lyons silk became a household word, and Jean-Philippe Worth recorded that 'when my father persuaded the Empress to wear the dress "like a curtain" he automatically increased the looms in operation in Lyons from 57,000 to 120,000.' Eugénie's passion for artificial flowers not only helped the silk-workers in Lyons, but the paper-makers of Angoulême and the jaconet-makers of Alsace.[15]

239

Eugénie was not the most daring or inspiring of Worth's clients. In about 1867, he decided that the crinoline was becoming absurd, and he invented a dress with a gored skirt. Eugénie was too timid to launch it. Someone else had to try it, before she bought a dress in the same style. 'Her Majesty,' wrote Jean-Philippe Worth, 'not only never initiated a fashion, but she was exceedingly reluctant to adopt new ideas, even after they were on the road to popularity. She also clung passionately to her likes and dislikes. When she became attached to a trimming, she wanted it on all her dresses. When she liked a certain colour or design, she never wanted to supplant it with something new.'[16]

A more demanding client was young Mme Octave Feuillet, the novelist's wife. One evening she and her husband were invited to dinner at the Tuileries. The dress she had ordered from some or other couturier had arrived the previous day, so dowager in style that she could not wear it. On the morning of the Imperial dinner, before the shops were open, she arrived at the rue de la Paix. Worth received her in his *robe de chambre*, and promised her a dress for that evening. Then he escorted her to his wife's room, where Mme Worth, who was still in bed, wanted to give advice.

While the two women were talking together, 'M. Worth leant against one of the bedposts, dreaming of the wonderful work which he was about to undertake. He soon told us about his plans,' so Mme Feuillet remembered, 'and we entirely approved of them. He wanted a dress of lilac silk, covered with puffs of tulle of the same shade, in which he would set sprays of lilies-of-the-valley. A veil of white tulle would be cast like a cloud over the puffs and flowers. Finally there would be a belt with floating ends, like the reins of the chariot of Venus . . .'[17]

That evening, at the Tuileries, Worth's latest achievement earned the delighted compliments of the Empress; and when, soon afterwards, Mme Feuillet was asked to the famous fancy-dress ball at the Hôtel d'Albe, she promptly ordered a Spanish costume from Worth. It was conjured up, a flamboyant creation of red and blue satin, 'covered with gold and silver lace, brilliant spangles, and fringes which fell like golden rain on the poppy-coloured bodice.'[18]

The former assistant at Swan & Edgar's had become the dictator of Paris fashion, and a suitably aesthetic figure. 'Oft-recorded Worth' had his unfailing sources of inspiration. 'When this truly great man is composing,' noted Felix Whitehurst, 'he reclines on a sofa, and one of the young ladies of the establishment plays Verdi to him. He composes chiefly in the evenings, and says that the rays of the setting sun gild his conceptions.'[19]

Sumptuous, extravagant, with a touch of grand opera, his conceptions matched *la vie parisienne*. Dedicated work, and inspiration, brought success, and success brought social significance. In 1868, Joseph Primoli, a nephew of Princess Mathilde, recorded a visit to the rue de la Paix.

'I have been with mother to Worth's. He is the great couturier in fashion. He charges sixteen hundred francs for a simple little costume! Ladies arrange to meet at Worth's, and they talk politics there as they sip tea. At Worth's, the faubourg Saint-Germain sits between two kept women, and the world of officialdom meets the faubourg

Saint-Germain. Perhaps M. Worth does not even realise what he is doing, but . . . he is reconciling all political parties, and mingling all social classes. An artistically rumpled bit of fabric has achieved what wit has been unable to contrive.

'And so M. Worth gives delightful matinées. I don't only mean on his first floor in the rue de la Paix, where all the young men look like embassy attachés with their English accents, curled hair, pearl tie-pins and turquoise rings . . . ; I don't only mean the apartment which exhales some atmosphere of degraded aristocracy, some heady fragrance of elegance, wealth, and forbidden fruit . . . Besides this apartment, I may add, M. Worth has a country house at Suresnes, and the noble faubourg aspires to the honour of being received there. This villa, it appears, is full of marvels of every kind. People go there in *séries*, as they do to Compiègne . . .'[20]

During the Second Empire, the rue de la Paix reached its utmost splendour.

'Every Friday,' remembered Jean-Philippe Worth, 'great ladies drove through it on the way to the Bois in gowns elaborate enough for ball dresses, gowns which were trimmed with miles of Valenciennes. They rode in open carriages, with footmen in powdered wigs and satin breeches. Mme Musard appeared in particularly fine specimens of the carriage-maker's art. These were always lined with white satin and drawn by the most magnificent horses procurable . . . And her jewels were equal in magnificence to her horses. They were in sets, as was the fashion, and every Friday she would send her emeralds or rubies to our workshop to be sewn on her bodices as trimming.'[21]

'I should not give it as my fixed opinion that Paris was a religious city. No, the men believe in the Bourse, and the women in Worth.'[22] So wrote an English journalist in April 1870: only a few months before the Empire fell. His witticism contained much truth. The religion of money, as Théophile Gautier observed, was the only one which had no unbelievers; and Worth, the king of fashion, kept his throne long after Napoleon III had been deposed.

Though Worth dictated Second Empire fashion, even he had had to defer to the idiosyncracies of the age. One of his more eccentric customers was a Mme Erazu: indeed, she almost symbolised the feckless extravagance of the time. Every Friday Worth sent her one, two, or three new dresses for the Opéra, and every Tuesday he sent her one for the Théâtre des Italiens. One day she confessed that she had made a religious vow never to wear silk again, but always to wear brown wool. Worth did not fail her. He had fabrics woven for her, so that she might keep her vow to Notre Dame du Mont Carmel.

If Mme Erazu was eccentric, society in general showed the opulence of the *nouveaux riches*. Women's clothes were no longer made to enhance their beauty, but to display their wealth. The materials which were used for full dress were very beautiful: velvet, silk and satin vied in richness with one another. But one wonders why, because the fabrics were completely hidden by the trimmings. Three or four trimmings were not enough for a single dress; when it had lace and garlands of flowers, ribbons and frills,

Madame Moitessier,
painted by Ingres in 1856.

'. . . they put a jewel in the centre of every bow. They sprinkled the garlands of flowers with precious stones. One saw, for example, a maize yellow crêpe dress embroidered in silver, starred with gold, garlanded with poppies and diamond ears of corn . . . And then it was that woman was able to satisfy one of her vanities: she could display a dress not just because it was beautiful, but because it was expensive, too.'[23]

Posterity may see these fashions as a sign of philistinism, and of social irresponsibility. Women's clothes disguised their wearers' figures beyond recognition; they revealed the unreality of social life. Like certain contemporary poets and novelists, who wrote about ancient or exotic worlds, women revealed the general need to escape reality.

In 1864, the Emperor and Empress gave a banquet and reception for the future Emperor and Empress of Mexico. 'I'm not going to say "What elegance!"' wrote a journalist in *La Presse*. 'I say: "What opulence!" Women do not dress, they dress up . . . The profusion of false hair has been followed by the profusion of jewels . . . Women are no longer content to wear one necklace, they wear three or four. Every woman to-day is a tempest. She cannot enter or leave a room without knocking over everything in her path; and, whenever she takes a step, it sounds like rain or hail, according to the stuff her dress is made of.'[24]

*The Duchesse de Morny: one of the beauties of Society,
seen through the rose-coloured glass of Winterhalter.*

Gustave Claudin saw women's fashions with the eye of a crabbed bachelor. 'The great couturiers of Paris are really only skilful magicians, who possess to the highest degree the art of anticipating every depravity.'[25] Felix Whitehurst smiled at some of the more striking innovations. At the first imperial ball of 1866, he noted:

'Short waists, *crêpé* hair, brocaded trains which would have gladdened the hearts of our grandmothers, over skirts which took up so much room that there was one perpetual rending of garments, splendid jewels, and perhaps just a little more than a suspicion of rouge and false ringlets – such were the outward and visible signs of the ball. Of course I cannot speak of individuals, yet I may say that the Empress was beautifully dressed in white trimmed with ivy; and the Rimsky-Korsakoff had a bird of paradise in her hair, a dress trimmed with feathers of the same, and looked quite fit to fly away home with that bird . . .'[26]

Soon afterwards, Baron Haussmann gave a ball at the Hôtel de Ville where the ostentation was even greater. 'As for the dresses,' wrote Whitehurst, '– impossible! I see now, in my mind's eye, a Polish princess in white tulle, dressed *en soufflé*, with a robe of black velvet reaching three of my paces . . . ; round her waist a girdle of gold, studded with emeralds any one of which would have raised a regiment in her country.'[27] The following year, at the ball at the Hôtel de Ville, 'the great event of the evening was the dress of Mme Rimsky-Korsakoff, the train of which took up standing room for about ten men.'[28] In 1868, Whitehurst reported that 'the last new thing in dress is a *puff petticoat*, which sticks out in a bunch, and causes the female form divine to look rather like the Gnathodon or the Dodo.'[29]

But we must be fair. The imperial Court did not just impose a general extravagance. André Blum, in his study of nineteenth-century fashion, records that it also encouraged the wearing of practical clothes in the country and at the seaside: cloaks, jackets, pilot-coats and boating-jackets, and, especially, short skirts, which made women less encumbered in their movements.[30] In November 1857, discussing the *séries* at Compiègne, Mme Baroche observed: 'This year, the women at Court have adopted a completely English fashion: a checkered woollen skirt which reveals the ankles, a Louis XIII hat, ... and patent boots with heels. This costume has the disadvantage of demanding well-shaped legs and pretty feet. However, it is spruce and smart, casual, convenient, and more suitable than anything else for walks in the woods.'[31] Mme de Metternich noted, at Biarritz, in 1859, that the Empress dressed with extreme simplicity. She wore 'a black silk skirt, with a shorter hemline all round. This had become the fashion, thanks to her, because the Empress had the good sense to dispense with trailing dresses in the country . . . With the short skirt she wore a simple red flannel blouse, held in at the waist by a black belt with a buckle.'[32]

Eugénie (an accomplished horsewoman) also showed her practical sense by wearing a white piqué riding-habit when, one summer, she reviewed some of her husband's troops.

The Second Empire was the age for elegant women riders. The *amazones* caracoled in the Bois in riding-habits of white piqué, cloth or alpaca; and this somewhat masculine

Amazone, *by Constantin Guys.*

dress later inspired the tailored costumes of the Third Republic. In the meanwhile, Parisian women indulged in less sober fashions.

'Do not the words "astrakhan and braiding" bring the whole period of the Second Empire before your eyes?' continued Uzanne, at the end of the century. 'Do you not see again, in memory, Gagelin's long narrow fashion plates, with ladies' figures, full face, back, and profile, displaying long wraps, overloaded with cords and openwork, and braids, and tasseled girdles, and heavy military-looking embroideries of every kind, and with huge facings of black astrakhan – the very acme, it was claimed, of comfort and of smartness!'[33]

Smart women sometimes enhanced their suits with frogging, epaulettes and shoulder-knots, like the grenadiers of the Imperial Guard. They even carried swagger-sticks. 'All they need is a busby,' said a critic in 1864. 'That will come next year.'[34] Which in fact it did.

The ceremonials and festivities of the Second Empire brought the jewellers un-
paralleled prosperity. On his marriage in 1853, the Emperor had some of the Crown
diamonds re-set in more modern style. He ordered an imperial crown; the Fannière
brothers designed the eagles for it, and it promised to be beautiful. But it was not
finished, because for political reasons the Coronation itself was abandoned. All that
existed of the crown was the diamond-studded cross made to surmount it. In 1887,
long after the fall of the Empire, this cross was separately sold, among the uncatalogued
items, at the sale of the Crown diamonds. The design of this crown is the same as that
of the crown which appears beside the Empress in the Winterhalter portrait.[35]

But while the Crown itself was not made, the jewels of the previous reign seem
modest beside the cascade of precious stones displayed at the Tuileries and at
Compiègne. The first years of the Second Empire brought tiaras into fashion.
Lemonnier, and Oscar Massin, created diamond bouquets and foliage which might
be compared with the finest work of the eighteenth century. The very photographs of
Massin's jewelled flowers and ears of corn, the sprays of eglantine and lilies-of-the-valley,
seem to shine with an iridescent light. The jewelled lilac-blossom which was bought by
the Empress, and shown at the Exhibition of 1867, is a triumph of the jeweller's art.
So are the generous shoulder-knots which were made for her by Bapst in 1863. The
Second Empire saw collections of jewels which were worthy of the Arabian Nights.

LEFT *A reliquary brooch made by Bapst in 1855, for Eugénie, and* RIGHT *the Empress in her robes of state.
A detail from a Gobelins tapestry after the painting by Winterhalter.*

In 1904, when the effects of Princess Mathilde were sold, one item fetched nearly half a million francs: the seven-string pearl necklace, composed of 384 pearls, which had been Napoleon's wedding-present to her mother. The sale catalogue also included 70 brooches, 59 bracelets, and 20 pairs of earrings, not to mention tiaras, combs, belt buckles and necklaces. At imperial and ministerial balls in the Second Empire, there had been a virtual battle of diamonds; at one fancy-dress ball in 1860, Mlle Erazu came 'completely enveloped in the light of her rubies', while Mme Jurawicz appeared as the Queen of Sheba, 'with at least a thousand precious stones flashing and shining'.[36]

Here, as elsewhere, the Second Empire showed its passion for the excessive. In the second half of the reign, there was a vogue for long earrings; these grew progressively longer until they reached the shoulder. These earrings were not only ridiculous in size (they were sometimes six inches long); in the last five years of the reign, they were also bizarre in design. Some of them represented hens brooding over eggs, others were in the shape of stable lanterns, wheelbarrows, windmills, panniers, scales, and watering-cans.

The Second Empire saw the triumph of the bracelet, and often several bracelets were worn together. Some women wore tartan dresses, and enamelled brooches and bracelets to match. When the French Court came to share the English love of racing, *le bijou sportif* made its appearance, and, when the first Grand Prix de Paris was run, men and women wore cravat-pins, cuff-links, chains and medallions, and jewels of every kind, representing horse-shoes, bits, nails, and spurs and stirrups. *Le bijou hippique* came into its own.

The jewellers who had shone at the Court of Louis-Philippe did not easily abandon their conceptions, but they had to sacrifice to the whims of fashion. They created jewellery in the English, Byzantine, Egyptian, Greek, and even the French styles. The Campana Collection, acquired by the Louvre in 1861, had an immediate effect on jewellery. Even before the collection was officially on view, the jewellers were under its charm and they were making a new fashion of it. One of the masters in the Greek and Etruscan style was Fontenay; he worked in filigree and light gold, and among his most remarkable creations was a pair of earrings in the Etruscan style, each containing a tiny bust in lapis-lazuli. A photograph of the Emperor's mistress, La Castiglione, dressed as the Queen of Sheba, shows her ostentatious parade of the current fashion.

All the elegant women of the time had jewels by Lemonnier, Massin or Fontenay, while less well-to-do women contented themselves with electro-plated imitations by Alexandre Gueyton, or with replicas by Savart: he produced jewels which could be mistaken for expensive gems. 'Artificial diamonds, turquoises and pearls are a common thing in high society,' reported Prosper Ménière in 1858. 'Quite recently, a great lady died, and her diamonds were valued at 500,000 francs. The estimate showed that they were worth 35,000 francs at the most.' And Ménière added a cautionary tale in his journal. 'A gentleman who was about to marry a rich heiress wanted to re-set a set of sapphires. It was proved that eighteen out of the twenty stones were fakes, and the marriage was therefore broken off.'[37] It was a sad comment on social values.

But appearance remained all that mattered to Parisian society; and Zola recorded this love of show in his novels of Second Empire life. During her love-affair with Maxime, Renée, the heroine of *La Curée*, indulged in the boldest, most fantastic dress.

'The season was a long triumph for her. Never had she been more daring or more imaginative in her hair-styles and clothes. It was then that she ventured to wear the famous dress of thicket-coloured satin, on which a whole deer-stalking was embroidered, complete with its accessories: powder-flasks, hunting horns, broad-bladed knives. It was then, too, that she brought classical hair-styles into fashion; Maxime had to go and draw them for her at the Musée Campana, which had just been opened . . .

'One of their great expeditions was when they went skating; skating was in fashion that winter, since the Emperor had been among the first to try the ice on the lake in the Bois de Boulogne. Renée ordered a complete polonaise costume in fur-trimmed velvet.'[38]

Dresses cost twelve hundred francs, hats cost a hundred and twenty. The life of luxury not only fostered the love of pleasure, it encouraged immorality. Women needed to have rich protectors. 'Few of them care about mental pursuits,' wrote an English observer. 'Ornamentation and decoration is the *ne plus ultra* of a Frenchwoman's life.' The ornamentation and decoration continued.

'Heads of the fashionable tints – yellow, tomato-red, mahogany, and every other impossible exaggeration of the true Venetian blonde – were crowned with hats and bonnets dubbed Trianon, Lamballe, Watteau, or Marie-Antoinette. Oh, those appalling tumbled heads!' remembered Uzanne. 'They may indeed, as the smart *lorettes* declared, have possessed a *sacré chien*, but, looking at them across the intervening years, we are fain to murmur: "Quelle dégringolade, mon Empereur!"

'Those untidy locks straying wildly about, mingled with false hair of every kind, burnt with acids, ruined with hot tongs, dried up with ammonia, those dead-looking tresses that drooped in curls, or looped in chignons, beneath those extraordinary hats and bonnets, were the most untempting sight man ever gazed upon. No other decadent epoch has offered more unlovely specimens of the wigmaker's art.'[39]

Félix was considered to be the supreme hairdresser of the age; Leroy dressed the Empress's hair. Both set examples which society followed. At one moment, chignons were small, and women wore vast hats; then enormous chignons came into fashion, and hats became Lilliputian. The Empress set a fashion for gold-dust on the hair, and for ringlets reaching to the shoulders. Cora Pearl, the *grande cocotte*, set a fashion for red hair and even pink hair, and some of the *demi-monde* had their poodles dyed pink to match their chignons. 'The smart ladies of that period really looked like monkeys,' wrote Uzanne, 'with their strange contortions and eager cunning faces; and the men, in their morning jackets and light trousers, with their Tyrolean hats and peacocks' feathers, were just as unlovely objects, worthy to bear them company . . . The *cocodès* and *petits crevés*, who had replaced the *Daims*, the *Lions* and *Gants jaunes*, were a pitiful race, weakly, unhealthy, smeared with pomades and scents, feeble of speech, and utterly absurd.'[40]

RIGHT Haute couture *of the 1860s, designed by Charles Frederick Worth.*
OVERLEAF Souper aux Tuileries, *from the painting by Henri Baron, 1867.*

H. BARON

However, pomades and scents, cosmetics and medicinal preparations were advertised by careful copy-writers. In the *Guide Général dans Paris pour 1855*, designed for visitors to the Exhibition, Mignot of the rue Vivienne advertised Crème des Barbades, 'which has the incontestable power of removing freckles permanently'. Women were also urged to try Eau des fleurs de lys; this not only made freckles disappear, 'it postponed wrinkles, whitened and softened the skin, and gave it a radiance which neither sun nor air could tarnish.'[41]

No doubt society tried such products; certainly they continued to dress with theatrical ostentation. At a gala performance in 1867, Princess Metternich entered her box, wearing pink tulle covered with jewels. She was preceded by two lackeys; they bore an immense silver candelabrum holding ten lighted candles. In 1869, at the Beauvais ball, the Duchesse de Mouchy wore nearly two million francs' worth of diamonds.

High society could afford to dress with magnificence. But Princess Caroline Murat, the niece of Princess Mathilde, remembered that 'the ostentation in dress and jewellery and the general rivalry in display weighed heavily upon those whose means were limited, and an invitation to a special Court function often came as a calamity . . . One of the lady guests at the first *séries* was heard to say, "I have been invited to Compiègne, and have had to sell a flour mill to meet the expense." '[42]

Journal des Tailleurs.

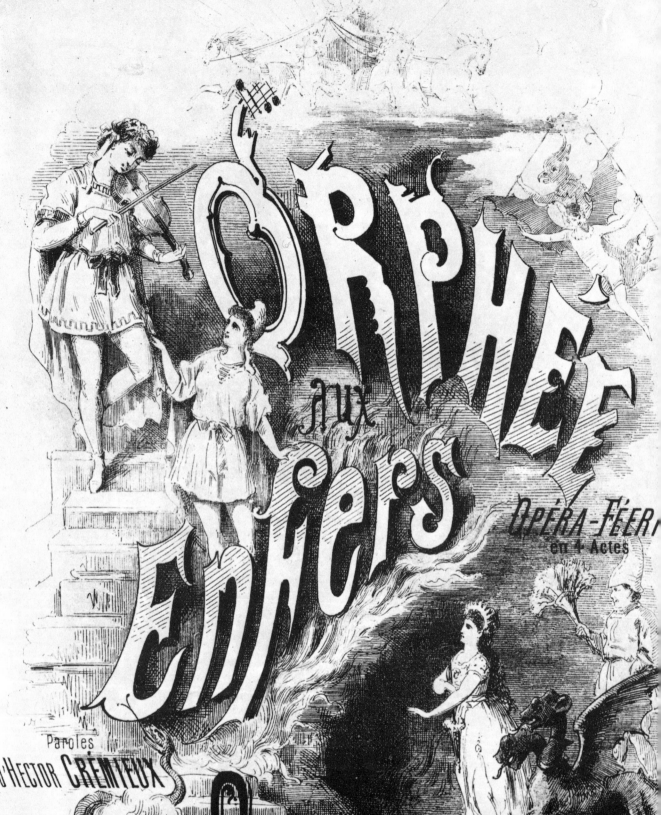

ORPHÉE aux ENFERS

OPÉRA-FÉERI
en 4 Actes

Paroles
d'HECTOR CRÉMIEUX

Musique de
J. OFFENBACH

14 Notes de Musique

In the mid-nineteenth century, Paris became the centre of musical Europe; but this was the result of chance rather than national interest. The greatest French composer at this time was Hector Berlioz, who introduced the Romantic spirit into French music.[1]

Berlioz had been born in 1803, the son of a doctor; the family had lived in the neighbourhood of La Côte-Saint-André, in the Isère, for centuries. When he was about twelve, he began to compose; his father found a music teacher for him, but he had decided that the boy was to be a doctor, like himself. In 1821, Berlioz duly went to Paris to study medicine. There was never any doubt of his true vocation, and three years later he dropped all pretence of a medical career.

One of his earliest compositions was his opera, *Les Francs-Juges*. Only the overture remains. In 1827 came an event which was to shape his life: an English company gave a Shakespearean season at the Odéon. Berlioz saw their first production, *Hamlet*, and he fell in love with Harriet Smithson, who was playing Ophelia. Soon afterwards he went to see *Romeo and Juliet*; the theme matured in his imagination, and years later it inspired one of his most typical works. In the meantime he was tortured by his passion for Harriet, and one result of his emotional crisis was the conception of *La Symphonie fantastique*.

Berlioz conferred many benefits on music, and the first of them was to give France some great symphonic works. The *Symphonie fantastique* was followed, in 1834, by the triumphant symphony, *Harold en Italie*. But applause was not enough; in 1833 Berlioz had married Harriet, and he now had responsibilities. He was still unable to earn his living by composition, and he was forced to turn to journalism and to be music critic on *Le Journal des Débats*. However, *Benvenuto Cellini* was finished in 1837, and that year his *Messe des Morts* set the seal on his reputation in Paris. His *Roméo et Juliette* was brilliantly produced at the Conservatoire in 1839.

In the summer of 1852, on the eve of the Second Empire, he had already written enough to establish himself as a great composer. But, as Adolphe Boschot has said, 'by

A music cover for Offenbach's Orphée aux Enfers.

255

some cruel irony he failed as a musician of genius, and succeeded as a skilful chronicler; his *Damnation de Faust* did not find a publisher, but his collection of whims and fancies, his *Soirées de l'orchestre*, found a buyer.'[2] Berlioz saw the new régime as an occasion for music; he prepared for a commissioned work, he solicited the honour, but no commission was given to him.

Late in July 1854, he finished his pastoral oratorio, *L'Enfance du Christ*. After the vast frescoes of the *Te Deum* and the *Messe des morts* he painted some delicate pictures for a missal.

On 10 December, *L'Enfance du Christ* won acclaim at its first performance. One of those who heard it was Dr Prosper Ménière. Berlioz, he wrote, 'has many more admirers in England and Germany than he has in Paris . . . His new work is of a very lofty order. There is skilful orchestration, there are delightful tunes, there is something great, impassioned and tender about it all.'[3]

On 30 April 1855, in the Église Saint-Eustache, Berlioz conducted his *Te Deum*, to mark the opening of the International Exhibition. Nine hundred performers took part, and he wrote triumphantly to Liszt: 'It was colossal, Babylonian, Ninivite.' In 1856, he was accepted by the Institut ('it is,' he declared, 'a coup-d'état in the empire of the arts'). But such official recognition did not bring him the particular success for which he longed. In April 1858 he finished his opera *Les Troyens*; but he could not get it performed. He approached the Emperor and Empress, Prince Napoléon, the Opéra, and the Ministère des Beaux-Arts, but he gained nothing except good wishes and dilatory promises. He struggled against the complexities of his private life (his marriage to Harriet had been a failure), he struggled against official indifference, and against the

Two composers in Second Empire Paris: Charles-François Gounod LEFT, *and Hector Berlioz.*

encroachments of ill-health. In 1862, when he prepared to conduct the first performance of his *Béatrice et Bénédict*, he was in such pain that he became indifferent to success. On 4 November 1863, after five years of postponement, *Les Troyens* was at last performed at the Théâtre-Lyrique. Since it would have taken five hours to perform in its entirety, Léon Carvalho only presented the second part. 'A wonderful success,' wrote Berlioz. 'The public were profoundly moved, they wept, and they applauded endlessly.' Bizet went repeatedly to applaud the masterpiece. Meyerbeer, too, was present night after night, 'for my pleasure,' he said, 'and my education.' Corot became a devotee, knew the score by heart and sang it at his easel. *Les Troyens* earned Berlioz fifty thousand francs, and it enabled him to resign his labours as a critic.

But if the élite showed their appreciation of the opera, it did not fill the theatre with admirers; and no-one from the official world troubled to attend a performance. Berlioz had no illusions about the state of Parisian musical culture. 'Everything is dead,' he said, 'save the authority of fools.' In 1864 he entered his sixty-second year. His music was hardly played anywhere and authority did nothing for him.

On 7 March 1866, at a popular concert, Pasdeloup boldly played the *septuor* from *Les Troyens*. Berlioz was anxious to see how his work would be received. He slipped into the Cirque Napoléon. The *septuor* was acclaimed and encored, and the applauding audience finally recognised the composer. They were moved to see this old man, who seemed a ghost from the past, a man who was overwhelmed by his triumph.

In 1868, they performed his work again at a Pasdeloup concert; Théophile Gautier, stirred by his old Romantic loyalty, confessed himself to be an admirer.

'They played *Roméo et Juliette*, not the whole symphony, but just "the ball at the Capulets'". What a wonderful and profoundly Shakespearian piece! . . . This great symphonic extract was warmly applauded; as one listened to it, one wondered how it was that a composer of Berlioz' power is hardly ever performed in France . . . How many works he could have produced, if the better part of his life had not been spent in obscure struggles, in futile tasks, in vain expectations! Certainly he has done enough to prove his genius . . . What a pity that he cannot come back to life in fifty years' time; he would see his works, now disdained in France, . . . figuring in classical concerts.'[4]

Such acclaim was heartfelt, but it came too late. Berlioz died on 8 March 1869.

Charles-François Gounod was a lesser but more popular composer. Born in Paris in 1818, he inherited music from his mother, who was a notable pianist. He studied at the Conservatoire, and won the Prix de Rome. In Rome he discovered his particular interest in church music, and, on his return to Paris, he became an organist and briefly considered entering the priesthood. His Solemn Mass, first performed in London in 1851, brought him the publicity which every composer needs. He was then thirty-four. On 28 November 1865, Anthony North Peat recorded: 'So great was the anxiety of the public to hear Gounod's Mass that as early as 10 o'clock this morning every available spot in the magnificent church of St Eustache was filled by a dense crowd, who patiently waited fully two hours before the first notes of the organ were heard.'[5]

A few months after the first performance of the Mass, the opera *Sappho* was produced in Paris. In 1858 *Le Médecin malgré lui*, a comic work based on Molière's play, was performed at the Théâtre-Lyrique. It was Gounod's first success in the theatre. But the work which was to bring him real fame was *Faust*, which appeared in 1859. Its stage-skill and flowing melody have made it one of the most popular operas ever written. Gounod also wrote other operas, a symphony or two, and a number of oratorios. The oratorios were especially popular in England. Gounod went there at the time of the Franco-Prussian War, and stayed there until 1875. He had a lyric gift, a dramatic gift, and a gift of very pleasant orchestration; in fact he had all the 'popular' qualities.

So had Léo Delibes, who was born in 1836. His mother was the daughter of Batiste, once the baritone of the Opéra-Comique. His uncle was Édouard Batiste, the organist at Saint-Eustache, who became professor at the Paris Conservatoire. After the death of Delibes *père*, Léo was brought to Paris, where his uncle helped him to enter the Conservatoire. In 1853, when Delibes was seventeen, Adolphe Adam, who taught him composition, had him appointed organist at Saint-Pierre de Chaillot and accompanist at the Théâtre-Lyrique.

The latter appointment brought Delibes into touch with some famous composers of the time. He was not attracted by pure music, but he was undoubtedly drawn to the theatre; and in 1856 his first work was heard at the Folies-Nouvelles: his music for a sketch called *Deux sous de charbon*. Delibes was now launched, and he was to write fourteen operettas in fourteen years, and a further two in collaboration. Most of them were performed at Offenbach's little theatre, the Bouffes-Parisiens, for Offenbach had recognised his gifts. It was Offenbach who arranged for him to write an operetta, *Les Eaux d'Ems*, in 1861.

The era of operettas was not over for Delibes, but more serious productions were now to alternate with his farces. On 15 August 1865, his cantata *Alger* was performed at the Opéra in honour of *la fête de l'Empereur*. It had been written at the request of Émile Perrin, director of the Opéra; and it was, again, at his request that Delibes composed part of a two-act ballet, *La Source*. But it was in the final days of the Second Empire, in *Coppélia*, that he revealed his stature. A two-act ballet based on a tale by Hoffmann, it was first performed at the Opéra on 2 May 1870. It was well received by the public and it remains high in favour today.

Georges Bizet, two years younger than Delibes, was born in 1838. It was a long time before he won recognition as an opera composer. He reached the height of his powers at the zenith of the Second Empire, when the Opéra was a conservative sort of club for the upper classes, and wanted no new forms of entertainment. Léon Carvalho commissioned him to write *Les Pêcheurs de Perles* for the Théâtre-Lyrique in 1863. It was an audacious move, and Carvalho made it on the strength of the state subsidy which he was not due to receive until the following year. However, on 20 September *Les Pêcheurs de Perles* had its first performance, and Berlioz declared in *Le Journal des Débats* that 'M. Bizet will have to be recognised as a composer in spite of his rare talent as a pianist.'

LEFT *Georges Bizet, the composer of* Les Pêcheurs de Perles, *and* RIGHT *Léo Delibes, who composed music for* Coppélia.

Despite the praise of Berlioz, *Les Pêcheurs de Perles* remained a comparative failure, and Bizet was obliged to earn his living as an accompanist. Gounod was seriously concerned about Bizet's despondency. He introduced him to the *salon* of Princess Mathilde, where he could broaden his social life, and profit from his gifts as a pianist.

In 1867, Bizet launched his new opera, *La Jolie Fille de Perth*. Gautier reviewed it kindly.

'M. Bizet belongs to the new school of music, and he has broken with . . . all the old formulas. He follows the melody right through the situation, and he does not cut it up into little themes which are easy to catch and hum as you come out of the theatre. Richard Wagner must be his favourite master, and we congratulate him on that. His aversion to straightforward music . . . may earn him the reproach that he lacks melody; but he will easily console himself. Melody does not consist of waltzes and popular songs. It merges with harmony, as drawing does with colour . . . M. Bizet's instrumentation is . . . full of ingenious combinations, new sonorities and unforeseen effects.'[6]

Gautier was generous, but *La Jolie Fille de Perth* had a mixed reception, and it was withdrawn after twenty-one performances.

Bizet's *Djamileh* was produced in 1872, after the Second Empire had fallen. He also wrote some incidental music for Daudet's *L'Arlésienne*. His *Carmen* was a setting of a libretto taken from the story by Mérimée. Its success was not immediate, and he died in 1875, a month or two after its first performance. It is now the most popular of all his works.

One pre-eminent name of the period is that of César Franck. Born in Liége in 1822, the son of a Belgian bank official, he entered the Paris Conservatoire in 1837. After his marriage in 1848, he established the routine to which he kept for the rest of his life. He gave lessons in order to earn his living. He composed his music between five and seven o'clock each morning, in the evenings, and during his annual holiday. His way of life was arduous; and when, in 1853, he finished his opera *Le Valet de Ferme*, he had a breakdown which made him unable to compose. Some time later, he was appointed organist at Saint-Jean-Saint-François-au-Marais. A magnificent new organ – 'an orchestra' he called it – had been installed there.

Franck worked happily, and in 1858 the urge for composition returned to him. He then became organist at Sainte-Clotilde, a position which he kept until his death. The organ was even larger than the 'orchestra' at Saint-Jean-Saint-François. He composed music for it; and if the general public failed to appreciate his extemporisation, the organ loft became a holy of holies, every Sunday, for his pupils and admirers. From 1860–62 he composed his famous *Six Pièces*. In 1865 he wrote an oratorio *La Tour de Babel*; in 1869 he embarked on his life's ambition and began to compose *Les Béatitudes*. Franck became a naturalised Frenchman in 1873. He lived on until 1890; he brought French music a new solidity, and a mystical feeling.

Another composer with a strong religious sense was Camille Saint-Saëns. He was little more than three when, in 1838, he composed his first work for the piano. When he was eighteen, his Symphony in E Flat was performed in Paris, and Gounod told him that he had 'contracted the obligation to become a great master'. Before he was twenty, Saint-Saëns' life had fallen into the pattern which it was to follow for sixty years. He spent his time between composition and giving virtuoso concerts to increase his modest stipend as the organist of Saint-Merry. In 1856, the year of his twenty-first birthday, he wrote his first big choral work, the *Messe*, and Liszt proclaimed: 'It is like a magnificent Gothic cathedral in which Bach himself would not disdain to conduct the orchestra.' Not long afterwards, Saint-Saëns succeeded Lefebure-Wély as organist at the Madeleine; it was a coveted position, and it brought him a handsome salary and prestige. 'High Mass at the Madeleine was an important social event where the congregation resembled a gala night audience at the Opéra. Saint-Saëns took up his appointment on 7 December 1857, and only laid it down nineteen years later.'

In 1859, he composed his First Violin Concerto in A major. That year he also wrote his Second Symphony in A minor; it was first performed in 1860, under a conductor who was one of the pioneers of symphonic music in France. This was Jules Pasdeloup, the founder of the Concerts populaires. To the same period belongs Saint-Saëns' First Piano Concerto in D major. Berlioz was on the jury which awarded Saint-Saëns the prize for musical composition at the time of the Exhibition in 1867. Yet, as Saint-Saëns' biographer writes, ' . . . although Saint-Saëns had been awarded the prize for his *Noces de Prométhée*, as the cantata was called, the authorities seemed oddly reluctant to have it performed. Musical life under the Second Empire was quite as plot-ridden as the political world, and since Berlioz' enemies had control of artistic affairs at the Exhibition, they certainly did not intend to help his protégé any further. By putting off performance they were able to avoid paying out the five thousand francs cash prize, and

LEFT *César Franck at the organ, and* RIGHT *Camille Saint-Saëns.*

Saint-Saëns was met with excuses that the delicate nature of his work would be lost in the gigantic Hall of Industry. At this stage a remarkable development took place. For a reason which is unknown, Rossini unexpectedly made a private call on the Emperor and persuaded him to accept his own work, the *Hymne à Napoléon III*, which was chosen for the ceremony in place of Saint-Saëns' cantata . . . On 1 July it was performed by twelve hundred executants.'[7]

Musical life was indeed plot-ridden; and no event had proved this more clearly than the first performance of *Tannhäuser* in Paris. This *première*, in 1861, was one of the *causes célèbres* of the Second Empire.

The Comtesse Tascher de la Pagerie recalled the famous evening.

'Love well sung was not,' she wrote, 'enough for M. Wagner; and so his operas are inspired by the Wartburg, Lohengrin, the Phantom-Ship, and other products of an extraordinary imagination. To try and make them cross the frontier, and to produce them in France, in a country so fond of clarity, was an impossible task. What happened, then?

'Madame de Metternich, one of the people passionately fond of this new music, intrigued so much and to such effect that Comte Walewski authorised M. Wagner to have his *Tannhäuser* performed at the Grand Opéra in Paris . . .

'One might have foreseen the fate of *Tannhäuser*; however, the whole of Paris wanted to attend the first performance.

'It began. The overture has some genuine beauty, and it was applauded; but once the opera was launched, no-one could understand it . . . The composer's friends went wild, and tried to ensure success by the loudness of their applause. People shouted and whistled. Mme de Metternich stood up and leant out of her box and applauded ostentatiously . . . Thenceforth, the opera was doomed, and, despite the reputation of M. Wagner, and the efforts of the singers, it ended in fiasco . . .

'At the second performance, the opera was booed. At the third, it was shameful for our own Académie Impériale de Musique to see such a scandal, and such an inhospitable reception given to a foreign artist . . .'[8]

Wagner had failed because of the conservative tastes of Parisians, because he was Germanic and alien, and because Mme de Metternich had attempted to impose him on the public. Mérimée found *Tannhäuser* 'a colossal bore. Some say,' he wrote, 'that M. Wagner has been sent to force us to admire Berlioz. Actually it was monstrous. I feel I could write something like it tomorrow, if my cat inspired me by walking over the piano. It was an enormous fiasco.' Gounod thought differently: 'God grant me a failure like that!'[9]

Soon after the *première*, Baudelaire published his article *Richard Wagner et* TANN-HÄUSER *à Paris*. 'To those who live far away from Paris, . . . the unexpected fate of *Tannhäuser* must seem like an enigma . . . Let us confess the main reason at once: Wagner's opera is a *serious work*, which demands concentrated attention.'[10]

The Second Empire had not always resisted musical progress. One happy innovation was the establishment of the Pasdeloup Concerts. What Cherubini had done for an élite through the Société des Concerts, Jules Pasdeloup determined to do for the general public. In 1861, he made arrangements with the owner of the Cirque du boulevard des Filles-de-Calvaire, and announced eight popular concerts of classical music. Tickets cost 3 francs, 2 francs 50, 1 franc 25, and 75 centimes. The first concert took place on 27 October. The success exceeded all expectation, and the eight concerts had to be followed by a further series of eight. The last took place on 13 April 1862.

Since then, wrote a critic in 1867, 'M. Pasdeloup has continued his concerts every year, during the winter season. They are given every Sunday, and at the same price. Only the music of the masters is played there: Beethoven, Mozart, Haydn, Weber, Meyerbeer, Mendelssohn, etc. The attendance is always enormous, and the success is growing. The *Popular Concerts* have become a Parisian habit.'[11]

The supreme composer of Second Empire Paris was Berlioz; and he, alas, was not appreciated in his lifetime. Yet, in some ways, Berlioz belonged to an earlier age: he was a great Romantic, living on in an era which scorned Romantic values. He was too profound for an epoch which concentrated largely on pleasure. Long before Delibes wrote the music for *Coppélia*, Paris had revelled in the waltzes of Olivier Métra

The popular concerts organised by Pasdeloup in 1861 became a feature of musical life in Paris.

(1839–89), and in those of Waldteufel and Strauss. It revelled, above all, in the work of Offenbach. The *opéra bouffe*, it has been said, was the one original art form bequeathed to posterity by the Second Empire; it corresponded to the Parisians' taste for farce and to their indifference to good music. Second Empire music is really summarised in the unappreciated grandeur of Berlioz and the triumphant frivolity of Offenbach: of this German composer who expressed the spirit of *la vie parisienne*.

On 20 June 1819, a son was born to the wife of Isaac Juda Eberst, a cantor at the synagogue in Cologne. Eberst was a native of the town of Offenbach-am-Main, and he had come to be known as Der Offenbacher – the man from Offenbach. His son was to make the name his own, and make it celebrated ever after. [12]

An immortal triumvirate: Jacques Offenbach CENTRE *with his librettists Ludovic Halévy* LEFT, *and* RIGHT *Henri Meilhac.*

Offenbach was by birth a German Jew, but he soon came to consider himself a Frenchman. Isaac Eberst was well aware of the anti-Semitism in Cologne. He felt that Paris offered more opportunities for his son who, even in his childhood, showed remarkable promise as a cellist. Late in 1833, when the boy was fourteen, Eberst took him to Paris. Cherubini, the director of the Conservatoire, recognised him as a prodigy, and accepted him as a pupil.

After a year as a cello student, Offenbach left the Conservatoire, and played in various theatre orchestras. For years he repressed his aspirations to write music for the stage; but he established himself as a virtuoso, and he already showed his capacity for relentless work, his ingenuity and his uncommon skill. He already exerted the power of his personality. 'People had an intimation that there was more in him than a mere cello virtuoso. What excited people about him was that he seemed a messenger from another, stranger world . . . His audience felt that there was something daemonic about him, a feeling that was accentuated by that curious glitter in his eye.'[13]

It has been said that his success lasted exactly as long as the Second Empire. It was, in fact, in 1850, when Louis-Napoleon was President of the Republic, that Arsène Houssaye, the director of the Théâtre-Français, asked Offenbach to conduct his

A music sheet for La Grande Duchesse de Gérolstein.

LA GRANDE DUCHESSE

de GEROLSTEIN

Opéra Bouffe en 3 Actes et 4 Tableaux.

Paroles de
Henri MEILHAC et Ludovic HALÉVY.

Musique de
J. Offenbach

Partition Piano et Chant

Arrangée
par Léon ROQUES.

Paris
G. BRANDUS & S. DUFOUR
103, Rue Richelieu.

France et Etranger

Imp Thierry frères Paris

orchestra. He offered him the modest salary of six thousand francs a year. As Offenbach remembered: 'I stayed at the Théâtre-Français for five years. It was then that the idea came to me of starting a musical theatre myself, because of the continued impossibility of getting my work produced by anybody else. I said to myself that the Opéra-Comique was no longer the home of comic opera, and that the idea of really gay, cheerful, witty music – in short, the idea of music with life in it, was gradually being forgotten. I felt sure that there was something that could be done by the young musicians who, like myself, were being kept waiting in idleness.'[14]

In 1855, just before the opening of the International Exhibition, someone mentioned to him that there was a little theatre vacant near the Palace of Industry. It would certainly draw the crowds while the Exhibition was on. Offenbach immediately applied for the licence. The opening of the Bouffes-Parisiens, as the theatre would now be called, was announced for 5 July. There was little time for preparation. Offenbach was obliged to turn to an unknown author for his libretti. As it happened, his name was Ludovic Halévy. There could not have been a more fortunate choice.

The Bouffes-Parisiens opened with *Les Deux Aveugles*, a one-act sketch about two supposedly blind beggars. It was a wild success. The tiny theatre – 'the chocolate box' some called it – became the rage, and Offenbach's career had begun in earnest. Luck continued to be with him. He had not only found his own theatre, and the ideal librettist. In the midst of all the Exhibition festivities a young girl arrived in Paris in search of fame.

Hortense Schneider was twenty-two, the daughter of a German master-tailor who had settled in Bordeaux, married a French wife and succumbed to drink. At the age of three, Hortense was already singing songs; at the age of twelve she had threatened to kill herself unless she were allowed to go on the stage. In the end, she had her own way, studied singing for several years, and joined a small provincial troupe. She now arrived in Paris, and immediately went to see Offenbach. Offenbach engaged her at two hundred francs a month.

Hortense Schneider made her début at the Bouffes in *Le Violoneux*, a sentimental piece based on a Breton legend. She was praised by *Le Figaro* for her grace and polish, and Offenbach's music was praised for its wit and feeling. Two months after the Bouffes was founded, it had become a recognised institution.

Yet though Offenbach's operettas played to full houses, his theatre did not prosper, because he was a bad businessman. He had lavish tastes, and it never occurred to him to economise. It soon became clear that only a resounding triumph would save him, and in 1858 he set all his hopes on the new operetta, *Orphée aux Enfers*, which he was composing. The sets were designed by Cambon, the costumes by Bertall and by Gustave Doré; Offenbach himself even worked at his operetta in the hotel bedrooms where he had to stay to escape his creditors.

The first performance of *Orphée aux Enfers* took place on 21 October 1858. It was not the success that he needed. Then, a few weeks later, a thunderbolt fell. It was hurled by Jules Janin, the critic, from his Olympus, *Le Journal des Débats*. *Orphée aux Enfers*, he

'None in grace and beauty's charms with our Grand Duchess can compare.'
Hortense Schneider as la Grande Duchesse de Gérolstein.

said, was a profanation of sacred antiquity. All Paris became convinced that mighty issues were at stake, and everyone felt it incumbent on him to see *Orphée* and to judge for himself.

Henceforward *Orphée aux Enfers* was performed to a full house every night. Offenbach was saved. As a critic wrote: 'When everyone finds what they want in a work, the general public and the connoisseur, there is no longer any doubt of its value. Jacques Offenbach is modern. His music is *daemonic*, like the century we live in – the century which rushes on, full steam ahead.'[15]

The music of *Orphée aux Enfers* set Paris dancing. The *voltigeurs* marched to it, and its waltzes and gallops became the rage, from the Tuileries to the smallest suburban taverns. After the 228th performance, the cast were so exhausted that the operetta had to be taken off. However, in April 1860, it was staged again at a gala evening at the Italian Opera. The Emperor had consented to be present on condition that it was on the programme.

Offenbach had found his first librettist, Ludovic Halévy. In 1860 he happened to come across an old schoolfriend, Henri Meilhac. Meilhac was a boulevardier with an eye for situations and a limitless ability to turn them into plays. Henceforward, he and Halévy were collaborators.

The profits from *Orphée aux Enfers* had enabled Offenbach to build himself a summer house at Étretat, which was then in fashion. The Villa d'Orphée, as it was called, became a meeting-place for his friends. The operetta also brought official recognition of all kinds. In 1860 he became a naturalised Frenchman. The following year he was awarded the Légion-d'honneur. But Offenbach was far from content. He wanted to write an even more successful operetta. Halévy wanted to write about Greek mythology, this time with Meilhac. The three of them agreed on the subject of Helen of Troy. *La Belle Hélène* was first performed at the Variétés on 17 December 1864.

La Belle Hélène reflected the contemporary régime without mercy. In fact it was shown up so pitilessly that its early end appeared inevitable. *Orphée aux Enfers* had contained no hint about the future, but, in *La Belle Hélène*, the revels are accompanied by a presentiment of doom. *La Belle Hélène* became the talk of Paris. 'La Belle Hélène,' wrote the critic Jules Lemaître, 'was one of the favourite diversions of an age which was, alas, very frivolous, but was also one of the most peaceful, lively, amusing and brilliant ages in our history.'[16]

On 24 June 1866, Halévy recorded: 'The Palais-Royal will take *La Vie Parisienne*.' Offenbach's latest operetta presented a series of characters in modern, cosmopolitan Paris; it gave a picture of the social turmoil. The first performance took place on 31 October 1866. Its reception exceeded even Offenbach's expectations. But Offenbach gave the age what it wanted. He understood its feverish tempo, its reckless love of pleasure, its brilliance and its immorality. He satirised the peacock Court of Napoleon III, and the vulgar love of money which was typical of the Second Empire. He was perfectly in tune with imperial Paris, and, as long as the Empire lasted, his triumph was assured. As if the success of *La Vie Parisienne* was not enough, the new year brought

RIGHT *La Discorde: a costume designed by Alfred Albert for the ballet* Coppélia, *1870.* OVERLEAF La Musique aux Tuileries, *by Édouard Manet, 1862.*

La Discorde.
Mlle Marquet.

Alf Albert
1870

yet another triumph. On 1 April 1867, in the midst of a political crisis over Luxembourg, Napoleon III opened the new International Exhibition in Paris. Most of the sovereigns of Europe, their heirs and ministers, would come to visit it. On 12 April, the curtain rose at the Variétés on the first act of *La Grande Duchesse de Gérolstein*.

'*La Grande Duchesse* was a great success,' recorded Halévy. 'Four operettas in two-and-a-half years, all of them successful . . . *La Belle Hélène* performed nearly three hundred times, . . . *La Vie Parisienne* nearly two hundred, and now *La Grande Duchesse*, which will be, if not the most fruitful, at least the longest and the most resounding of our successes. For this is where luck comes in, and politics come to our aid, and M. de Bismarck is working to double our takings. This time we are laughing at war, and war is at our gates, and the Luxembourg crisis comes just in time to give the spice of topicality to our play.'[17] Ernest Vizetelly, an English resident in Paris, remembered: '*La Grande Duchesse* was essentially a satire on the petty German states which Prussia had been annexing or mediatising since her victory over Austria at Sadowa. There is a story that Bismarck, in Paris that year, remarked to a high French personage: "We are getting rid of the Gérolsteins, there will soon be none left. I am indebted to your Parisian artistes for showing the world how ridiculous they were." '[18]

Once again Offenbach caught the mood of the moment. Gustave Claudin recorded: 'The Czar of Russia, on his way to the Exhibition, sent a telegram from Cologne to book two stage-boxes at the Variétés. On the evening he reached Paris, he greeted the Emperor of the French and went with his sons, the Grand Dukes, to hear *La Grande Duchesse*.'[19] Schneider's most conspicuous admirer was, however, the Viceroy of Egypt; during the six weeks he spent in Paris he patronised the Variétés forty times.

After *La Grande Duchesse de Gérolstein*, the form and content of Offenbach's operettas changed. He began to drop contemporary satire, and sought to approach the comic opera form. In 1868 *La Périchole* had shown the way in which he was going. *La Princesse de Trébizonde*, produced at Baden in 1869, resembled it in style. In it he plunged into a fantasy world. Offenbach was to write other works, including *Les Contes Fantastiques d'Hoffmann*, before his death in 1880; but in 1870, when the Second Empire fell, his world really ended.

Hortense Schneider.

LEFT *A music cover for a* La Vie Parisienne *quadrille, by Charles Marriott.*

Epilogue

In the winter of 1869 to 1870, remembered Albert Verly, there was a break in the social life which had been so hectic for the past fifteen years. It seemed almost like a premonition of the doom to come. 'People had a sort of intuition of the end, of disasters which were as yet unknown. An indefinable unease reigned almost everywhere.'[1] The general unease was also observed by the new American Minister, Mr Washburne, who had arrived in Paris in 1869. He was aware of a still more profound and widespread unrest.

'In Paris, during the last years of the Empire, . . . there were certain appearances of prosperity, happiness and content; but they were like the fruit of the Dead Sea, and to the last degree deceptive. Beneath all the outside show there was to be heard rumbling popular discontent. The people were dissatisfied, restless and uneasy. They considered that their rights and liberties had been trampled upon, and their discontent was often made manifest in Paris by their turbulent gatherings on the Boulevards . . . Night after night large numbers would be arrested as rioters and revolutionists, and locked up in the prison of Mazas, or sent to the casemates of Fort Bicêtre.'[2]

In November 1869, Washburne was invited to one of the last *séries* at Compiègne. 'As the Emperor spoke English quite fluently, I had,' he wrote, 'much conversation with him, particularly as to the state of things then existing in France. He expressed his regret that the French people were not better fitted for more liberal institutions and for the concessions which he desired to make to them. The great trouble with the French, he said, was that they always looked to the government for everything, instead of depending on themselves. In their estimation, the ruler was responsible for everything.'[3]

North Peat had made the same observation five years earlier. 'A Frenchman is, more or less, born to be rode roughshod over, and he himself is positively happier when ruled with a rod of iron.'[4] Du Camp, in his survey of Paris, went somewhat deeper:

'The Parisian, like Diogenes, is looking for a man, not to study this rare curiosity, but to admire him, and if necessary, obey him. In time of danger, . . . he reposes all his hopes, all his destiny, in a man; he chooses him, he imagines him according to his desires and not according to reality, then he sets the burden on his shoulders. If the improvised hero bows beneath the weight, he is accused of treachery.'[5]

The Emperor himself maintained that public opinion always won the final victory. 'Lead the ideas of your country, and they follow you and support you. March behind them, and they drag you after them. March against them, and they overthrow you.'[6] He had determined that he would yield to the growing demand for liberty by granting it while he could of his own free will; and, on 8 May 1870, a liberalised constitution for the Empire was approved in a plebiscite by an overwhelming vote of more than seventy million. It was a noble and original experiment, and it might have succeeded if the Franco-Prussian War had not destroyed it in its infancy.

On 21 May, in the great Salle des États at the Louvre, Napoleon III was presented with the result of the plebiscite; and the programme which he announced, that day, to the assembled dignitaries of France, remains an unexceptionable document. To posterity, which knows that it was not to be fulfilled, it is deeply touching.

'We must,' he said, 'have but one object in view. To rally the honest men of all parties round the Constitution which has just been sanctioned by the country; to insure public security; to calm party passions; to preserve social interests from the contagion of false doctrines; to inquire, with the aid of all intellects, into the means of increasing the greatness and prosperity of France; to diffuse education everywhere; to simplify the administrative machinery; to carry activity from the centre, where it superabounds, to the extremities, where it is wanting; to introduce into our codes of law . . . the improvements justified by time; to multiply the general agencies of production and wealth; to promote agriculture and the development of public works; and, lastly, to consecrate our labour to this problem, constantly solved and constantly presenting itself anew – to find the best mode of distributing the burdens which press upon the taxpayers. Such is our programme. In realising it, our nation . . . will advance the progress of civilisation.'

And then, wrote an English journalist, 'His Majesty bowed, and there arose such a cheer as certainly is seldom heard in Paris . . . It was a brief ceremony, but it was one I shall never forget.'[7]

Almost at the same moment, Miss Bicknell, the former governess to the Tascher de la Pageries, bade farewell to the palace of the Tuileries. 'I left the palace,' she recalled, 'with sorrowful forebodings – a sort of threatening cloud seemed to hang over it, nay, over Paris itself. As I saw Paris recede in the distance on the day of my departure, I thought of the doomed cities in Scripture . . . The next time that I stood before the palace of the Tuileries, it was in ruins.'[8]

In 1872, in a melancholy album of photographs, *Paris incendié*, an observer surveyed 'the apartments of the Empress and the Prince Imperial, destroyed by fire and blackened by petroleum. The grand entrance of the Pavillon de l'Horloge is nothing, now,' he wrote, 'but a heap of ruins. The ceiling of the Salle des Maréchaux has fallen in, and the room is just an enormous gulf.'[9]

The sacking of the Tuileries seems a final comment on the Paris of the Second Empire;

The ruins of the Tuileries, 1871. The shell of the imperial apartments.

and yet, perhaps, there is more to be said. Imperial Paris was not only the symbol of a discredited régime, of unhappy *folie de grandeur*. It was not only, in Zola's words, the décor 'of a dead reign, of a strange epoch of folly and shame.' It had, for some eighteen years, been the capital of Continental Europe.

It had been the home of some of the greatest figures in French literature. If Hugo had been exiled, and chosen to remain in exile, Baudelaire had taken Paris as his inspiration, and Verlaine had written poems in Haussmann's Hôtel de Ville. Leconte de Lisle had presided over his Parnassian *salon* in the boulevard des Invalides, and Gérard de Nerval had wandered round the Paris streets, with the manuscript of *Aurélia* in his pocket. Flaubert had come to Paris, to enjoy the popularity which he had earned with his *Madame Bovary* and *Salammbô*; the Goncourts had based their novels on experiences of Paris life, and they had recorded the imperial city in all its splendour and its squalor, all its vividness and diversity, in their *Journal*. Taine and Renan had worked in Paris, and given new, disturbing directions to thought. Gautier had proved himself a poet and a novelist, and made criticism itself a work of art. Sainte-Beuve, his friend and contemporary, had given criticism intellectual depth in his literary *causeries*, his *Lundis*. If the Second Empire Press had suffered from political censorship, it had also been a forum for remarkable writing; and, under the dynamic influence of Girardin, the popular Press had been firmly established.

The Second Empire had been a notable age for the theatre: the age of Ponsard and Augier, the age of Dumas *fils* and Sardou. During the Second Empire, Rachel had given her last performance, and Sarah Bernhardt had given her first. *Coppélia* had been added to the repertoire of ballet. Berlioz was still composing, Bizet, Saint-Saëns and Gounod were beginning their careers; the Pasdeloup concerts were spreading a taste for classical music, and popular music had come into its own, in a Paris which applauded Strauss, encouraged Waldteufel, and took Offenbach to its heart.

Ingres and Delacroix were still painting during the Second Empire, Millet was recording his hieratic peasants, Courbet and Manet were shaking the critics with their realism; and, in the work of Monet and Renoir, Impressionism, though not christened, was already born. In his high-relief, *La Danse*, on the new Opéra, and in his imperial portrait sculptures, Carpeaux showed himself to be the pre-eminent sculptor of the age; he caught its fever and its outward grandeur. Garnier, the architect of the Opéra itself, symbolised again, in a single work, the tinsel glory of *la fête impériale*. Haussmann, *le Grand Préfet*, transformed the whole capital beyond recognition.

Many achievements of the Second Empire lie beyond the scope of this study. During the Second Empire, Victor Duruy (1811–94) reformed French education.[10] He introduced secondary education for the twenty-four million Frenchmen occupied in agriculture and the thirteen million in industry and commerce.

'As for those who . . . are called to move in the first rank of society, let us,' he wrote, 'assure them, with literature and science, with philosophy and history, the widest and the most fruitful culture of the mind. Let us strengthen the intellectual aristocracy in the midst of a people who want no other aristocracy . . . Let us raise the moral level of the bourgeoisie by a vigorous secondary classical education, and by a higher education, which we must shake out of its lethargy and its weakness.'[11]

In the years of Duruy's ministry (1862–9), much was achieved, but the achievement was most important for the movement it began, and the direction which it set.

While Duruy revolutionised the educational system, medicine and science made significant progress. Jean-Martin Charcot (1825–93) transformed la Salpêtrière, the geriatric hospital for women, into one of the leading research centres of the world; he emerged as the creator of modern neurology.[12] Claude Bernard (1813–78) threw light on the cause of diabetes, and proved himself one of the great physiologists of the century.[13] During the Second Empire, Jean-Henri Fabre was studying insect life, and Urbain-Jean-Joseph Leverrier, who had deduced the existence of the planet Neptune, was directing the Paris Observatory. During the Second Empire, the ubiquitous Nadar founded the Société d'encouragement de la locomotion aérienne; he remains a legendary figure in the history of the conquest of the air.

One figure still bestrides the world of Second Empire science like a colossus. It is that of Louis Pasteur (1822–95).[14] In 1857 he published a paper on fermentation, which marked the beginning of scientific microbiology. That year, he was appointed director of scientific studies at the École normale supérieure. Despite his title and prestige, he still had few facilities for work: he was forced to convert two attics into a laboratory, and equip them with money from the family budget; only later was he allowed to move his laboratory into a little building designed for it by the school architect. This building was so cramped that he had to improvise an incubator under the stairs. But here he kept all the flasks he used to prove his theory of germs: to show that there was no such thing as 'spontaneous generation'. These experiments helped him to establish the science of bacteriology.

The achievements were magnificent, and they were manifest; but there still remained much to criticise in Second Empire Paris. The first cause for criticism was the irresponsibility of the age. 'The society of the Second Empire is absolutely different from those which preceded it,' wrote the Vicomte de Beaumont-Vassy in 1860. 'They say that grave diseases need drastic cures. The remedy for our society would be to suppress half their way of life.'[15] 'All hail, noble races of the future!' wrote Gastineau in 1863. 'God preserve you from our pettiness, our physical and moral ugliness, our nothingness!'[16] Maxime du Camp deplored the superficial nature of the Parisian; and, when he ended his survey of nineteenth-century Paris, he drew some sharp but not unfair conclusions. The Parisians, he wrote, '. . . do not reason, they feel; they do not discuss, they are carried away: they do not act, they flutter about. Paris is a nervous aggregation, governed by impressions, in short it lacks character . . . Efforts have been made in vain, tentatives have remained sterile. Drawn by the weight of its tradition, Paris has always fallen back again to the level of recklessness where it is happy.'[17]

Among the large majority of Parisians, there was clearly no concern for graver issues; true patriotism was forgotten in the search for *la gloire*, political problems were tossed aside, social injustice was blatant, and it was frequently ignored. While Napoleon III determined to better the condition of the working classes, the Empress could still spend fifteen hundred francs on a dress, while a laundress earned two francs a day. There was a chasm between poor and rich. There was also an unbridgeable chasm between the deserving and the undeserving. Daumier could not earn his living when he turned to serious painting. Millet sometimes knew starvation. Gautier, at the height of his renown, could not afford to stop his journalism. Yet when Cora Pearl made her brief appearance as Cupid in *Orphée aux Enfers*, the soles of her shoes were one mass of diamonds.

Imperial Paris was not a place for the unhappy or the unsuccessful. Those who could not stand the febrile pace of living turned, all too often, to the Left Bank cafés and brasseries. The Bohemian world was full of social misfits, of would-be writers and artists who had fallen by the way. Second Empire Paris was a place for the *parvenu* and the *nouveau riche*. It was a place for the dynamic, the resolute and versatile, for the *arriviste* and the unscrupulous. It was a place for those who remained undisturbed by graver issues, and could afford to live a life of pleasure.

For them it was a perfect place, at an incomparable time. A woman could be dressed by Worth, and spend her day in indulgent preparation for her carriage drive in the Bois,

The end of the Second Empire: the Imperial Family in exile in England.

her *souper intime* at the Maison d'Or. A man might linger at the Jockey Club, smoke his cigar at the Café Riche, dine at Magny's and pay court (if he could afford the cost) to one of the great demi-mondaines of the age.

And here, it seems we reach a symbol of Second Empire Paris. For we remember the place, at this time, not so much for its contribution to art and letters, to music and to scholarship, to medicine and science. We remember it for its glitter and its *joie de vivre*. When we think of Imperial Paris, we recall the Cent-Gardes lining the staircase at the Tuileries, the chamberlains in scarlet coats, the prefects of the palace in wine-red, and the Grand Master of Ceremonies in violet; we recall a Winterhalter world dancing to the music of Strauss, and refreshing themselves with truffles and champagne. We remember the fancy-dress balls, and La Castiglione dressed as Salammbô, and Princess Mathilde unhappily disguised as a Nubian. We remember the *séries* at Compiègne, and Pasteur's frogs escaping from their boxes, and Baron Haussmann, at the breakfast table, giving Mrs Moulton a slice of the Bois de Boulogne. We remember the table-turning, and M. Worth, still in his dressing-gown, urgently devising some new creation for an imperial dinner-party that evening.

There remains much to criticise in those 'eighteen years of luxury, pleasure, recklessness and gaiety, . . . those poor years of corruption.' And yet, as the Comte de Maugny said, who could recall them and not repress a feeling of pleasure? Only in Second Empire Paris could one drive down a brand-new boulevard by Haussmann to attend the *première* of *La Vie Parisienne*. Paris has never been more Parisian than it was in the days of Napoleon III.

Notes

The following abbreviations have been used:

GJ Goncourt *Journal*   JO *Le Journal officiel*   MU *Le Moniteur universel*   La P *La Presse*

1 THE IMPERIAL FAMILY

Napoleon III

1 Joanna Richardson: *Princess Mathilde*, 8
2 Ibid: 19
3 Ibid: 24
4 Princess Caroline Murat: *My Memoirs*, 108
5 Richardson: op. cit., 69
6 E. Crane (ed.): *The Memoirs of Dr Thomas W. Evans*, I, 40 – 1
7 Dr E. Barthez: *The Empress Eugénie and her circle*, 240–3
8 For the Emperor's theories, *see* F. A. Simpson: *The Rise of Louis Napoleon*; and *Louis-Napoleon and the Recovery of France*
9 G. P. Gooch: *The Second Empire*. Preface, v
10 Quoted by Gooch: op. cit., 33
11 Ibid.
12 A. Houssaye: *Les Confessions*, III, 71–2
13 Crane: op. cit., I, 174
14 Général Comte Fleury: *Souvenirs*, I, 201–2
15 Crane: op. cit., I, 44
16 M. du Camp: *Souvenirs d'un demi-siècle*, I, 146
17 L. Halévy: *Carnets*, I, 106
18 MU, 16 July 1870
19 Ibid.
20 L. Halévy: op. cit., I, 224
21 *The Times*, 5 September 1870
22 Ibid, 6 September 1870
23 MU, 5, 6, September 1870
24 MU, 5 September 1870; GJ, IX, 29. *See also* G. Bapst: *Histoire des joyaux de la couronne de France*
25 Quoted by Gooch: op. cit., 32
26 Ibid.
27 Ivor Guest: *Napoleon III in England*, 195

Princess Mathilde

1 For the most complete account of the Princess, *see* Joanna Richardson: op. cit.
2 GJ, VII, 183–4
3 *L'Artiste*, 1 April 1870
4 La P, 13 May 1863
5 Ibid, 24 November 1863
6 Ibid, 7 March 1864, 20 January 1866
7 Felix M. Whitehurst: *Court and Social Life in France under Napoleon III*, I, 262
8 La P, 5 November 1864

9 GJ, XI, 155
10 La P, 1 June 1864
11 Primoli Diary, 1867 (Primoli)
12 Ibid.
13 Ibid.
14 18 October 1862 (Primoli)
15 Primoli Diary: IV, 74–5 (Primoli)
16 Primoli Diary, 1869 (Primoli)

Prince Napoleon

1 For Prince Napoleon, *see*: *Le Prince Napoléon*, by Ferdinand Bac (whose father was the illegitimate son of King Jerome); *see also* F. Berthet-Leleux: *Le Vrai Prince Napoléon*
2 Berthet-Leleux: op. cit., 45–6
3 Bac: op. cit., 203
4 du Camp: op. cit., I, 184–5, 186
5 Houssaye: op. cit., IV, 163 sqq.
6 Baroche: op. cit., 141
7 Houssaye: op. cit., V, 172–3
8 Whitehurst: op. cit., I, 88, 176
9 Houssaye: op. cit., IV, 170
10 Whitehurst: op. cit., I, 91, 170
11 du Camp: op. cit., I, 179–80, 197
12 Vicomte de Beaumont-Vassy: *Histoire intime du Second Empire*, 199
13 Anna Bicknell: *Life in the Tuileries under the Second Empire*, 64–5

2 LIFE AT COURT

1 Bicknell: op. cit., 31–2
2 For a full account of Court Life under Napoleon III, *see* Jacques Boulenger: *Les Tuileries sous le Second Empire*. In *Souvenirs du Second Empire. De Notre-Dame au Zululand*, pp. 100 sqq., Albert Verly lists the various imperial households in 1870
3 Albert Verly: *Souvenirs du Second Empire. I. L'Escadron des Cent-Gardes*, passim; *L'Indépendance belge*, 10 September 1870
4 Boulenger: op. cit., 131, 142
5 Verly: *Souvenirs du Second Empire. De Notre-Dame au Zululand*, 94–5
6 Mme Carette: *Souvenirs intimes de la Cour des Tuileries*, 228–9
7 La P, 6 January 1869
8 Mme Carette: op. cit., 245
9 Bicknell: op. cit., 32–3
10 Ibid: 40
11 Ibid: 140–1
12 Ibid: 52–3
13 Ibid: 53

14 Ibid: 30, 88

15 Boulenger: op. cit., 137 sqq.

16 Murat: op. cit., 133

17 Boulenger: op. cit., 144–5, 150

18 Bicknell: op. cit., 139

19 Benson and Esher (ed.): *The Letters of Queen Victoria, 1854–1861*, 173

20 La P, 9 March, 27 April 1864

21 La P, 12 June 1867

22 MU, 11 June 1869, 22 February 1870

23 Crane: op. cit., I, 42–3

24 H. Clouzot: *Des Tuileries à Saint-Cloud*, 165, 197–8

25 Mme Octave Feuillet: *Quelques années de ma vie*, 225, 322

26 The best account is given by Boulenger: op. cit.

27 Whitehurst: op. cit., II, 23 sqq.; Général Comte Fleury: *Souvenirs*, II, 194 sqq.

28 Henri Bouchot: *Les Élégances du Second Empire*, 209, note

29 Mme Octave Feuillet: op. cit., 291, 298–9

30 L. de Hegermann Lindencrone: *In the Courts of Memory*, 96–102

31 Émile Zola: *Son Excellence Eugène Rougon*, 192–3

32 Hegermann Lindencrone: op. cit., 103–6

33 Ibid: 138

3 LA VIE PARISIENNE

1 Philibert Audebrand: *Un Café de journalistes sous Napoléon III*, 29

2 Houssaye: op. cit., V, 213

3 A. Villemot: *La Vie à Paris*, 2e série, 199–200

4 *L'Artiste*, 1 February 1860

5 *L'Artiste*, 15 February 1865

6 Whitehurst: op. cit., I, 39–40

7 Ibid: I, 285

8 Beaumont-Vassy: op. cit., 327–9

9 Baroche: op. cit., 59, 150

10 Dabot: op. cit., 120

11 Baroche: op. cit., 225

12 Whitehurst: op. cit., I, 44 sqq.

13 Anthony B. North Peat: *Gossip from Paris during the Second Empire*, I, 153 sqq.

14 La P, 10 February 1866; G. Bapst: *Le Maréchal Canrobert*, IV, 24–5; North Peat: op. cit., 162

15 La P, 11 February 1863, records her appearance as Salammbô.

16 Anon.: *Life in Paris before the War and during the Siege*, 23

17 Whitehurst: op. cit., I, 178

18 P. d'Ariste: op. cit., 255–6

19 Viel-Castel: op. cit., IV, 38 sqq.

20 É. Bergerat: *Souvenirs d'un Enfant de Paris*, II, 298

21 Anon.: *What's What in Paris*, 1867, 58

22 Mané: *Paris mystérieux*, 77

23 GJ: II, 72–3

24 du Camp: *Paris*, III, 460–4

25 A. Wolff: *Mémoires d'un Parisien*, 251 sqq.

26 *La Revue de Paris*, 20 November 1864

27 A. Delvau: *Les Plaisirs de Paris*, 145–6

28 Dabot: op. cit., 68, 72, 129, 130–1

29 North Peat: op. cit., 100; P. d'Ariste: *La Vie et la monde du boulevard*, 152–3

30 North Peat: op. cit., 101

31 Anon.: *Life in Paris before the War and during the Siege*, 46

32 du Camp: *Paris*, VI, 389–90

33 Baroche: op. cit., 64

34 Dabot: op. cit., 26, 123

35 North Peat: op. cit., 101, 178

36 Delvau: *Les Heures parisiennes*, 5

37 Quoted in É. Thévenin: *Entretiens populaires*, 221–3

38 G. Claudin: *Paris*, 72–3

39 R. Desarbres: *Paris Partout*, 77–9

40 *La Vie parisienne*, 3 October 1868, p. 723

41 Ibid.

42 H. Taine: *Notes sur Paris*, 1–2, 9, 31

43 J. Claretie: *La Vie moderne au théâtre*, 1re série

44 Taine: op. cit., 170

45 Bicknell: op. cit., 170–1

46 W. Blanchard Jerrold: *At Home in Paris*, I, 146–7

47 Taine: op. cit., 31

48 W. Blanchard Jerrold: op. cit., I, 148–9

49 Henri Dabot: *Griffonnages quotidiens d'un bourgeois du Quartier Latin*, p. 6, note

50 W. Blanchard Jerrold: *On the Boulevards*, II, 11–12

51 Eugène Delacroix: *Journal*, II, 167–8

52 Ibid, 332–3

53 J. Vallès: *Le Tableau de Paris*, 187

54 Crane: op. cit., I, 138–9

4 PARIS INCONNU

1 L. Lespès: *Les Quatre Coins de Paris*, 73, 74–5, 80–1

2 Anon.: *Life in Paris before the War and during the Siege*, 26

3 R. Desarbres: *Paris Partout*, 21, 24–5, 67–8

4 For a comprehensive study of commerce and working-class life, *see* E. Levasseur: *Histoire des Classes ouvrières et de l'industrie en France de 1789 à 1870*

5 Mané: *Paris amoureux*, 4

6 B. Gastineau: *Sottises et scandales du temps présent*, 154–6

7 Anon.: *Paris illustrée*, 35–6

8 Anon.: *Eight days in Paris*, 24 sqq.

9 Anon.: *Paris illustrée*, 35–6

10 P. Leroy-Beaulieu: *La Question ouvrière au XIXe siècle*, 301–3

11 W. Blanchard Jerrold: *Imperial Paris*, 65; Anon.: *Life in Paris before the War and during the Siege*, 24

12 GJ: II, 79

13 L'Abbé Isidore Mullois: *Livre des classes ouvrières*, 31, 131–2

14 A. Corbon: *Le Secret du peuple de Paris*, 35, 45, 406–7

15 Leroy-Beaulieu: op. cit., 331

16 Anon.: *Realities of Paris Life*, I, 125–6

17 P. Leroy-Beaulieu: *Le Travail des femmes au XIXe siècle*, 107 sqq.

18 A. Privat d'Anglemont: *Paris inconnu*, 36–7, 38–9, 51

19 J. Vallès: *Les Réfractaires*, 7, 13

20 Joanna Richardson: *The Bohemians*, 77–8

5 LA VIE DE BOHÈME

1 Whitehurst: op. cit., I, 130–2

2 G. Guillemot: *Le Bohème*, passim.

3 Ibid.

4 E. Daudet: *Souvenirs de mon temps*, 27–8

5 GJ: I, 246

6 J. Chabannes: *La Sainte Bohème: Albert Glatigny*, 50–8

7 GJ: II, 111

8 Ibid: II, 118

9 F. Calmettes: *Leconte de Lisle et ses amis*, 125 sqq.

10 Privat d'Anglemont: op. cit., 78–9, 80

11 C. Monselet: *La Lorgnette littéraire*, 22

12 Joanna Richardson: *The Bohemians*, 142–5

13 Guillemot: op. cit., passim.

14 Richardson: op. cit., 148–50

15 For Glatigny, *see* Chabannes: op. cit., and Richardson, op. cit., 78 sqq.

16 B. Roosevelt: *Life and Reminiscences of Gustave Doré*, 264 sqq.

17 For Mme Sabatier, *see* A. Billy: *La Présidente et ses amis*; Joanna Richardson: *The Courtesans*, 171 sqq.

18 E. Feydeau: *Théophile Gautier. Souvenirs intimes*, 153 sqq.

6 HUNTING, FISHING, AND CRIKETT

1 British Officer, A: *Napoleon III.* Preface, v–vi
2 W. Blanchard Jerrold: *Imperial Paris*, 6–7
3 Anon.: *Guide Général dans Paris pour 1855*, 182
4 Whitehurst: op. cit., I, 244
5 Philippe de Massa: *Souvenirs et impressions*, 143–4
6 Mané: *Paris amoureux*, 130–1
7 Alfred Delvau: *Les Plaisirs de Paris*, 217 sqq.
8 Gustave Claudin: *Paris*, 64–5
9 Ibid, 92, 119
10 Charles Yriarte: *Les Cercles de Paris*, 4–5
11 Ibid, 61, 64
12 Ibid, 116–7
13 Ibid, 108
14 Ibid, 155 and passim
15 Ibid, 215, 216
16 Ibid, 302–3
17 Anon.: *What's What in Paris*, 1867, 24–5
18 H. Taine: *Notes sur Paris*
19 Gustave Claudin: *Paris*, 204
20 Delvau: op. cit., 229 sqq.
21 Anon.: *Paris illustrée*, 410–11
22 Delvau: loc. cit.
23 H. Dabot: *Souvenirs et impressions*, 170, 173
24 North Peat: op. cit., I, 96
25 Dabot: op. cit., 177
26 Henry A. de Conty: *Paris en Poche*, 261
27 du Camp: *Paris*, VI, 385–6
28 Anon.: *Paris illustrée*, 423–4
29 Beaumont-Vassy: op. cit., 332
30 W. Blanchard Jerrold: *Paris for the English*, 1867, 54
31 Denis Bingham: *Recollections of Paris*, I, 91–2
32 Whitehurst: op. cit., II, 24 sqq.
33 Émile Zola: *La Curée*, 232
34 Anon.: *Paris illustrée*, 428–30
35 A. Delvau: *Les Plaisirs de Paris*, 247 sqq.
36 É. Gourdon: *Le Bois de Boulogne*, 208–10
37 H. Dabot: op. cit., 269
38 Joanna Richardson: *Princess Mathilde*, 79
39 P. d'Ariste: *La Vie et le monde du boulevard*, 269

7 LA CUISINE CLASSIQUE

1 Philibert Audebrand: *Un Café de Journalistes*, 26
2 Haussmann: *Mémoires*, I, 101
3 Whitehurst: op. cit., I, 7
4 Joanna Richardson: *Princess Mathilde*, 107–8
5 Alfred Delvau: *Les Plaisirs de Paris*, 129–30
6 Ibid: 128
7 Gustave Claudin: *Mes Souvenirs*, 249–50
8 H. de Villemessant: *Mémoires d'un journaliste*, 3e série, 131
9 Ibid: 133
10 H. de Villemessant: op. cit., 132
11 R. Boutet de Monvel: *Les Variétés*, 170–1
12 *Paris-Guide*, II, 1547
13 GJ: III, 106
14 Ponson du Terrail: *Les Nuits de la Maison Dorée*, 1
15 P. d'Ariste: op. cit., 52
16 H. de Villemessant: loc. cit.
17 A. Delvau: *Histoire anecdotique des cafés et cabarets de Paris*, 254–6
18 GJ: II, 190; R. Boutet de Monvel, op. cit., 172–5
19 Boutet de Monvel: op. cit., 162 sqq.
20 Villemessant: op. cit., 218–9
21 Boutet de Monvel: loc. cit.

22 H. de Conty: op. cit., 24
23 Zed: *Le Demi-monde sous le Second Empire*, 51–2
24 G. Claudin: *Mes Souvenirs*, 310 sqq.
25 G. Claudin: *Paris*, 102–3, 124 sqq.
26 Ibid, 127 sqq.
27 Dabot: *Souvenirs et impressions*, 20
28 Ménière: op. cit., 217–8
29 Anon.: *Paris illustrée*, 17
30 H. de Conty: op. cit., 23
31 Whitehurst: op. cit., I, 120–1
32 North Peat: op. cit., I, 54–5, 192, 200, 208
33 Anon.: *Paris illustrée*, 25
34 Anon.: *Life in Paris before the War and during the Siege*, 16–17
35 Quoted by W. Blanchard Jerrold: *On the Boulevards*, I, 152–3
36 W. Blanchard Jerrold: *Imperial Paris*, 93
37 North Peat: op. cit., I, 170
38 H. Taine: op. cit., 81
39 North Peat: op. cit., I, 111
40 Whitehurst: op. cit., I, 68, II, 92, 301

8 THÉÂTRES DIVERS

1 G. Claudin: *Mes Souvenirs*, 222–3
2 For Gautier's dramatic criticism, *see* Joanna Richardson: *Théophile Gautier: His Life and Times*, 54 sqq.
3 MU, 10 March 1862
4 E. Daudet: op. cit., 116–7
5 Houssaye: op. cit.
6 Viel-Castel: op. cit., II, 34–5
7 A. Dumas *fils*: *Le Demi-monde*, II, ix
8 JO, 29 August 1870
9 Ibid.
10 For her career, *see* Joanna Richardson: *Rachel*
11 Ibid, 157
12 MU, 9 July 1855
13 For her career, *see* Joanna Richardson: *Sarah Bernhardt*
14 Ibid, 33
15 JO, 18 January 1869
16 MU, 11 June 1866
17 MU, 6 August 1866
18 MU, 16 and 17 August 1863
19 MU, 13 July 1863
20 La P, 23 October 1848
21 Ibid: 15 October 1849
22 For an authoritative account, *see* Ivor Guest: *The Ballet of the Second Empire*
23 Théophile Gautier: *Portraits contemporains*, 429
24 Guest: op. cit., 92
25 Théophile Gautier: undated letter to Carlotta Grisi (Henriot)
26 *See* F. C. Green: *A Comparative View of French and British Civilization*, passim
27 A. Vandam: *Undercurrents of the Second Empire*, 333
28 La P, 21 February 1867; GJ: VII, 237
29 W. Blanchard Jerrold: *Paris for the English*, 1867, passim
30 Halévy: op. cit.
31 *Revue de Paris*, 1 November 1867
32 Comtesse Stéphanie Tascher de la Pagerie: op. cit., 247–8
33 Cole: op. cit., 21–2
34 Ibid: 12
35 Cole: op. cit., 13
36 Ibid: 95–7
37 H. de Conty: op. cit., 260

9 LITERATURE AND THE PRESS

1 Ménière: op. cit., 81
2 *The Times*, 8 September 1870
3 For a complete account of Gautier, *see* Joanna Richardson: *Théophile Gautier: His Life and Times*
4 The best account of Baudelaire is given by Enid Starkie in *Baudelaire*
5 Quoted by Joanna Richardson in *Verlaine*
6 F. Coppée: *Mon Franc parler*, 3e série, 62 sqq.
7 C. Mendès: *La Légende du Parnasse contemporain*
8 For the most complete account of Verlaine, *see* Joanna Richardson: *Verlaine*
9 E. Daudet: op. cit., 134
10 J. Claretie: *Peintres et sculpteurs*, 200
11 É. Zola: *La Fortune des Rougon*. Preface, 5–6
12 The standard work on Flaubert is Enid Starkie's two-volume critical biography
13 Primoli Diary, V, 97–8 (Primoli)
14 W. Blanchard Jerrold: *On the Boulevards*, I, 38–9
15 Mme Juliette Adam: *Mes Sentiments et Nos Idées avant 1870*, 167
16 E. Renan: *Vie de Jésus*. Introduction, li sqq.
17 Ibid: 457, 459
18 C. Simond: *Paris de 1800 à 1900*, II, 731–2
19 Jerrold: op. cit., I, 143–4
20 For Girardin, *see*: M. Reclus: *Émile de Girardin. Le Créateur de la Presse Moderne*; and Odysse-Barot: *Émile de Girardin*
21 *Gazette anecdotique*, 1881, 257 sqq.
22 Odysse Barot: op. cit., 132 sqq.
23 For Girardin and Princess Mathilde, *see* Richardson: *Princess Mathilde*, passim
24 G. Claudin: *Mes Souvenirs*, 250 sqq.

10 LES BEAUX-ARTS

1 T. Gautier: *Portraits contemporains*, 287–8
2 Ibid: 322
3 Ibid: 321
4 J. Claretie: *Peintres et sculpteurs*, 106–7
5 Ibid.
6 For Millet, and for general survey of the period, *see* L. Dimier: *Histoire de la peinture française au XIXe siècle*
7 Claretie: op. cit., 254, 259
8 MU, 11 May 1868
9 H. Dabot: *Griffonnages . . .*, 26, and note, 26–7
10 For Manet, *see* P. Courthion: *Édouard Manet*
11 MU, 11 May 1868
12 Typescript copy of undated letter (Primoli)
13 For Monet, *see* W. C. Seitz: *Claude Monet*
14 For Boudin, *see* G. Cahen: *Eugène Boudin. Sa Vie et son Œuvre*; G. Jean-Aubry: *Eugène Boudin*
15 Quoted by Jean-Aubry: op. cit., 74
16 J. Rewald: *Camille Pissarro*, 18. *See also*: A. Vollard: *La Vie et l'Œuvre de Pierre-Auguste Renoir*; F. Daulte: *Frédéric Bazille et son temps*; J. Bouret: *Degas*
17 For Fantin-Latour, *see* A. Jullien: *Fantin-Latour. Sa Vie et ses Amitiés*
18 W. Blanchard Jerrold: *On the Boulevards*. I, 187
19 For Guys, *see* G. Geoffroy: *Constantin Guys*; C. G. Holme (ed.): *The Painter of Victorian Life*
20 C. Baudelaire: *L'Art Romantique*, 45–6, 59–60
21 Ibid, 67–8
22 For Daumier, *see* C. Holmes (ed.); *Daumier and Gavarni*
23 Ibid.
24 Baudelaire: op. cit., 44
25 For Doré, *see*: B. Roosevelt: *Life and Reminiscences of Gustave Doré*; E. Tromp: *Gustave Doré*; J. Valmy-Baysse: *Gustave Doré*
26 MU, 31 July and 1 August 1861
27 Tromp: op. cit., 52
28 For Carpeaux, *see* E. Chesneau: *Le Statuaire J.-B. Carpeaux. Sa Vie et son Œuvre*
29 Primoli Diary, VI, 22 April 1869 (Primoli)
30 H. Dabot: op. cit., 5, 8
31 For Nadar, *see*, J. Prinet and A. Dilasser: *Nadar*

11 THE TRANSFORMATION OF PARIS

1 For Haussmann's career, *see* his own *Mémoires*, and G. Lameyre: *Haussmann, 'Préfet de Paris'*
2 Haussmann: op. cit., II, xiii, 53
3 Ibid: II, xii. Report of 20 May 1868
4 Lameyre: op. cit., 52
5 Crane: op. cit., I, 175
6 Haussmann: op. cit., I, xi–xii
7 Fournel: op. cit., 113
8 Ibid: 115
9 H. de Conty: op. cit., 147; MU, 9 December 1861
10 G. Claudin: *Paris*, 175
11 Gourdon: op. cit., 281
12 *The Athenaeum*, 22 June 1861, p. 831
13 Ibid.
14 Gourdon: op. cit., 62, 83
15 Ibid: 93–4
16 Beaumont-Vassy: op. cit., 188–90
17 Crane: op. cit., I, 42–3
18 For Alphand, *see* Massillon Rouvet, op. cit.; *see also* Alphand: *Les Promenades de Paris*
19 Haussmann: op. cit., II, 117
20 La P, 6 December 1866
21 Crane: op. cit., I, 178–9
22 Houssaye: op. cit., IV, 219
23 Haussmann: op. cit., II, 91–2
24 Dabot: op. cit., 2, 59
25 Ibid: 59, 62
26 Crane: op. cit., I, 179–80
27 Gourdon: op. cit., 85–7
28 Gastineau: op. cit., 152
29 Fournel: op. cit., 15, 71–2
30 L. Veuillot: op. cit., vii–ix
31 Fournel: 105
32 Dabot: 133–4
33 Whitehurst: I, 56–7
34 Ibid, I, 85–6
35 Anon.: *Life in Paris before the War and during the Siege*, 44–5
36 Fournel: 47–8
37 J. Ferry: *Comptes fantastiques d'Haussmann*, 7–8, 67–8
38 Verly: *Souvenirs du Second Empire. De Notre-Dame au Zululand*, 122–3
39 *The Times*, 7, 8 January 1870
40 Halévy: II, 40
41 Haussmann: I, v–vi, xii

12 LE STYLE NAPOLÉON III

1 L. Veuillot: *Les Odeurs de Paris*
2 Quoted by E. Levasseur: op. cit., II, 530–1
3 V. Fournel: *Paris nouveau et Paris futur*, 60–1
4 Ménière: op. cit., 217–8
5 Levasseur: op. cit., II, 526
6 H. Clouzot: *Des Tuileries à Saint-Cloud. L'Art décoratif du Second Empire*, 12 sqq.
7 E. Rouyer: *Les Appartements privés de S. M. l'Impératrice . . .*, 9–10

8 C. Daly: *L'Architecture privée sous Napoléon III*, 8
9 E. Delacroix: *Journal*, III, 371–3
10 G. Claudin: *Paris*, 146
11 Ibid.
12 Massillon Rouvet: *Viollet-le-Duc et Alphand au Siège de Paris*, 7, 10–11, 12–14
13 H. Clouzot: op. cit., 57
14 Ibid: 12 sqq.
15 Whitehurst: op. cit., II, 111
16 G. Bapst: *Essai sur l'histoire du théâtre*, 604–7
17 Delacroix: op. cit., II, 353
18 Claudin: op. cit., 135–6
19 *L'Artiste*, 5 September 1858, 7–8
20 Claudin: op. cit., 139–40, 141
21 E. Daudet: *Souvenirs de mon temps*, 89–90
22 [M. Liénard]: *Spécimens de la décoration et de l'ornementation au XIXe siècle*. Avant-propos, 3–4
23 Clouzot: op. cit., 34–6, 37–8, 40–1; Clouzot: *Le Style Louis-Philippe–Napoléon III*, 8
24 Ibid, 38–9; *see also*: L. Dimier: op. cit., 172–3
25 J. Claretie: *La Vie moderne au théâtre*, 1re série, 55
26 Clouzot: op. cit., 44–51; H. Bouilhet: *L'Orfèvrerie française aux XVIIIe et XIXe siècles*, II, 286 sqq.
27 Anon.: *Wagons composant le train impérial . . .* [pages un-numbered]
28 Claudin: op. cit., 142

13 THE WORLD OF M. WORTH

1 Octave Uzanne: *Fashion in Paris*, 127
2 Ibid: 128–9
3 Ibid.
4 Quoted by A. Blum and C. Chassé in *Les Modes au XIXe siècle*, 66–7
5 P.-L. de Giafferri: *L'Histoire du costume féminin français*
6 Uzanne: op. cit., 129–30
7 H. Defontaine: *Du costume civil officiel . . .*, 212
8 Uzanne: op. cit., 129–30
9 Cabris: *Le Costume de la Parisienne au XIXe siècle*, 169–71
10 Uzanne: op. cit., 138; J.-P. Worth: *A Century of Fashion*, 51
11 La Comtesse Dash: *Comment on fait son chemin dans le monde*, 73, 282
12 The best account of Charles Frederick Worth is given by his son, Jean-Philippe, in *A Century of Fashion*; *see also* W. F. Lonergan: *Forty Years of Paris*
13 Worth: op. cit., 26
14 Ibid, 28–9
15 Ibid, 39–43; J. Boulenger: op. cit., 162–3
16 Worth: op. cit., 56
17 Mme Octave Feuillet: op. cit., 199 sqq.
18 Ibid: 207, 208
19 Whitehurst: op. cit., II, 85
20 Primoli Diary, 1868, 50 sqq. (Primoli)
21 Worth: op. cit., 66–7
22 Whitehurst: op. cit., II, 322
23 Cabris: op. cit., 154–6
24 La P, 9 March 1864
25 G. Claudin: *Paris*, 90–1
26 Whitehurst: op. cit., I, 147 sqq.
27 Ibid: I, 165
28 Ibid: I, 241
29 Whitehurst: op. cit.,
30 Blum et Chassé: op. cit., 134

31 Baroche: op. cit., 83
32 Blum et Chassé: op. cit., 67
33 Uzanne: op. cit., 132–4
34 Blum et Chassé: op. cit., 67–8
35 H. Vever: *La Bijouterie française au XIXe siècle*, II, 41–2; *see also* G. Bapst: *Histoire des joyaux de la couronne de France*, 656 sqq.
36 Vever: op. cit., II, 103–4
37 Ménière: op. cit., 367
38 Émile Zola: *La Curée*, 228–9
39 Uzanne: op. cit., 134–5
40 Uzanne: op. cit., 136
41 *Guide Général dans Paris pour 1855*, 143 and passim.
42 Murat: op. cit., 167

14 NOTES DE MUSIQUE

1 For Berlioz, *see* J. H. Elliot: *Berlioz*; A. Boschot: *Hector Berlioz*
2 Boschot: 234
3 Ménière: 117–8
4 *MU*, 23 March 1868
5 North Peat: 136
6 *MU*, 6 January 1868
7 J. Harding: *Saint-Saëns and his circle*, 97
8 Tascher de la Pagerie: 142–5
9 M. Curtis: *Bizet and his World*, 108
10 Baudelaire: 201
11 P. Feval [et al.]: *Paris-Guide*, II, 999
12 For Offenbach, *see* S. Kracauer: *Jacques Offenbach ou le secret du Second Empire*; L. Schneider: *Offenbach*
13 Kracauer, op. cit., Offenbach was said to have the evil eye
14 Kracauer, op. cit.
15 A. Wolff in introduction to Offenbach: *Offenbach en Amérique*, xxv
16 J. Lemaître: *Impressions de théâtre*. 1re série, 217 sqq.
17 Halévy: I, 153–5
18 E. A. Vizetelly: *Paris and her People under the Third Republic*, 35–6
19 G. Claudin: *Mes Souvenirs*, 240–1

EPILOGUE

1 A. Verly: *Souvenirs du Second Empire. De Notre-Dame au Zululand*, 118–9
2 E. B. Washburne: *Recollections of a Minister to France*, 1869–1877, I, 6–7, 34
3 Ibid: I, 16–17
4 North Peat: op. cit., I, 38–9
5 du Camp: *Paris*, VI, 385–6
6 For the most useful accounts of his policies, *see* G. P. Gooch and F. A. Simpson
7 Whitehurst: op. cit., II, 344–5
8 Bicknell: op. cit., 210
9 E. Dangin: *Paris incendié* [pages un-numbered]
10 E. Lavisse gives a good account of him in: *Un Ministre, Victor Duruy*
11 Ibid: 66–9
12 For the most complete life, *see* G. Guillain: *J.-M. Charcot*
13 A sound assessment of his work may be found in J. M. D. Olmsted: *Claude Bernard. Physiologist*
14 *See* R. Vallery-Radot: *La Vie de Pasteur*
15 Beaumont-Vassy: op. cit., 338–40
16 Gastineau: op. cit., 152
17 du Camp: *Paris*, VI, 401

Bibliography

French books have been published in Paris,
English books in London, unless otherwise stated.

ADAM, Mme Juliette *Mes Sentiments et Nos Idées avant 1870.* (Lemerre, 1905)

ALLEM, Maurice *La Vie quotidienne sous le Second Empire.* (Hachette, 1948)

ALMÉRAS, Henri d' *La Vie Parisienne sous le Second Empire.* (Albin Michel, 1933)

ALPHAND, A. *Les Promenades de Paris.* (Rothschild, 1867–73)

ANON. *Guide Général dans Paris pour 1855, suivi d'une visite à l'Exposition.* (Imprimerie Wiesener, 1855)

ANON. *Paris illustrée.* (Hachette, 1858)

ANON. *Eight Days in Paris; or, Paris in the Hand.* (Ledot, 1866)

ANON. *Realities of Paris Life.* (Hurst & Blackett, 1859)

ANON. *What's What in Paris, 1867, addressed to Who's Who in London.* (Baily, 1867)

ANON. *M. le Baron Haussmann jugé par ses œuvres.* (Dentu, 1870)

ANON. *Life in Paris before the War and during the Siege.* Together with Reasons why the Germans beat the French. (Diprose & Bateman, 1871)

ANON. *Wagons composant le train impérial offert à LL.MM. l'Empereur et l'Impératrice par la Compagnie du chemin de fer d'Orléans.* (Bance, 1857)

ARISTE, Paul d' *La vie et le monde du boulevard (1830–1870).* Un Dandy: Nestor Roqueplan. (Tallandier, 1930)

AUDEBRAND, Philibert *Romanciers et viveurs du XIXe siècle.* (Calmann-Lévy, 1905)

AUDEBRAND, Philibert *Un Café de Journalistes sous Napoléon III.* (Dentu, 1888)

AUDIGANNE, M. [*et al.*] *Paris dans sa splendeur.* (Charpentier, 1861)

AVENEL, H. *Histoire de la Presse française depuis 1789 jusqu'à nos jours.* (Flammarion, 1900)

BAC, Ferdinand *La Cour des Tuileries sous le Second Empire.* (Hachette, 1930)

BAC, Ferdinand *Le Prince Napoléon.* (Éditions des Portiques, 1932)

BAPST, Germain *Histoire des joyaux de la couronne de France d'après des documents inédits.* (Hachette, 1889)

BAPST, Germain *Essai sur l'histoire du théâtre.* (Hachette, 1893)

BAPST, Germain *Le Maréchal Canrobert. Souvenirs d'un siècle.* (Plon, Nourrit, 1898–1913)

BAROCHE, Mme Jules *Le Second Empire. Notes et Souvenirs.* (Crès, 1921)

BARTHEZ, Dr E. *The Empress Eugénie and her circle.* Translated by Bernard Miall. (T. Fisher Unwin, 1912)

BAUDELAIRE, Charles *L'Art Romantique.* (Grasset, 1931)

BAUDELAIRE, Charles *Les Fleurs du mal.* Edited by Enid Starkie. (Blackwell, Oxford, 1943)

BEAUMONT-VASSY, Vicomte de *Les Salons de Paris et la Société parisienne sous Napoléon III.* (Sartorius, 1868)

BEAUMONT-VASSY, Vicomte de *Histoire intime du Second Empire.* (Sartorius, 1874)

BEAUVOIR, Roger de *Les Soupeurs de mon temps.* (Achille Faure, 1868)

BELLANGER, Marguerite *Confessions. Mémoires anecdotiques.* (Librairie populaire, 1882)

BENSON, A. C. and ESHER, Viscount (editors) *The Letters of Queen Victoria, 1854–1861.* (Murray, 1907)

BERLIOZ, Hector *Lettres intimes.* Avec une préface par Charles Gounod. (Calmann-Lévy, 1882)

BERTHET-LELEUX, François *Le Vrai Prince Napoléon.* (Grasset, 1932)

BICKNELL, Anna L. *Life in the Tuileries under the Second Empire.* (The Century Co, New York, 1895)

BILLY, André *La Présidente et ses amis.* (Flammarion, 1945)

BINGHAM, Hon. Denis *Recollections of Paris.* (Chapman & Hall, 1896)

BLUM, André, et CHASSÉ, Charles *Les Modes au XIXe siècle.* (Hachette, 1931)

BOSCHOT, Adolphe *Hector Berlioz. Une Vie romantique.* (Plon, 1942)

BOUCHOT, Henri *Les Élégances du Second Empire.* (Librairie illustrée, 1896)

BOUILHET, Henri *L'Orfèvrerie française aux XVIIIe et XIXe siècles.* (Laurens, 1908–12)

BOULENGER, Jacques *Les Tuileries sous le Second Empire.* (Calmann-Lévy, 1932)

BOUTET DE MONVEL, Roger *Les Variétés, 1850–1870.* (Plon, 1905)

BRITISH OFFICER, A *Napoleon III.* (Longman, Brown, 1857)

BURY, J. P. T. *Napoleon III and the Second Empire.* (English Universities Press, 1964)

BUSQUET, Alfred *Almanach-Album des Célébrités contemporaines.* (Pagnerre, 1869)

BYAM, Edward Colby *Théodore Barrière, Dramatist of the Second Empire.* (The Johns Hopkins Press, Baltimore, Maryland, 1938)

CABRIS *Le Costume de la Parisienne au XIXe siècle.* (Société Anonyme des Publications Scientifiques et Industrielles, 1901)

CAHEN, Gustave *Eugène Boudin. Sa Vie et son Œuvre.* (Floury, 1900)

CALMETTES, Fernand *Leconte de Lisle et ses amis.* (Librairies-Imprimeries réunies, 1902)

CARETTE, Mme *Souvenirs intimes de la Cour des Tuileries.* (Ollendorff, 1889)

CASSAGNE, Albert *La Théorie de l'Art pour l'Art en France.* (Hachette, 1906)

CASTELLANE, Maréchal de *Journal, 1804–1862.* (Plon, 1895–7)

CASTILLE, Hippolyte *Émile de Girardin.* (Sartorius, 1858)

CASTILLE, Hippolyte *Les Journaux et les Journalistes depuis 1848.* (Sartorius, 1858)

CHABANNES, Jacques *La Sainte Bohème: Albert Glatigny.* (Grasset, 1948)

CHESNEAU, Ernest *Le Statuaire J.-B. Carpeaux. Sa Vie et son Œuvre.* (Quantin, 1880)

CLARETIE, Jules *La Vie moderne au théâtre.* 1re et 2e série. (Barba, 1869, 1875)

CLARETIE, Jules *Peintres et sculpteurs.* (Librarie des Bibliophiles, 1882)

CLAUDIN, Gustave *Mes Souvenirs. Les Boulevards de 1840–1870.* (Calmann-Lévy, 1884)

CLAUDIN, Gustave *Paris.* (Faure, 1867)

CLOUZOT, Henri *Des Tuileries à Saint-Cloud. L'Art décoratif du Second Empire.* (Payot, 1925)

CLOUZOT, Henri *Le Style Louis-Philippe – Napoléon III.* (Larousse, 1939)

COLE, Charles Augustus (editor) *The Imperial Paris Guide.* (Hotten, 1867)

CONTY, Henry A. de *Paris en Poche.* (Faure, 1865)

COPPÉE, François *Mon Franc parler.* 3e série. (Lemerre, 1895)

COQUIS, André *Léo Delibes. Sa Vie et son œuvre (1836–1891).* (Richard-Masse, 1957)

CORBON, A. *Le Secret du Peuple de Paris.* (Pagnerre, 1863)

COURTHION, Pierre *Édouard Manet.* (Thames & Hudson, 1962)

CRANE, Edward A. (ed.) *The Memoirs of Dr Thomas W. Evans. Recollections of the Second French Empire.* (T. Fisher Unwin, 1905)

CURTISS, Mina *Bizet and His World.* (Secker & Warburg, 1959)

DABOT, Henri *Griffonnages quotidiens d'un bourgeois du Quartier Latin du 14 mai 1869 au 2 décembre 1871.* (Quentin, Péronne, 1895)

DABOT, Henri *Souvenirs et impressions d'un bourgeois du Quartier Latin de mai 1854 à mai 1869.* (Quentin, Péronne, 1899)

DALY, César *L'Architecture privée au XIXe siècle, sous Napoléon III. Nouvelles Maisons de Paris et des environs.* (Morel, 1864)

DANGIN, E. *Paris incendié, 1871. Album historique.* (Jarry, 1872)

DASH, la Comtesse *Comment on fait son chemin dans le monde. Code du savoir-vivre.* (Michel Lévy, 1868)

DAUDET, Ernest *Souvenirs de mon temps. Débuts d'un homme de lettres, 1857–1861.* (Plon, 1921)

DAULTE, François *Frédéric Bazille et son temps.* (Cailler, Genève, 1952)

DAYOT, Armand *Le Second Empire.* (Flammarion, 1900)

DEFONTAINE, Henri *Du costume civil officiel et de l'uniforme militaire des officiers à la Cour ou auprès des Chefs d'État français depuis 1804 jusqu'à nos jours.* (Geoffroy, 1908)

DELACROIX, Eugène *Journal.* (Plon, Nourrit, 1893, 1895)

DELVAU, Alfred *Les Dessous de Paris.* (Poulet-Malassis et de Broise, 1860)

DELVAU, Alfred *Histoire anecdotique des cafés et cabarets de Paris.* (Dentu, 1862)

DELVAU, Alfred *Les Heures parisiennes.* (Librairie centrale, 1866)

DELVAU, Alfred *Les Plaisirs de Paris. Guide pratique et illustré.* (Faure, 1867)

DEMUTH, Norman *César Franck.* (Dobson, 1949)

DESARBRES, Renée *Paris Partout.* (Librairie Centrale, 1865)

DIMIER, L. *Histoire de la peinture française au XIXe siècle (1793–1903).* (Delagrave, 1914)

DU BLED, Victor *La Société française depuis cent ans. Quelques salons du Second Empire.* (Bloud & Gay, 1923)

DUBOIS, Urbain, et BERNARD, Émile *La Cuisine classique.* (Dentu, 1864)

DU CAMP, Maxime *Paris. Ses organes, sa fonction et sa vie dans la seconde moitié du XIXe siècle.* 6 tomes. (Hachette, 1869–76)

DU CAMP, Maxime *Souvenirs littéraires.* (Hachette, 1892)

DU CAMP, Maxime *Souvenirs d'un demi-siècle.* (Hachette, 1949)

DUMAS, Alexandre père [et al.] *Paris et les Parisiens au XIXe siècle. Mœurs, arts et monuments.* (Morizot, 1856)

DUMAS, Alexandre fils *Le Demi-monde.* (Michel Lévy, 1855)

ELLIOT, J. H. *Berlioz.* (Dent, 1938)

FERRY, Jules *Comptes fantastiques d'Haussmann.* (Le Chevalier, 1868)

FEUILLET, Mme Octave *Quelques Années de ma vie.* (Calmann-Lévy, 1894)

FÉVAL, Paul [et al.] *Paris-Guide.* II La Vie. (Librairie internationale, 1867)

FEYDEAU, Ernest *Théophile Gautier. Souvenirs intimes.* (Plon, 1874)

FLAUBERT, Gustave *Correspondance.* (Conard, 1926–1930)

FLEURY, Général Comte *Souvenirs.* (Plon, Nourrit, 1897–8)

FLEURY, Comte, et SONOLET, Louis *La Société du Second Empire.* (Albin Michel, n.d.)

FOSCA, François *Histoire des Cafés de Paris.* (Firmin-Didot, 1934)

FOURNEL, Victor *Paris nouveau et Paris futur.* (Lecoffre, 1865)

GASTINEAU, Benjamin *Sottises et scandales du temps présent.* (Pagnerre, 1863)

GAUTIER, Théophile *Histoire de l'Art Dramatique en France depuis Vingt-Cinq ans.* (Hetzel, 1858–9)

GAUTIER, Théophile *Émaux et Camées.* (Droz, Genève, 1947)

GAUTIER, Théophile *Portraits contemporains.* (Bibliothèque-Charpentier, Fasquelle, n.d.)

GAUTIER, Théophile *Souvenirs de Théâtre.* (Charpentier, 1883)

GEOFFROY, Gustave *Constantin Guys. L'Historien du Second Empire.* (Crès, 1920)

GIAFFERRI, P.-L. de *L'Histoire du costume féminin français. Les Modes du Second Empire, 1852 à 1870.* (Nilsson, 1922)

GIAFFERRI, P.-L. de *The History of French Masculine Costume. Appearance of the Second Empire Fops.* (Foreign Publications, New York, 1937)

GIGAULT DE LA BÉDOLLIÈRE, Émile *Le Nouveau Paris.* (Barba, 1860)

GONCOURT, Edmond et Jules de *Journal. Mémoirs de la vie littéraire.* (Les Éditions de l'Imprimerie nationale, Monaco, 1956)

GOOCH, G. P. *The Second Empire.* (Longmans, 1960)

GOT, Edmond *Journal.* (Plon, Nourrit, 1910)

GOUNOD, Charles *Mémoires d'un artiste.* (Calmann-Lévy, 1896)

GOURDON, Édouard *Le Bois de Boulogne.* (Bourdilliat, 1861)

GREEN, F. C. *A Comparative View of French and British Civilization, 1850–1870.* (Dent, 1965)

GUEST, Ivor *Napoleon III in England.* (British Technical and General Press, 1952)

GUEST, Ivor *The Ballet of the Second Empire, 1858–1870.* (A. & C. Black, 1953)

GUILLAIN, Georges *J.-M. Charcot, 1825–1893. His Life – His Work.* Edited and translated by Pearce Bailey. (Pitman Medical Publishing Company, 1959)

GUILLEMOT, Gabriel *Le Bohème.* (A. le Chevalier, 1868)

GUYS, Constantin *Dessins. Pages de Baudelaire. Catalogue de Bruno Sieff.* (Mermod, Lausanne, 1957)

HALÉVY, Ludovic *Carnets. Publiés avec une introduction et des notes par Daniel Halévy.* (Calmann-Lévy, 1935)

HARDING, James *Saint-Saëns and his Circle.* (Chapman & Hall, 1965)

HAUSSMANN, Baron G.-E. *Mémoires.* (Victor-Havard, 1890)

HEGERMANN-LINDENCRONE, L. de *In the Courts of Memory, 1858–1875.* (Harper & Bros, 1912)

HOLME, Charles (ed.) *Daumier and Gavarni.* (The Studio, 1904)

HOLME, C. Geoffrey (ed.) *The Painter of Victorian Life.* A study of Constantin Guys, with an introduction and a translation of Baudelaire's Peintre de la Vie Moderne by P. G. Konody. (The Studio, 1930)

HOUSSAYE, Arsène *Souvenirs de Jeunesse, 1850–1870.* (Flammarion, 1890)

HOUSSAYE, Arsène *Les Confessions. Souvenirs d'un demi-siècle, 1830–1890.* (Dentu, 1885–1891)

IBROVAC, Miodrag *José-Maria de Heredia. Sa Vie – Son Œuvre.* (Les Presses Françaises, 1923)

JEAN-AUBRY, G. *Eugène Boudin.* Translated from the French by Caroline Tisdall. (Thames & Hudson, 1969)

JERROLD, W. Blanchard *At Home in Paris: at Peace and at War.* (W. H. Allen, 1871)

JERROLD, W. Blanchard *Imperial Paris; including new scenes for old visitors.* (Bradbury & Evans, 1855)

JERROLD, W. Blanchard *On the Boulevards.* (W. H. Allen, 1867)

JERROLD, W. Blanchard *Paris for the English, 1867.* (Bradbury & Evans, 1867)

JOLLIVET, Gaston *Souvenirs d'un Parisien.* (Tallandier, 1928)

JULLIEN, Adolphe *Hector Berlioz. Sa vie et ses œuvres.* (À la librairie de l'art, 1888)

JULLIEN, Adolphe *Fantin-Latour. Sa Vie et ses Amitiés.* (Laveur, 1909)

KRACAUER, S. *Jacques Offenbach, ou le secret du Second Empire.* (Grasset, 1937)

KURTZ, Harold *The Empress Eugénie, 1826–1920.* (Hamish Hamilton, 1964)

LAMEYRE, Gérard *Haussmann, 'Préfet de Paris'.* (Flammarion, 1958)

LAVISSE, Ernest *Un Ministre. Victor Duruy.* (Colin, 1895)

LAVISSE, Ernest *Souvenirs.* (Calmann-Lévy, 1912)

[LEFUEL, H.] *Palais du Louvre et des Tuileries. Motifs de Décorations tirés des Constructions exécutées au Nouveau Louvre et au Palais des Tuileries sous la direction de H. Lefuel Architecte de l'Empereur.* (Baudry/Morel, 1870–5)

LEMAÎTRE, Jules *Impressions de Théâtre.* 1re série. (Lecène & Oudin, 1888)

LEROY-BEAULIEU, Paul *La Question ouvrière au XIXe siècle.* (Charpentier, 1872)

LEROY-BEAULIEU, Paul *Le Travail des femmes au XIXe siècle.* (Charpentier, 1873)

286

LESPÈS, Léo *Les Quatre Coins de Paris.* (Dentu, 1863)

LEVASSEUR, E. *Histoire des Classes ouvrières et de l'industrie en France de 1789 à 1870.* (Rousseau, 1903-4)

[LIÉNARD, Michel] *Spécimens de la décoration et de l'ornementation au XIXe siècle, par Liénard.* (Claesen, Liége et Leipzig, 1866)

LONERGAN, W. F. *Forty Years of Paris.* (T. Fisher Unwin, 1907)

MAILLARD, Firmin *Les Derniers Bohèmes. Henri Murger et son temps.* (Sartorius, 1847)

MANÉ, *Paris aventureux.* (Dentu, 1860)

MANÉ *Paris mystérieux.* (Dentu, 1861)

MANÉ *Paris amoureux.* (Dentu, 1864)

MASSA, le Marquis Philippe de *Souvenirs et Impressions, 1840-1871.* (Calmann-Lévy, 1897)

MENDÈS, Catulle *La Légende du Parnasse contemporain.* (Brancart, Bruxelles, 1884)

MÉNIÈRE, Dr Prosper *Journal.* (Plon, Nourrit, 1903)

MÉRIMÉE, Prosper *Correspondance générale.* Établie et annotée par Maurice Parturier. (Édouard Privat, Toulouse, 1953)

MONSELET, Charles *La Lorgnette littéraire.* (Poulet-Malassis et de Broise, 1857)

MULLOIS, l'Abbé Isidore *Livre des classes ouvrières.* (Lecoffre, 1852)

MURAT, Princess Caroline *My Memoirs.* (Eveleigh Nash, 1910)

NADAR [Félix Tournachon, known as], *Mémoirs du Géant.* Avec une introduction par M. Babinet, de l'Institut. (Dentu, 1864)

ODYSSE-BAROT *Émile de Girardin. Sa vie – ses idées – son œuvre – son influence.* (Michel Lévy, 1866)

OFFENBACH, Jacques *Offenbach en Amérique. Notes d'un musicien en voyage.* Précédées d'une notice biographique par Albert Wolff. (Calmann-Lévy, 1877)

OLMSTED, J. M. D. *Claude Bernard. Physiologist.* (Cassell, 1939)

PEAT, Anthony B. North *Gossip from Paris during the Second Empire. Correspondence (1864-1869).* Selected and arranged by A. R. Waller. (Kegan Paul, 1903)

PONSON DU TERRAIL, Vicomte *Les Nuits de la Maison Dorée.* (Dentu, 1862)

PRINET, Jean, et DILASSER, Antoinette *Nadar.* (Armand Colin, 1966)

PRIVAT D'ANGLEMONT, A. *Paris inconnu.* (Delahays, 1861)

PROD'HOMME, J.-G., et DANDELOT, A. *Gounod (1818-1893). Sa Vie et ses Œuvres.* (Delagrave, 1911)

RAITT, A. W. *Prosper Mérimée.* (Eyre & Spottiswoode, 1970)

RECLUS, Maurice *Émile de Girardin. Le Créateur de la Presse moderne.* (Hachette, 1934)

RÉGNIER, Henri de *Portraits et Souvenirs.* (Mercure de France, 1913)

RENAN, Ernest *Vie de Jésus.* (Michel Lévy, 1863)

REYMOND, Jean *Albert Glatigny.* (Droz, 1936)

RICHARDSON, Joanna *Rachel.* (Reinhardt, 1956)

RICHARDSON, Joanna *Théophile Gautier: His Life and Times.* (Reinhardt, 1958)

RICHARDSON, Joanna *Sarah Bernhardt.* (Reinhardt, 1959)

RICHARDSON, Joanna *The Courtesans.* (Weidenfeld & Nicolson, 1967)

RICHARDSON, Joanna *Princess Mathilde.* (Weidenfeld & Nicolson, 1969)

RICHARDSON, Joanna *The Bohemians.* (Macmillan, 1969)

RICHARDSON, Joanna *Verlaine.* (Weidenfeld & Nicolson, 1971)

ROOSEVELT, Blanche *Life and Reminiscences of Gustave Doré.* (Sampson Low, 1885)

ROUFF, Marcel, et CASEMITZ, Thérèse *La Vie de Fête sous le Second Empire. Hortense Schneider.* (Jules Tallandier, 1931)

ROUVET, Massillon *Viollet-le-Duc et Alphand au Siège de Paris.* (Librairies-Imprimeries réunies, 1892)

ROUYER, Eugène *Les Appartements privés de S. M. l'Impératrice au Palais des Tuileries décorés par M. Lefuel, architecte de S. M. l'Empereur, publiés par Eugène Rouyer, architecte.* (Baudry, 1867)

RUDE, Maxime *Confidences d'un Journaliste.* (André Sagnier, 1876)

SAINTE-BEUVE, Charles-Augustin *Correspondance générale.* Recueillie, classée et annotée par Jean Bonnerot. (Privat Didier, Stock, 1935)

SCHNEIDER, Louis *Offenbach.* (Perrin, 1923)

SELTZ, William C. *Claude Monet.* (Thames & Hudson, 1960)

SIMOND, Charles *Paris de 1800 à 1900.* (Plon, Nourrit, 1900)

SIMPSON, F. A. *The Rise of Louis-Napoleon.* (Longmans, Green, 1950)

SIMPSON, F. A. *Louis-Napoleon and the Recovery of France.* (Longmans, Green, 1951)

STARKIE, Enid *Baudelaire.* (Faber, 1957)

STARKIE, Enid *Flaubert. The Making of the Master.* (Weidenfeld & Nicolson, 1967)

STARKIE, Enid *Flaubert the Master. A critical and biographical study, 1856-1880.* (Weidenfeld & Nicolson, 1971)

TAINE, H. *Introduction à l'histoire de la littérature anglaise.* Edited from the original text with a preface by H. B. Charlton. (Manchester University Press, Manchester, 1936)

TAINE, H. *Notes sur Paris. Vie et opinions de M. Frédéric-Thomas Graindorge.* (Hachette, 1867)

TASCHER DE LA PAGERIE, Comtesse Stéphanie *Mon Séjour aux Tuileries. Deuxième série. 1859-1865.* (Ollendorff, 1894)

THÉVENIN, Évariste (ed.) *Entretiens populaires.* (Hachette, 1864)

TROMP, Édouard *Gustave Doré.* (Rieder, 1932)

UZANNE, Octave *Fashion in Paris. The various phases of feminine taste and aesthetics from 1797 to 1897.* Translated from the French by Lady Mary Loyd. (Heinemann, 1898)

VACQUER, Théodore *Le Bois de Boulogne architectural.* (Caudrilier, 1860)

VALLERY-RADOT, R. *La Vie de Pasteur.* (Hachette, 1900)

VALLÈS, Jules *Les Réfractaires.* (Faure, 1866)

VALLÈS, Jules *Le Tableau de Paris.* (Gallimard, 1932)

VANDAM, Albert *An Englishman in Paris. Notes and Recollections.* (Chapman & Hall, 1892)

VANDAM, Albert *Undercurrents of the Second Empire. Notes and Recollections.* (Heinemann, 1897)

VERLY, Albert *Souvenirs du Second Empire. I. L'Escadron des Cent-Gardes.* (Ollendorff, 1894)

VERLY, Albert *Souvenirs du Second Empire. De Notre-Dame au Zulu-land.* (Ollendorff, 1896)

VEUILLOT, Louis *Les Odeurs de Paris.* (Palmé, 1867)

VEVER, Henri *La Bijouterie française au XIXe siècle (1800-1900).* (Floury, 1906-1908)

VIEL-CASTEL, Comte H. de *Mémoires sur le règne de Napoléon III (1851-1864).* (Chez tous les libraires, 1883)

VILLEMESSANT, H. de *Mémoires d'un journaliste.* 3e série. (Dentu, 1873)

VILLEMOT, Auguste *La Vie à Paris. Chroniques du Figaro.* 1re et 2e séries. (Michel Lévy, 1858)

VITRY, Paul *La Danse de Carpeaux.* (Documents d'art Alpina, 1938)

VIZETELLY, Ernest Alfred *Paris and her People under the Third Republic.* (Chatto & Windus, 1919)

VIZETELLY, Henry *Glances back through seventy years.* (Kegan Paul, 1893)

WASHBURNE, E. B. *Recollections of a Minister to France, 1869-1877.* (Sampson Low, 1887)

WHITEHURST, Felix M. *Court and Social Life in France under Napoleon III.* (Tinsley, 1873)

WOLFF, Albert *Mémoires d'un Parisien. La Gloriole.* (Victor-Havard, 1888)

WORTH, Jean-Philippe *A Century of Fashion.* Translated by Ruth Scott Miller. (Little, Brown, Boston, 1928)

YRIARTE, Charles *Les Cercles de Paris, 1828-1864.* (Dupray de la Mahérie, 1864)

ZED (le Comte de Maugny) *La Société Parisienne.* Librairie illustrée, 1888)

ZED (le Comte de Maugny) *Le Demi-Monde sous le Second Empire.* (Kolb, 1892)

ZOLA, Émile *La Fortune des Rougon.* (Lacroix, Verboeckhoven, 1871)

ZOLA, Émile *La Curée.* (Lacroix, Verboeckhoven, 1871)

ZOLA, Émile *Son Excellence Eugène Rougon.* (Charpentier, 1876)

List of Monochrome Illustrations

AND PHOTOGRAPHIC CREDITS

256 RIGHT Hector Berlioz in 1865. Sirot Collection.

259 LEFT Georges Bizet. The Mander and Mitchenson Theatre Collection.

259 RIGHT Léo Delibes. The Mander and Mitchenson Theatre Collection.

261 LEFT César Franck at the organ, by J. Rongier. *Photo: Rainbird.*

261 RIGHT Camille Saint-Saëns. The Mander and Mitchenson Theatre Collection.

263 *Concerts Populaires.* The concert at the Cirque Napoléon, on 3 November 1861. Bibliothèque Nationale, Paris.

264 LEFT Ludovic Halévy. Sirot Collection.

264 CENTRE Jacques Offenbach, by Nadar. Sirot Collection.

264 RIGHT Henri Meilhac. Sirot Collection.

265 A music cover for *La Grande Duchesse de Gérolstein.* Bibliothèque de l'Opéra, Paris.

267 Hortense Schneider as 'La Grande Duchesse'. Enthoven Collection, Victoria and Albert Museum, London.

273 Hortense Schneider. Enthoven Collection. Victoria and Albert Museum, London.

276 The ruins of the Tuileries, 1871. Bibliothèque Nationale, Paris. *Photo: Viollet.*

279 The Imperial Family. Sirot Collection.

The decorations reproduced at the heads of chapters are from Dubois and Bernard's *La Cuisine classique*, 1864.

The endpapers show a design of bees, the Bonaparte emblem, surrounding the cipher of Napoleon III.

ACKNOWLEDGMENTS FOR COLOUR ILLUSTRATIONS

Bulloz: frontispiece, 45 BELOW, 48, 120, 154–155, 156, 165, 183, 193, 223 ABOVE and BELOW.

Cliché des Musées Nationaux: 196.

Connaissance des Arts: 73, 206.

R. B. Fleming: half title, 91.

Françoise Foliot: 153, 269.

John Freeman: 205, 272.

Giraudon: 20, 45 ABOVE, 46–47, 92, 117, 166, 184, 250–251, 252.

Michael Holford: 19.

Derrick Witty: 249.

Index

Figures in **bold type** indicate pages carrying illustrations in colour; figures in *italic type* indicate pages carrying illustrations in black and white.

293

295